The Korean Wave

Since the late 1990s South Korea has emerged as a new center for the production of transnational popular culture – the first instance of a major global circulation of Korean popular culture in history. Why popular (or not)? Why now? What does it mean socially, culturally and politically in a global context?

This edited collection considers the Korean Wave in a global digital age and addresses the social, cultural and political implications in their complexity and paradox within the contexts of global inequalities and uneven power structures. The emerging consequences at multiple levels – both macro structures and micro processes that influence media production, distribution, representation and consumption – deserve to be analyzed and explored fully in an increasingly global media environment.

This book argues for the Korean Wave's double capacity in the creation of new and complex spaces of identity that are both enabling and disabling cultural diversity in a digital cosmopolitan world.

The Korean Wave combines theoretical perspectives with grounded case studies in an up-to-date and accessible volume ideal for both undergraduate and postgraduate students of Media and Communications, Cultural Studies, Korean Studies and Asian Studies.

Youna Kim is Associate Professor of Global Communications at the American University of Paris. Previously from 2004 she taught at the London School of Economics and Political Science, after completing her PhD at the University of London, Goldsmiths College. Her books are *Women, Television and Everyday Life in Korea: Journeys of Hope* (Routledge, 2005); *Media Consumption and Everyday Life in Asia* (Routledge, 2008); *Transnational Migration, Media and Identity of Asian Women: Diasporic Daughters* (Routledge, 2011); *Women and the Media in Asia: The Precarious Self* (Palgrave Macmillan, 2012); *Global Nannies: Minorities and the Digital Media* (in preparation).

Internationalizing Media Studies

Series Editor: Daya Kishan Thussu
University of Westminster

Internationalizing Media Studies
Edited by Daya Kishan Thussu

Popular Media, Democracy and Development in Africa
Edited by Herman Wasserman

The Korean Wave: Korean Media Go Global
Edited by Youna Kim

The Korean Wave

Korean Media Go Global

Edited by
Youna Kim

LONDON AND NEW YORK

First published 2013
by Routledge
2 Park Square, Milton Park, Abingdon, Oxon, OX14 4RN

and by Routledge
711 Third Avenue, New York, NY 10017

Routledge is an imprint of the Taylor & Francis Group, an informa business

© 2013 Youna Kim for selection and editorial matter; individual contributions the contributors

The right of Youna Kim to be identified as author of the editorial material, and the individual contributors for their contributions has been asserted in accordance with sections 77 and 78 of the Copyright, Designs and Patents Act 1988.

All rights reserved. No part of this book may be reprinted or reproduced or utilised in any form or by any electronic, mechanical, or other means, now known or hereafter invented, including photocopying and recording, or in any information storage or retrieval system, without permission in writing from the publishers.

Trademark notice: Product or corporate names may be trademarks or registered trademarks, and are used only for identification and explanation without intent to infringe.

British Library Cataloguing in Publication Data
A catalogue record for this book is available from the British Library

Library of Congress Cataloging in Publication Data
The Korean wave : Korean media go global / edited by Youna Kim.
pages cm. – (Internationalizing media studies)
Includes bibliographical references and index.
1. Mass media–Korea (South) 2. Mass media–Technological innovations–Korea (South) 3. Korea (South)–Popular culture. 4. Digital media–Korea (South) 5. Mass media–Social aspects. I. Kim, Youna, editor of compilation.
P92.K6K67 2014
302.23'095195–dc23
2013021569

ISBN: 978-0-415-71278-1 (hbk)
ISBN: 978-0-415-71279-8 (pbk)
ISBN: 978-1-315-85906-4 (ebk)

Typeset in Bembo
by Taylor & Francis Books

To Oh, Sooan
and
Oh, Jeill

Contents

List of figures and tables	ix
Notes on contributors	x
Acknowledgments	xiii
Foreword	xiv
ELAINE H. KIM	

Introduction: Korean media in a digital cosmopolitan world   1
YOUNA KIM

PART I
Power and politics of the global   29

1 Soft power and the Korean Wave   31
JOSEPH NYE AND YOUNA KIM

2 Korean Wave and inter-Asian referencing   43
KOICHI IWABUCHI

3 Reconfiguring media and empire   58
OLIVER BOYD-BARRETT

PART II
Popular media and digital mobile culture   73

4 Korean Wave pop culture in the global Internet age: why popular? Why now?   75
YOUNA KIM

5 For the eyes of North Koreans? Politics of money and class in *Boys Over Flowers*   93
SUK-YOUNG KIM

viii Contents

6 K-pop female idols in the West: racial imaginations and erotic
  fantasies   106
  EUN-YOUNG JUNG

7 Negotiating identity and power in transnational cultural
  consumption: Korean American youths and the Korean Wave   120
  JUNG-SUN PARK

8 Digitization and online cultures of the Korean Wave: "East Asian"
  virtual community in Europe   135
  SANG-YEON SUNG

9 Hybridization of Korean popular culture: films and online gaming   148
  DAL YONG JIN

10 K-pop dance trackers and cover dancers: global cosmopolitanization
  and local spatialization   165
  LIEW KAI KHIUN

PART III
Perspectives inside/outside   183

11 Cultural policy and the Korean Wave: from national culture to
  transnational consumerism   185
  HYE-KYUNG LEE

12 Re-worlding culture?: YouTube as a K-pop interlocutor   199
  KENT A. ONO AND JUNGMIN KWON

13 The Korean Wave as a cultural epistemic   215
  ANANDAM KAVOORI

14 The Korean Wave and "global culture"   219
  YUDHISHTHIR RAJ ISAR

  Index   230

List of figures and tables

Figures

9.1	Subscription to MMORPGs	158
10.1	Cover dance of SNSD *Hoot* by WondershiDae and STARREseconds	175
10.2	Girls' Generation (SNSD) cover dance flash mob organized by Samsung	176
10.3	Flash mob for petition to bring SMTown concert to Singapore on June 25, 2011	176
10.4	Singaporean Style by Dee Kosh	177

Tables

9.1	Top 10 grossing movies in 2006	153
9.2	Top 10 grossing films in 2012	154
10.1	The sound tracker and dance tracker	168
10.2	Official and cover dances	170

Notes on contributors

Oliver Boyd-Barrett is Professor at the School of Media and Communication, Bowling Green State University, Ohio. His books include *The International News Agencies* (Sage, 1980), *Le Trafic des Nouvelles* (with Michael Palmer, 1981), *Contra-Flow in Global News* (with Daya Thussu, 1992), *The Globalization of News* (with Terhi Rantanen, 1998), *News Agencies in the Turbulent Era of the Internet* (2010), *Hollywood and the CIA* (with David Herrera and Jim Baumann, 2011).

Yudhishthir Raj Isar is Professor of Cultural Policy Studies at the American University of Paris, and Eminent Research Visitor at the Institute for Culture and Society, University of Western Sydney. He is the founding co-editor of the *Cultures and Globalization Series* (Sage), and advisor to international organizations, associations and foundations; President of *Culture Action Europe*, 2004–8. Earlier, at UNESCO, he was *inter alia* Executive Secretary of the World Commission on Culture and Development.

Koichi Iwabuchi is Professor of Media and Cultural Studies of Monash University and the Director of Monash Asia Institute. His recent publications include *East Asian Pop Culture: Analyzing the Korean Wave* (co-edited with Chua Beng-Huat, Hong Kong University Press, 2008); "Culture and National Border Administration in Twenty-First Century Japan," in Marwan Kraidy (ed.), *Communication and Power in the Global Era: Orders and Borders*, New York: Routledge (2013).

Dal Yong Jin is Associate Professor at Simon Fraser University. His major research interests are on globalization, social media and game studies, transnational cultural studies, and the political economy of media. He is the author of several books, including *De-Convergence of Global Media Industries* (Routledge, 2013), *Korea's Online Gaming Empire* (MIT Press, 2010), and *Hands On/Hands Off: The Korean State and the Market Liberalization of the Communication Industry* (Hampton Press, 2011).

Eun-Young Jung is Assistant Professor of Integrative Studies, Music Department, at the University of California, San Diego. She received her PhD from the University of Pittsburgh in 2007 and served as the Assistant

Director at the Center for East Asian Studies, University of Wisconsin-Madison. Her research focuses on transnational dynamics of music in and from East Asia and on music, media, race and ethnicity in Asian American communities.

Anandam Kavoori is Professor at the University of Georgia, Grady College, working in the area of International Communication, New Media and Media Literacy. He is the author or editor of ten scholarly books and over 40 journal articles and book chapters. Amongst his recent book publications are *Reading YouTube* (Peter Lang, 2011), *The Logics of Globalization* (Rowman & Littlefield, 2009), and *Global Bollywood* (New York University Press, 2008). He is also the author of two books of fiction, including a critically acclaimed novel, *The Children of Shahida*.

Suk-Young Kim is Professor of Theatre at the University of California at Santa Barbara. She is the author of *Illusive Utopia: Theater, Film, and Everyday Performance in North Korea* (University of Michigan Press, 2010), which was the 2013 winner of the Association for Asian Studies James Palais Book Prize. She is also a co-author (with Kim Yong) of *Long Road Home: A Testimony of a North Korean Camp Survivor* (Columbia University Press, 2009).

Youna Kim is Associate Professor of Global Communications at the American University of Paris. Previously she taught at the London School of Economics and Political Science, after completing her PhD at the University of London, Goldsmiths College. Her books are *Women, Television and Everyday Life in Korea: Journeys of Hope* (Routledge, 2005); *Media Consumption and Everyday Life in Asia* (Routledge, 2008); *Transnational Migration, Media and Identity of Asian Women: Diasporic Daughters* (Routledge, 2011); *Women and the Media in Asia: The Precarious Self* (Palgrave Macmillan, 2012); and *Global Nannies: Minorities and the Digital Media* (in preparation).

Hye-Kyung Lee is Lecturer in Culture, Media & Creative Industries at King's College London. She researches cultural policy, cultural industries and cultural consumption within European and East Asian contexts. She has published papers in major journals including the *International Journal of Cultural Policy*, and *Media, Culture & Society*. She is currently co-editing a book, *Cultural Policies in East Asia: Dynamics between the State, Arts and Cultural Industries* (Palgrave Macmillan, 2014 forthcoming).

Liew Kai Khiun is Assistant Professor at the Wee Kim Wee School of Communication and Information at the Nanyang Technological University, Singapore. His research interests include the transnational circulation of popular media and culture around East and Southeast Asia. He has published several articles on the Korean Wave and is also looking into the use of the social media by teenage fans of Korean popular music. He is also

xii Notes on contributors

developing research on the politics of transnational remembrance of popular icons in the social media across the region of the Asia-Pacific.

Jungmin Kwon is a doctoral candidate in the Institute of Communications Research at the University of Illinois at Urbana-Champaign. Her thesis explores the complex relationship between the Korean media industry and transnationally mediated queer texts that represent the homosexual body and are produced by young heterosexual Korean women. Her interests include critical/cultural studies, gender and sexuality, Asian media studies, and the new media.

Joseph Nye is Professor and former Dean of the Kennedy School, Harvard University. He is an expert on Asia, diplomacy, leadership and international politics. In 2004, he published *Soft Power: The Means to Success in World Politics*; *Understanding International Conflict* (5th edition); and *The Power Game: A Washington Novel*. In 2008 he published *The Powers to Lead*, and in 2011 *The Future of Power*.

Kent A. Ono is Chair of the Department of Communication at the University of Utah. He has authored/co-authored: *Contemporary Media Culture and the Remnants of a Colonial Past* (Peter Lang, 2009); *Asian Americans and the Media* with Vincent Pham (Polity, 2009); *Shifting Borders: Rhetoric, Immigration, and California's Proposition 187* with John Sloop (Temple University Press, 2002). He edits *Critical Studies in Media Communication* with Ronald L. Jackson II.

Jung-Sun Park is Professor of Asian-Pacific Studies at the California State University, Dominguez Hills. As a cultural anthropologist, she has conducted research on (trans)nationalism, (im)migration, citizenship, race/ethnicity, Korean/Asian popular culture, Asian Americans, politics of identity, and community power relations. She is author of *Chicago Korean Americans: Identity and Politics in a Transnational Community* (Routledge, forthcoming) and co-editor of *The Borders in All of Us: New Approaches to Three Global Diasporic Communities* (New World African Press, 2006).

Sang-Yeon Sung teaches at the Department of East Asian Studies, University of Vienna, Austria. She earned a PhD in Ethnomusicology from Indiana University in 2008, with a doctoral thesis on the Korean Wave in the Construction of Taiwanese Identities and Asian Values. Her current research interests include ethnographic study on K-pop music reception in Europe, Austria in particular.

Acknowledgments

Ever since Daya Thussu invited me to contribute a chapter on the Korean Wave in his well-received volume (Routledge, 2007) *Media on the Move: Global Flow and Contra-Flow*, I have closely observed the Korean Wave phenomenon in global contexts. I want to express my personal gratitude to Daya Thussu for extending his continual support and intellectual resources; and to Natalie Foster at my publisher Routledge for taking care of this book project which expands on this important moment in global media culture.

I am grateful to Anthony Giddens for his valuable advice and friendship, as always. Special thanks to Charles Armstrong, Chris Berry, Joseph Man Chan, Nick Couldry, John Downing, Terry Flew, Johan Fornas, Gerard Goggin, Jonathan Gray, David Hesmondhalgh, Matt Hills, Theodore Hughes, Karim Karim, Michael Keane, Elaine Kim, Heonik Kwon, Jin-Kyung Lee, Toby Miller, Eugene Park, Gi-Wook Shin, Michael Shin, Ella Shohat, Julian Stringer and Liesbet Van-Zoonen for their encouraging words and support when much needed.

I have also appreciated the interesting events, networks and talks that have stimulated the production of this book – especially, the invitations from the University of California at Berkeley, San Diego and Irvine, the University of Michigan, the University of Heidelberg in Germany, the University of Cambridge in the UK, and the Universitat Autonoma de Barcelona in Spain. As always, heart-felt thanks to my dedicated PA and friend Diane Willian for helping me wherever I am.

I am deeply appreciative of the contributors in this book for collaborating so willingly and delightfully. Thank you all.

Youna Kim
Paris, April 2013

Foreword

Elaine H. Kim

Since the early 1990s, many of my students have told me that when they go home for weekends and holidays, they end up staying up all night with their mothers watching Korean dramas, episode after episode, all night long. Returning to school, they find themselves falling asleep in class, not because they have been up all night studying or partying with their friends but because, like their mothers, they knew better but just had to watch the Korean serial drama until the end.

The same thing happened to me about eight years ago. Not bilingual like many of my students, I had not been able to follow Korean dramas that didn't have subtitles, so I didn't even watch *Sandglass* (*Moresigye*) when everyone I knew was glued to their television sets because of it. With the advent of really excellent and colloquial English subtitling, though, I started first with *Phoenix* (*Bulsae*), then *Jewel in the Palace* (*Daejanggueum*), which had more than 40 episodes, then *Winter Sonata* (*Kyeoul Yonga*). I told myself that I was practicing my Korean comprehension in preparation for a conference I was planning to attend in Seoul. But when I found myself staying up all night in front of the TV, ignoring phone calls and the fact that I was supposed to go to work the next day, I realized that I was hooked.

My problem with Korean dramas was the same as anyone's problem with addiction. The world in the drama is seductively beautiful. On television, the Korean landscapes and even the sparkling lights of the Seoul cityscape seen from a slum apartment look more fabulous than the legendary beauty of the San Francisco Bay Area, where I live. Every South Korean apartment looks nicer than mine. Korean TV characters of every age are infinitely better looking than I am – or my friends and colleagues, for that matter. My friends tease each other that it's hard to look at the husband snoring in the bed beside you after spending several hours gawking at Hyun Bin, Min-Ho Lee, or Song Il-Kook. And as with addiction, the worse your city, apartment, friends and colleagues, and husband looks, the more likely you are to turn on your TV, which makes your life look even worse, and on and on! Finally I had to force myself to stop renting DVDs. But then streaming made Korean dramas even easier to get. So I try to ration and rationalize my viewing. I tell myself that I am analyzing – the gender and family relations, for instance, or how time travel themes address the contradiction of nostalgia for a Korea that has long since disappeared and everyone's desperation to not be seen as backward or formerly poor. Or I try to justify watching by telling myself that everyone, especially work-obsessed Americans, should be allowed some ostensibly harmless guilty pleasures.

The other problem that's more specific to me as a Korean American of my generation is that I had to spend so many years grappling with the omissions and distortions of media representations of Asians and, to a lesser but no less objectionable extent, women in U.S. and other Western media. I have heard of elderly Japanese Americans – men and women in their 80s – who are addicted to Korean dramas. One colleague told me that his mother-in-law insists on playing the theme songs of Korean dramas she enjoys whenever she rides in his car and that an elderly uncle's most treasured possession is his large collection of Korean DVDs. Japanese Americans of this age group suffered for most of their lives from either cultural invisibility or demonization as undesirable foreigners because Asian Americans were few and because overt racism against Asians was acceptable in every aspect of American life until only relatively recently. In my case, I just got tired of being bombarded with images of white people as the most or only important people in the world. It got to the point that I could barely watch television, and by the early 1990s, the only time I went to a movie theater was to watch a film from Hong Kong, China, or Taiwan or to see a film with an African American central character.

Korean films and television are interesting to me in many ways and for many different reasons. As head of Asian American and Asian Diaspora Studies at my university (UC Berkeley), I introduced a class on "Hallyu" as part of a series of classes on Asian Popular Culture. This course attracted both male and female students of various ethnicities and from many different departments, from literature and media studies to engineering and business. Although at first they might have wanted a class that would involve pleasurable viewing and gossip about South Korean celebrities, they were inspired by the instructor to consider questions of performance history, production structures and conditions, gender, viewerships and cultural "content." Korean popular culture exists at the nexus of many issues of importance at this particular moment.

The Korean Wave: Korean Media Go Global anticipates and addresses key questions about social, cultural and political implications of contemporary Korean popular culture. What are the bases of its global appeal? How does the concept of South Korean "soft power" operate today in relation to the history of West-centered media dominance? Does K-pop help de-Westernize cultural production, decentralize male power, pluralize and de-essentialize Asia, and encourage creative translations, inspiring reformulations and alternative imaginings that might contribute to the transformation of inequalities and the emergence of new forms of culture? Or does K-pop mostly render the West more palatable to non-Western viewers by deploying Hollywood signifiers in the commercialization of Korean issues and values? Does Korean popular culture promise a new kind of multi-directionality in which Korean culture influences the West and technological interactivity allows diverse viewers to rearticulate their own versions of Korean cultural production beyond the rigid confines of its manufacture, or does it instead show us the limits of cosmopolitanism, as Korean planners target foreign viewers who view Korean performers according to Orientalist stereotypes and Korean diaspora viewers give up their futile attempts to gain acceptance in Western countries by locking themselves up in front of their Korean TV programs?

This comprehensive collection of provocative essays by scholars and cultural critics from around the world grapples with such questions as the relationship between the global and the local, what happens to cultural production when it is placed under profit-motivated state control, the organic links between diversity and excellence and who and what gets excluded in the process of the globalization of cultures, and the widening gap between democratization in Asia and market values in U.S.-dominated neoliberalism.

The Korean Wave: Korean Media Go Global is a welcome and valuable book that has something to offer to a wide variety of readers. It will be immensely valuable to the study of transnational popular cultures. As a whole, the collection provides the rich context we need to understand the significance and complexity of the Korean Wave in particular and our current moment in general.

Elaine H. Kim, Professor of Asian American Studies
University of California at Berkeley

Introduction

Korean media in a digital cosmopolitan world

Youna Kim

> The success of the K-pop is primarily a marketing success ... The capitalist marketing kills art and true artists. However, as they attack with the same weapons that the U.S. audiovisual market uses, it adds a little diversity in French panorama.
>
> (Online talk, after *Le Monde* coverage of the K-pop concert in Paris, 2011)

> It's fantastic that music from Korea is reaching ears in the UK. We've been too far stuck into our own music to even care what other countries have to offer. But K-pop is breaking down that barrier and squeezing its way into our hearts!
>
> (Online talk, after *Guardian* coverage of K-pop entry in Europe, 2011)

> I rather prefer the North Korean patriotic songs than these things.
>
> (Online talk, after *Le Figaro* coverage of the K-pop concert in Paris, 2011)

> Who cares ... "Korean" is an unknown word here (Europe). If people stop telling me that China and Japan are the only countries in Asia, I will do their promotion.
>
> (Online talk, after *Le Monde* coverage of the K-pop concert in Paris, 2011)

Since the late 1990s South Korea (hereafter Korea) has emerged as a new center for the production of transnational popular culture, exporting its own media products into Asian countries including Japan, China, Taiwan, Hong Kong and Singapore (Kim 2007 and 2011b). The spread of Korean popular culture overseas is referred to as the "Korean Wave" or "Hallyu" – a term first coined by Chinese news media in the middle of 1998 to describe Chinese youth's sudden craze for Korean cultural products. Initiated by the export of TV dramas, it now includes a range of cultural products including Korean pop music (K-pop), films, animation, online games, smartphones, fashion, cosmetics, food and lifestyles. While its popularity is mainly concentrated in neighboring Asian markets, some of the products reach as far as the U.S., Mexico, Egypt, Iraq and, most recently, Europe. This is the first instance of a major global circulation of Korean popular culture in history.

In June 2011, Korea's production company held its first European concert in Paris, singing for fans from France, the UK, Germany, Spain, Italy and so on. The company initially scheduled only one show at Le Zénith de Paris concert hall which seats about 6,000, but the tickets sold out in 15 minutes, prompting hundreds of fans to organize flash mobs in front of the Louvre museum to demand an extra show (*Le Figaro* 2011; *Le Monde* 2011). The company thus decided to arrange a second concert, then again the tickets sold out in minutes. An online-based fan club in the UK organized similar flash mobs in London's Trafalgar Square to demand shows from K-pop acts (*Guardian* 2011). In 2012, Korean singer Psy became a global phenomenon with his song *Gangnam Style* and horse-riding dance move – the most watched video of 2012 on YouTube (1.5 billion views as of April 2013). There are an estimated 460,000 fans of the Korean Wave across Europe, concentrated in the UK and France. The trend is spreading to Europe through digital social networking services facilitated by the provision of information in English.

A revival of the Korean Wave is being anticipated by the development of digital media forms, the use of the Internet and online marketing. While the rise of satellite broadcast fueled the spread of the Korean Wave in the 1990s, social networking services and video-sharing websites such as YouTube, Facebook and Twitter are now playing a primary role in expanding "digital Hallyu" to Asia, the U.S., Europe and elsewhere. Korean dramas are being uploaded to the Internet and available with subtitles in various languages including English, Japanese, Chinese and Spanish. Driven by a desire to "help" their idols, fans do real-time translations of idols' performances on the social media. Soompi.com, a dominant source of Korean pop culture, has 6 million monthly users, who are consumers and creators of K-pop and Korean drama news. Allkpop.com, another English-based website with 4 million monthly readers, has seen a growth in its European readership: the Europeans made up 1% of the readers when the website launched in 2007, but close to 25% in 2011 (*Guardian* 2011).

The interest in Korean popular culture has further triggered an increase in foreign tourists visiting the locations where their favorite dramas and acts had been filmed. Its impact has reached into communist North Korea (Kim 2007 and 2011b). In 2005, a 20-year-old North Korean soldier defected across the demilitarized zone and the reason given, according to South Korean military officials, was that the soldier had grown to admire and yearn for South Korea after watching its TV dramas which had been smuggled across the border of China (*New York Times* 2005). Similar cases have continued to occur, while the means of access to the Korean Wave media culture has expanded through the use of the Internet and cellular phones in North Korea (*Daily NK* 2011). According to recent interviews with North Korean refugees, young people from the wealthy families of Pyongyang are willing to pay around $20 a month for private lessons to learn the fashionable dances of Girls' Generation (*Sonyosidae*), one of the most popular girl groups in the Korean Wave music (Lee and Seo 2012).

In the past, national images of Korea were negatively associated with the demilitarized zone, division and political disturbances, but now such images are gradually giving way to the vitality of trendy, transnational entertainers and cutting-edge technology. The success of Korean popular culture overseas is drawing an unfamiliar spotlight on a culture once colonized or overshadowed for centuries by powerful countries. The Asian region has long been under the influence of Western and Japanese cultural products. In the European imagination, Korea was once thought to be sandwiched between Japan and China and known only for exporting cars and electronics products, but now has made itself known through its culture (*Le Monde* 2011). The Korean government sees this phenomenon as a way to sell a dynamic image of the nation through soft power, the ability to entice and attract. The sudden attraction of the Korean Wave culture has presented a surprise: Why has it taken off so dramatically at this point?

Why popular (or not)? Why now? What does it mean socially, culturally and politically in global contexts? This book argues for the Korean Wave's double capacity in the creation of new and complex spaces of identity that are both enabling and disabling cultural diversity in a digital cosmopolitan world. While not denying the obvious power of Western, particularly American, dominance over the international media landscape and the continuing significance of Western media imperialism, this book considers the Korean Wave in the global digital age and addresses the social, cultural and political implications in their complexity and paradox within the contexts of global inequalities and uneven power structures. Even the processes of contraflows today, such as the Korean Wave, are multiply structured, mutually reinforcing and sometimes conflicting, while reconfiguring the asymmetrical relations of power within hybridization processes. The emerging consequences at multiple levels – both macro structures and micro processes that influence media production, distribution, representation and consumption – deserve to be analyzed and explored fully in an increasingly global, cosmopolitan media environment.

Globalization of the Korean culture industry

The Korean culture industry was developed for socio-economic, cultural and political reasons in the late 1990s (Kim 2007). The modernization process and transformation of Korea has been rapid and condensed – a compressed modernity that has taken place in a short period of time and mainly in the urban centers anchored on familism (Chang 2010) with a turbo capitalism without much space for self-reflexivity and cultural reflection (Cho 2005). Since the 1997 Asian financial crisis, the Korean government has thoroughly re-examined the process of modernization and targeted the export of popular media culture as a new economic initiative, one of the major sources of foreign revenue vital for the country's economic survival and advancement. Korea, with limited natural resources, sought to reduce its dependence on a manufacturing base under competitive threat from China. Trade experts have called for the nation to shift its key development strategy to fostering overseas marketing for culture, technology and services, including TV programs, popular music, online games, movies and distribution services. The government has striven to capitalize on Korean popular culture and given the same national support in export promotion that was once provided to electronics and cars. The Korean Wave started from the efforts of private sectors, but the government has played a key role in the speed of growth. A systematic political infrastructure set by the government and institutional strategies developed by the industry have combined to produce the pretext to the rise of the Korean Wave.

The Korean culture industry has been developed as a national project competing within globalization, not against it. In the late 1990s, the rise of Korean popular culture was facilitated by the opening of the Korean market to global cultural forces. Historically, Korea faced Japanese colonialism (1910–45), the arbitrary division by Western powers into opposed states, North and South (1948), the Korean War (1950–53), and the military rule and successive authoritarian regimes (1961–93) that involved infringements of freedom in "political and artistic expression," as evident in the film industry (Paquet 2010). Globalization had long been accompanied by the fear of Western cultural invasion, "a kind of cultural totalitarianism" (Tomlinson 1997), and the fear was amplified by the uncertainty of the competitiveness of Korean popular culture. Japanese popular culture was equally feared and banned in Korea due to colonial history between the two countries. Only in 1998, more than 50 years after Japanese colonial rule ended, did the Korean government begin to lift a ban on cultural imports from Japan. At the same time, in 1998, the government carried out its first five-year plan to build up the domestic culture industry and encourage exports. By the time nearly all restrictions on Japanese culture had been lifted (January 2004), the Korean Wave had spread across Asia. The sense of crisis coming from the opening of the market to the West and Japan has rather strengthened and benefited the Korean culture industry.

In the era of neoliberal globalization, characterized by market deregulation and reduced state intervention in economic and cultural affairs, the Korean government has pursued a proactive, not passive, cultural policy (Jin 2006). Due to the pressures from IMF and WTO, many countries in Asia opened up their cultural markets in the 1990s and media cultural products began to flow freely among Asian countries, while the Korean culture industry took advantage of this changing market situation. In 1995, the Korean government enacted the Motion Picture Promotion Law, which encouraged business conglomerates (*chaebol*) to invest in the film industry. Korea may be the first nation to consciously recognize and, more importantly, form official policy and take action towards becoming a dream society of icons and aesthetic experience (Dator and Seo 2004).

The culture industry has taken a center stage in Korea, with an increased recognition that the export of media cultural products not only boosts the economy but also strengthens the nation's image and "soft power" (Nye and Kim in this volume). Popular culture can be an effective instrument of soft power, the ability to attract and influence international audiences without coercion. The current focus on "culture" by governments in Northeast Asia is the product of a neoliberal ideology espousing a global free market and the linking of globalized consumerism to individual freedom and social well-being (Berry *et al.* 2009).

The seemingly sudden rise of the Korean Wave is a labored coincidence and amalgamation of the strategic export policy at a time when the Asian media market is rapidly growing, fueled by the emergence of the affluent urban middle class in Asia and the globalized consumer culture. The media culture and technological change is socially constructed and does not emerge itself without the involvement of the users who have to accept it as relevant in everyday life (Kim 2008). A dramatic growth in globalized consumerism has been identified among a youth segment called "lifestyle consumers" and the "new rich" in East Asia (Chua 2000). In Muslim Southeast Asia, despite a different history and economic development, roughly similar demographic, social and economic trends – urbanization, dependency on media technology, extended periods of education, later marriage and the rapid expansion of the middle class – are apparently ripe for distinctively Islamic and transnational cultural products and massive growth in middle-class consumerism (Nilan 2008). Media consumption has become another element of social distinction, a search for a different future by younger Asians and the transformation of identity in everyday life (Kim 2008). Typically, they are imagined to be younger generations under age 30, "urban-middle, rural-rich" classes, linked to global economic and cultural circuits as a result of digital communication networks, travel or overseas education. These mobile generations are seen to be culturally cosmopolitan and technologically literate.

Today's diasporic communities use digital communication networks to maintain strong ties back to their homelands, while engaging in complex cultural exchanges in host societies. Recently in Indonesia, home to the world's largest Muslim population, the number of consumers of the Korean Wave culture has been growing rapidly, partly because the Korean community is now among the biggest foreign communities in Indonesia, with approximately 50,000 people (*Jakarta Post* 2011). The interest in the Korean Wave is kept alive by a flexible, cultural citizenry of consumers who comprise both ethnic Korean communities and non-Koreans in Asia, the U.S. and elsewhere, unsettling boundaries concerning the definitions of diasporic consumption and identity (Yin and Liew 2005). Digital mobile generations look for diverse sources of entertainment and identity, not necessarily American or European. Popular culture, which was once considered as emotional, low culture in Korea, is now a potent export force providing significant underpinning for the generation of high value and meaning for the nation.

Export of meaning

Korea has experienced breathtaking export growth in its media cultural productions. The economic value of the Korean Wave is estimated to increase from $10 billion in 2012 to $57 billion in 2020 (Korean Ministry of Culture, Sports and Tourism 2013). The amount was so insignificant before 1998 that the government could not provide figures. From 2000 to 2002, Korean cultural content exports hovered at around $500 million, but rose to $610 million in 2003, and $800 million in 2004. It took only four years for the value of exports to double to $1.8 billion in 2008, and then rise to $4.42 billion in 2010. Korea has become the "Hollywood of the East," churning out entertainment that is coveted by millions of fans stretching from Japan to Indonesia (CNN World 2010). Driven by TV dramas, K-pop music, films and online games in a digital age, the Korean Wave has expanded beyond Asia to the Americas, Europe and the Middle East.

TV dramas

The first major, yet unplanned and accidental, impact of the Korean Wave started with the export of Korean TV dramas that were not produced for international audiences but for domestic audiences. TV dramas have been the major driving force of the Korean Wave, accounting for about 90% of the total TV program exports, $252 million in 2011 (Korean Ministry of Culture, Sports and Tourism 2013). The total amount of TV program exports increased more than five-fold between 1995 ($5.5 million) and 2002 ($28.8 million). In contrast, imported TV programs decreased 70% between 1996 ($69.3 million) and 2001 ($20.4 million). By 2004, the exports of Korean TV programs reached $71.5 million, more than twice the imports of foreign TV programs, $31 million. The export of TV dramas was on a rising curve from $105 million in 2008 to $107 million in 2009, and $133 million in 2010. The three nationwide TV networks – MBC, KBS and SBS – lead overseas sales for their dramas, typically called mini-series of 16 to 24 episodes. China has rapidly emerged as the largest cultural market in Asia. In 1997 China accounted for 5.8% of Korean TV programming sales, but in 2001 it made up the largest share (24.8%), followed by Taiwan (20.5%). Since 2004, the leading importers of Korean TV dramas have shifted: Taiwan (24.5%), Japan (19%), China (18.6%), Hong Kong (3.3%) and Southeast Asian countries.

The Korean Wave reached its peak in Japan when a Korean romance drama, *Winter Sonata* (2002), became a national phenomenon in 2004 (Kim 2007 and 2011b). It was first broadcast by NHK in 2003 and has been repeatedly aired four times due to popular demand. Almost 40% of the entire Japanese population has seen the drama at least once. *Winter Sonata* proved so popular that its lead actor was nicknamed by the Japanese as "*Yon-sama*" (a deferential word reserved for royalty). This tragic love story features beautiful winter scenery and pure love between a young woman and her boyfriend suffering from amnesia. The hero's unconditional love for a woman – faithful and devoted to one lover, sensitive and understanding of woman's emotional needs – captivated many Japanese women in their 30s to 50s. The delicate way of representing emotions and intense romantic passion without overt sexuality resonates further with viewers in the Middle East where displays of physical sexuality can draw censorship and protest (Ravina 2009).

The Korean Wave reached a new peak with the airing of a historical drama, *Jewel in the Palace* (*Dae Jang Geum*, 2003), which was sold to over 120 countries in Asia, Americas and Europe. Set in Korea's Chosun Dynasty (1392–1910), *Jewel in the Palace* depicts a story about royal physician Jang Geum, who rose from being an orphaned kitchen cook to the king's first female physician. The heroine goes through tough times of palace politics, court intrigue and persecution, but she endures and upholds all the virtues of Confucian values. *Jewel in the Palace* became the most-watched television show in Hong Kong history. The series finale reportedly drew a record of 3.2 million of Hong Kong's 6.9 million potential viewers – more than 40% of the total population (*Korea Times* 2005).

Boys Over Flowers (2009), which originated from a Japanese manga, became a recent hit around the world, as well as in North Korea. North Korean viewers can also relate to the subversive politics of money, the culture of the open market economy, the logic of class struggle and social hierarchy as captured in the South Korean drama, and these ideological concerns and the pleasure of subjective identification profoundly attract them to *Boys Over Flowers* (S. Kim in this volume). The illegal consumption of the Korean Wave media culture is perhaps triggering North Koreans' self-reflexivity about their society and outside (Kim 2007 and 2011b).

The extent of the Korean Wave has presented a surprise, and even the local Koreans have trouble explaining the sudden craze for Korean popular culture. However, the first common response is that Korean TV dramas are emotionally powerful and self-reflexive (Kim 2005; Kim in this volume). While Korean producers do not pay particular attention to a global formula for the success of TV drama, nevertheless they have found its affective form useful to touch the sensibilities of disparate audiences. Yet, a French industry expert predicts that Korean drama may not be suitable for French audiences because it is "too emotional, with too many crying scenes" (*Francezone* 2011). The affective impact, which may be assumed to be universal and transparent, is neither uniform nor even, as it cannot escape culturally coded constraints (Tan 2011). Asians are often seen as being more reserved in the realms of expressing about their love, emotion and sexuality, and this conservatism could be one common denominator among audiences, the young and the old, who favor Korean dramas (Leung 2004). For many Asian audiences, things "American" are dreams to be yearned for, but things "Korean" are their "accessible future," examples to be emulated and commodities to be acquired (Iwabuchi 2002).

8 Youna Kim

K-pop music

With the rapid ascent of K-pop and the recent success of Psy's *Gangnam Style* the Korean Wave in a digital age is expanding into a new stage, gaining more visible recognition all over the world. K-pop music exports are growing rapidly, with the value of exports about $177 million in 2011. Global sales were worth over $30 million in 2009, and that figure quickly doubled to $60 million in 2010 (Korean Ministry of Culture, Sports and Tourism 2013). Compared to Korean TV dramas, K-pop music is a much more deliberately planned industry targeting international audiences from its start. Most K-pop stars including idol groups are not accidentally discovered but have been recruited and systematically produced by entertainment management firms and their "star system" that was born in the early 1990s and consolidated in the mid-1990s (Shin 2009). This system integrates production and management including marketing of stars through digital communication networks. Especially, YouTube is a driving force of K-pop today (Jung; Liew; Ono and Kwon in this volume).

K-pop is not just a random response to neoliberal globalization, but a systematically planned, monitored, manifestation of "entrepreneurial self." Young talents have been recruited, sometimes from an early age of 12, and trained to become multi-purpose, transnational performers who "can do everything" through Spartan training. Years of training include singing lessons, synchronized dance moves, acting, learning foreign languages (English or Japanese), and Korean language training for group members recruited from China, Thailand and so on. K-pop is an environment of relentless newness, both in participants and in style (*New York Times* 2011). Like manufacturing cars and televisions, this star system is also criticized as an assembly-line of similar, robot-like teen stars whose every word and move is rigorously pre-scheduled by entertainment management agents (*Independent* 2011). Some of K-pop's biggest success stories were built on the back of so-called slave contracts, which tied its trainee-stars into long exclusive deals, with little control or financial reward (BBC News 2011).

The success of K-pop stars, such as Rain (*Bi*), BoA, Girls' Generation (*Sonyosidae*), Wonder Girls, Super Junior, Dong Bang Shin Ki and so on, is a direct outcome of the star system's rigorous training to deliver a very polished and easily identifiable show. K-pop is not just music but a complete show, close to total entertainment that is uniquely appealing to international fans: "I like the way Korean artists perform on stage. It's the whole package – their appearance, moves and singing" (an Indonesian fan, quoted in *Jakarta Post* 2011). "This is the main difference from French singers who mainly prefer to focus on lyrics and almost never dance" (a French fan, quoted in *Guardian* 2011). "It's pleasant to hear and see!" (online talk, after *Le Figaro* coverage of the K-pop concert in Paris, 2011). K-pop performers exemplify a sort of pop perfectionism – catchy tunes, good singing, attractive bodies, cool clothes, mesmerizing movements, and other attractive attributes in a non-threatening, pleasant package (Lie 2012). This pleasurable experience can make international fans feel how difficult it is not to enjoy it, even when they may be fully aware of its addictiveness and extremely photogenic, visual illusion.

While girl and boy groups produced by the K-pop industry tend to be fair skin "East Asian" looking singers, its fan bases have a significantly more diverse, inclusive, cosmopolitan profile, including under-represented and invisible groups (Liew in this volume). In Europe, the initial growth of the Korean Wave is due to the familiar domain of Japanese popular culture, as the fans who seek Japanese manga, anime and music are likely to encounter the Korean Wave culture without excessive foreignness: "I read manga. I then discovered the Korean television series and then the music" (a French fan, quoted in *Le Monde* 2011). "With the HUGE manga wave, people who are at first interested in Japanese stuff (manga, anime, drama, actors, singers), get to know about Korean stuff!" (Allkpop online talk, after French TV coverage of K-pop, 2011). Due to its proliferation through the digital communication networks, K-pop is becoming a viable leader of the Korean Wave now.

Korean films

From the late 1990s until it experienced a slump in recent years, the film industry had played a key role in the Korean Wave (Jin in this volume). Export sales of Korean films were a meager $472,000 in 1997, but leaped to $11 million in 2001, $31 million in 2003, and $76 million in 2005. Korean cinema was considered as one of the most successful film industries in the world. However, starting in 2006, the export of Korean films had decreased, from $24.5 million in 2006 to $13.5 million in 2010, although it slightly increased to $15.8 million in 2011.

Korea has a vibrant film industry which has challenged the dominant position of Hollywood films in the local market. The dominance of Korean film in its own domestic market is an extraordinary cultural triumph, one shared with few other national cinemas, notably India, China and France (Yecies and Shim 2011). The market share of domestic films was as low as 16% in 1993, but increased to 25% in 1998, 50% in 2001, and 64% in 2006, outperforming their Hollywood competitors at Korean box offices. No cultural alternatives could effectively challenge the hegemony of Hollywood until Korean commercial films – ironically, a Korean pastiche that emulated much of Hollywood's aesthetic – began to build their own audience base in the late 1990s (K. Kim 2011). However, the situation changed after 2006, immediately following the FTA with the U.S.: the market share of domestic films dropped to 42% in 2008, although it increased to 52% in 2011.

The creation of a status comparable to that of Hollywood was enabled by the proactive government policy and the capital investment of business conglomerates (*chaebol*) such as Samsung, Hyundai and Daewoo in the film industry of the mid-1990s (Jin 2006). However, *chaebol*-funded films were also criticized as being another version of Hollywood movies for their focus on violence and sexuality, the commercially driven standardization of cultural expression. With blockbuster-style contents, *chaebol*-funded films soared to the top of the box-office charts. *Shiri* (1999), known as Korea's first Hollywood-style, big-budget ($3.1 million) action thriller, attracted 5.8 million viewers – bigger than the Hollywood film *Titanic*'s Korean box-office record of 4.7 million viewers. *Shiri* is about a romance between a female secret agent from North Korea and a male secret agent from South Korea. It was exported to Japan for $1.3 million in 1999 and earned $14 million at the Japanese box office, as well as reaching out to large audiences in Hong Kong, Taiwan and Singapore. *Joint Security Area* (2000), another action blockbuster film about illicit friendship between North and South Korean soldiers in the demilitarized zones, was exported to Japan for $2 million in 2001. *Friend* (*Chingu*, 2001), a gangland saga, set a new box-office record of 8.2 million viewers, and *Taegukgi* (2004), with the Korean War theme, drew 13 million viewers in the domestic market.

The visibility of Korean cinema in Asia has expanded to the West, as some Korean films have received recognition and awards at renowned international film festivals. For example, in 2002 Im Kwon-taek's *Chihwaseon* (2002) won the Best Director award at the Cannes Film Festival; in 2003 Lee Chang-dong's *Oasis* (2002) won the award for Best Direction at the Venice Film Festival; in 2004, director Park Chan-wook's *Oldboy* (2003) won the Grand Prix at Cannes; and recently, director Kim Ki-duk won the Golden Lion at Venice for his film *Pieta* (2012). The Pusan International Film Festival, one of the biggest film festivals in Asia, was launched in Korea in 1997 to promote a pan-Asian film industry as well as Korean cinema itself.

The emergence of the Korean Wave is a story of what happened when filmmakers finally escaped their confinement from the authoritarian regimes, and became free to realize a politically and socially informed cinema, but also to look beyond this to a new era when films were no longer obligated to speak for their nation or people (Paquet 2010). Cultural identity in the pre-cariousness of Korean cinema's success is an ambiguous signifier, increasingly facing a dilemma in reconciling issues around the construction of national and local identities on screen, while at the same time trying to sustain a viable and popular film industry in the face of competition from Hollywood, capitalism and neoliberalism. By fully embracing Hollywood, rather than rejecting it, successful Korean films display hybridity that equally engages both national identity and global aesthetics, art and commercialism, conformity and subversion (K. Kim 2011).

Do the Korean Wave films constitute a counter-cinema that seeks to resist global/Hollywood power and create a unique space? Or, while resisting the global power, has the contemporary Korean cinema made another form of Hollywood that is continuously negotiated in interactions of differential power? (Jin in this volume). The power relationships found whenever filmmakers from different parts of the world simultaneously cooperate and compete with each other are structured by a range of push-and-pull factors that penetrate filmmaking of a high international standard; and these circumstances are delicate and fragile, ongoing and contingent, at an interpersonal level as well as at other linked levels of the economic and the political (Stringer 2012). On one hand, the term "Planet Hallyuwood" can be seen as a counter to worldwide cultural standardization by the global Hollywood industry, and as the Korean Wave's goal of avoiding a similar type of replication of uniformity (Yecies and Shim 2011). Yet at the same time, many Korean filmmakers have blended Hollywood styles and genres with characteristically Korean stories and themes, such as the division of the nation, the Korean War, democracy, Confucian values and the struggles of people in the nation, which uniquely appeal to international audiences and critics on the global digital visual scene.

Online games

Building upon existing strengths in the film and animation industry, the Korean Wave has been expanding with the dramatic growth of digital culture, particularly online gaming. The export of Korean online games has far exceeded that of other cultural sectors such as TV dramas, K-pop music and films (Jin in this volume). The online game industry has substantially increased its exports, from $182 million in 2003 to as much as $2.1 billion worth of games in 2011. While Western countries and Japan have emphasized console games, which are the largest in terms of the global market share in the video game sector, Korea has fundamentally developed and exported online games. Since the mid-1990s, the Korean government's neoliberal cultural policies have supported the globalization of the game industry in the context of a competitive market structure, a rapid development of information and communication technologies, both competition and collaboration with global game developers including Microsoft, Nintendo and Sony. The creation of a competitive league for players of computer games has shifted the public perception of game-playing from an idle leisure pursuit to a respectable professional career, to some extent.

The game industry itself is a hybrid sector with the complex mixing of format, style and content within games. In the process of competing and collaborating with Western game developers, the Korean online game industry has adopted hybridization strategies in both structure and content, while not necessarily diminishing asymmetrical cultural power between the West and Korea but reproducing the hegemonic relations. Korean online games have been developed mainly for international users through content hybridization, de-nationalized borderless storytelling and the creation of relatively identity-less games to minimize any possible antagonism or resistance towards foreign cultural products. Unlike TV dramas and films, the Korean online game industry has primarily exported products to the U.S. and Western Europe, as well as Asian countries. Its export primarily to the Western markets raises a question of whether digital culture has substantially changed the Korean Wave from a regionally focused Asian cultural flow to a Western-focused "contra-flow," a decentralizing subaltern flow from the non-West to the West, albeit embedded in the asymmetrical relations of power.

Nation branding

The Korean Wave is not just a cultural phenomenon but fundamentally about the creation of soft power, nation branding and sustainable development, albeit with its limits, through transnational meaning-making processes (Nye and Kim in this volume). The growing export of Korean media culture has improved the national image and led to heightened awareness of general Korean products. Overseas sales of Korean consumer goods, including televisions, mobile phones, cars, clothing and cosmetics, have risen from the strategic appropriation of the Korean Wave. For instance, in Vietnam where Korean dramas are among the highest-rated shows, a Korean electronics company has provided the latest Korean TV dramas to local broadcasting stations free of charge, even covering the cost of dubbing. A Korean cosmetics company has become a global market leader in Vietnam, as more and more Vietnamese youths have become influenced by trendy images of Korean TV dramas. Korea's cosmetics exports to China rose to $127 million in 2009, but after K-pop fever swept the country in 2010, the figure nearly tripled to $336.8 million (KBS World 2012).

The growing interest in the Korean Wave, especially TV dramas, has further triggered a drastic increase in foreign tourists visiting the locations where their favorite dramas had been filmed (Kim 2007 and 2011b). The economic impact of the Korean Wave on the tourism industry amounted to $825 million in 2004, attracting 3 million tourists. Two-thirds (67%) of the visitors were influenced by Korean TV dramas. In 2012, about 11 million foreign tourists visited Korea (Korean Ministry of Culture, Sports and Tourism 2013). The Korean Wave has further prompted an interest in learning the Korean language. Each year, more than 100,000 international students come to Korea, and a significant motive is their sudden interest in, and imagination about, Korea generated by the Korean Wave popular culture (*Yonhap News* 2013). The Korean Wave has become a cultural resource for the growing mass-mediated popular imagination, which is situated within a broader process of global consumerism and a new sphere of digital fan culture.

Digital fan culture

The global expansion of the Korean Wave today can be attributed to the power of the Internet and the social media – aided by fans' participatory culture and voluntary labor in prompt uploading, forwarding and sharing with wider audiences, while significantly shaping the production, distribution and reception of the Korean Wave cultural contents. Most fans in Europe, South America and the Middle East, unlike their East Asian counterparts, have little direct access to the Korean Wave culture via mainstream television and music stores, but appropriate the proliferation of Hallyu cultural contents through the social media. There are an estimated 182 Hallyu fan clubs worldwide, with approximately 3.3 million members; specifically, 84 fan clubs in Asia, 70 in Europe, and 25 in the Americas (Korean Ministry of Culture, Sports and Tourism 2013). The data are based on a survey of membership of official fan clubs, suggesting that the inclusion of data on unofficial fan clubs would show much higher numbers.

What is significant here is not just the numbers, but the active roles played by marginal, largely invisible yet devoted fans in shaping the Korean Wave's staying power. The power of the social media should not be understood as technological determinism or technological utopianism implying that technology itself determines outcomes. It is the power of digital fan labor, both material and immaterial, that encourages fellow fans and new users to participate in transnationally imagined fan communities. Some fans create a service for the larger K-pop community, and even an entrepreneurial business in the process (*Wall Street Journal* 2012). Entrepreneurs in popular culture – both individuals and companies, within and outside of the established industry – are constantly carving new marketing channels and looking for new producible materials (Otmazgin 2011). The web has enabled fans to start their own small-scale, and sometimes pirate, operations to help import, translate and distribute foreign popular culture – a case with Japanese manga and anime in the West (Jenkins 2006). Fansubbing, or amateur subtitling, has been critical to the growth of foreign popular culture and fandom in the West, based on an implicit understanding that fans from around the world contribute their individual linguistic knowledge for the greater good of the collective. The work of linguistic translation is indicative of fans' voluntary labor, collective emotional investment and "affective translation communities" (Hu 2010).

Subtitle files are made by fan site members themselves, almost as soon as dramas are aired and songs are released. Versions of Korean dramas, and lyrics for songs within the dramas, are now available in 15 to 20 different languages. In Turkey, a fan club produces and distributes an Internet magazine, a daily newspaper and radio broadcasts about Hallyu (Korean Ministry of Culture, Sports and Tourism 2013). Many international fans appropriate English-language websites, such as the U.S.-based Soompi.com and Allkpop.com, whose members generate millions of contents for posting and interactive communications on interests from K-pop music and dramas to food and language. In France, fans visit the French-language website Kpop France for Korean Wave information and news.

The multi-faceted, digital fan culture in various locations implies that the Korean Wave is not simply a flow that originates from Korea and transnational corporates, but it is a multi-directional flow and a highly inter-active ongoing process that is created, and possibly sustained, by digitally empowered fan consumers. In an era of narrowcasting reflected in the rise of digital media technologies, the fan as a specialized yet dedicated consumer has become a centerpiece of foreign niche media producers' marketing strategies. Fan audiences are now wooed and championed by niche cultural industries, as long as their activities do not divert from principles of capitalist exchange and recognize industries' legal ownership of the object of fandom (Gray *et al.* 2007). Fans, whether of ethnic Korean backgrounds or not, turn to the social networking services to proclaim their devotion and may further enact the fantasies of these imagined worlds through language learning, travel to Korea, and the purchase of Korean cultural products through eBay and web chats on the Internet discussion boards (Yin and Liew 2005). In Europe, can the Korean Wave make the transition from being an Internet-based phenomenon, with a self-selecting if hugely active fan-base, to crossing over into the main-stream media? (*Guardian* 2011). Perhaps it is unlikely to reach anything resembling a mass audience, yet fandom is central to how the Korean Wave operates and creates cultural diversity.

Fandom is typically associated with cultural forms that the mainstream, dominant value system denigrates. It is thus associated with, but not confined to, the cultural tastes of subordinated formations of people, particularly with those disempowered by any combination of race, gender, age and class (Fiske 1992). One unique appeal of the Korean Wave personality is that there seems "no diva attitude" as stars are taught to be humble and friendly with their fans (*NY Daily News* 2011). The oft-repeated claim about K-pop performers' politeness – their clean-cut features as well as their genteel demeanors – has near-universal appeal, whether to Muslim Indonesians or Catholic Peruvians (Lie 2012). Fans steadily construct knowledge communities by archiving, annotating and circulating moments of their favored stars and performances, while producing their own vernacular discourses and explanations for why their fan culture matters so much to them (Jenkins 2006).

Fan communities activate multiple, transnational sites of engagement that not only aggregate collective intelligence but also come into conflict with mainstream identities. For instance, the poor English spoken by lead actors in a Korean drama can generate an anxiety and contestation of a racial identity that is sensitive to the stigma of linguistic inauthenticity: "I cringe at the sound of every English word they try so hard to pronounce. It's like taking your fingernails and running it across the blackboard. Jeez … they just do not take into consideration of the viewers outside Korea. Have some sympathy for the US audience!!" (online talk about a Korean drama, quoted in Hu 2010). Although Korean dramas are rarely intended for audiences in the West, they can nevertheless reach out globally through the ease of the Internet, evoking online fan communities to contest racial, national or other important markers of identity that matter to them deeply. Fans, for better or for worse, tend to engage with popular media texts not in a rationally detached but in an emotionally involved and invested way (Gray *et al.* 2007). As social agents and performers, fans activate imaginative and emotional engagements with cultural texts, which come to carry subjective significance as well as being embedded in the historically specific, embodied and lived experiences of these fans (Hills 2002). The Korean Wave culture in online communities may allow fans to imagine new identities and practices at the heart of their social realities, hierarchies and inequalities. As an important interface between the dominant macro and micro forces, digital fan culture can be seen as alternative spaces of identity in which a different voice can be raised and a self can be expressed, contested, re-articulated or reaffirmed in relation to global cultural Others.

Spaces of identity: what is "Korean" in the Korean Wave?

Cultural flows in the international media today are not necessarily one-way from the core to the periphery, due to the increasing contra-flows (Thussu 2007). Those flows are apt to be multi-directional, creating temporary portals or contact zones between geographically dispersed cultures in an age of media convergence (Jenkins 2006). The Korean Wave phenomenon can be viewed as a counterweight to Western cultural influence, "a periphery's talking back to the central West" (Hannerz 1997), "a sign of resilience of the subaltern" (Shim 2006), or "a rebellion by Asian people against the images of Caucasian good looks that dominate much of the international media" (*Wall Street Journal* 2005).

Inside Korea, there is still a real insecurity and worry, despite all the amazing triumphs of the Korean culture industry: Korea is a small country and Koreans fear their accomplishments are not real and can be taken away at any time (Russell 2008). Nevertheless, the rapid growth of the Korean Wave has spurred the imagination of the power of Asia, vernacular modernities and modernizing desires. People located in different parts of Asia are adept in using Korean popular culture to imagine their own multiple, at times conflicting, subjectivities, and to negotiate what they see as their distinctive modern identities (Lin and Tong 2008). Arising as part of the historical milieu of decolonization, the significance of its popularity is reflective of a region-wide reassertion or imaginary of Asianism, and a key site of decolonization work that may self-reflexively interrogate and unsettle the global hegemony of Euro-America.

With the economic rise of Asia, "Asia as method" has increasingly become an inescapable demand and an issue of subjectivity in dealing with the globe and with the mistake of the "catching up Euro-America" sentiment that has repressed an alternative horizon, perspective or method (Chen 2010). Using Asia as an imaginary anchoring point can allow societies in Asia to become one another's reference points, so that the understanding of the self can be transformed, and subjectivity rebuilt. The mediating site for these movements is the imaginary Asia. Inter-Asian referencing is not just a matter of academic research but also of the advancement of people's cross-border dialogue as mundane practice (Iwabuchi in this volume). The Korean Wave is an imagination of a new regional cultural formation (Chua and Iwabuchi 2008), or a source of new definitions of the cultural geography of East Asia and East Asian sensibilities that are constantly re-imagined and reinvented via pan-Asian pop cultures (Cho 2011). Although the motives of pop cultures and entrepreneurs are often commercial, their activities have important consequences of spurring feelings of "Asian-ness" (Otmazgin 2011).

In Europe, East Asian migrants find it difficult to integrate themselves into their host society in the face of social exclusion and banal racism which does not respect cultural diversity (Kim 2011a). East Asian immigrants construct an independent, regional identity by consuming "Asian values" via the Korean Wave culture, thereby possibly making their integration more difficult and unsustainable in Europe (Sung in this volume). In the U.S., many Korean Americans feel that they have been marginalized and their identity has been simultaneously denied and imposed, while at the same time Korean popular culture has become a new source of shared reference and connection among some East Asian American youths (Park in this volume). Culture and the cultural industries of East Asia are gaining a global profile and helping to constitute a new sense of the region as "New Asia," the imagination and mobilization of a regional identity and affiliation (Berry *et al.* 2009).

The Korean Wave is constructing a regional hegemony to some extent, but also co-existing with Western media domination and unequal power relations that mediate the regulations and representations of media flows. The inequality and imbalance in the media flows between Western countries and Korea has not decreased significantly. Rather, the dominance of the U.S. has increased even more rapidly in the Korean cultural market today through the flows of cultural products and capital in the forms of joint ventures, direct investment and program affiliations as well as the reorganization of the industry, thereby continuing to instil dependence on the part of Korea (Jin 2007). The Korean Wave is not a counter-argument to the classic, Western media imperialism – in a current, digital world of media pluralism with the evolving formation of the neoliberal world economic order which is a transnational capitalist power and corporate-driven network of interests, more intensely present in some territories in the digital age (Boyd-Barrett in this volume). Although the rise of Asian media flows is a testimony to the relative decline of American media power, this does not mean that a new center is emerging to take the place of the U.S. nor that Asian media culture de-Westernizes media globalization (Iwabuchi 2009).

Even in the case of complex hybrid formations, it demonstrates the ongoing play of power in a postcolonial world, the idea of culture and identity in relation to residual ideologies of empires and "Empire" in its contemporary manifestations, and the power relations that structure hybrid formations in the realm of culture (Boyd-Barrett in this volume). Culture is always relational – an inscription of communicative processes that exist historically between subjects in uneven and interlocking relations of power – and thus understanding culture cannot be separated from processes of historical and contemporary colonialisms (Kavoori 2007). The foregrounding of hybridity in present postcolonial conditions calls attention to the mutual imbrication of, and the mutual constitution of, central and peripheral cultures within asymmetrical relations of power (Shohat and Stam 1994). The current phenomenon of K-pop is both worlding and un-worlding simultaneously, through the complex hybridization and the multi-directionality of flow in a digital age of YouTube (Ono and Kwon in this volume).

The Korean Wave culture embedded in dramas, K-pop music, films, online games and so on is in essence all things hybrid – a fusion of local, regional and Western cultures, forms, styles, genres, narratives or identities, in part accelerated by the developments in information and communication technologies, yet without necessarily eliminating the best of Korea's distinct traditional values, emotional aesthetics and expressive performances. Having accommodated foreign cultures from China, Japan and America for a long time, Koreans have historically acquired experience of embracing, appropriating and reinventing cultures with their own flair at a conscious and subconscious level. Such a process can create a new, dialogical space where intercultural practices, discourses and representations are variously articulated and continuously negotiated in tensions and interactions of differential power.

The Korean Wave, with the hybrid nature of cultural products, flows, audiences and identities, ineluctably poses a question: Precisely, whose culture is represented? What is "Korean" in the Korean Wave? Korean popular culture is not really Korean in the sense that it has not evolved from Korean traditional values but is a mixture of influences; furthermore, this hybridization process partly hurts Korean national and local identities although it proves to be a commercially viable contra-flow (Jin in this volume). K-pop music, in particular, has been growing rapidly in recent years, but the reasons have relatively little to do with aesthetic and cultural values that can be identified as typically Korean (Jung 2009). To European listeners, K-pop music is seen to be "a cocktail, total entertainment" (*Le Figaro* 2011), or a futuristic pastiche that sounds like a utopian blending of all contemporary musical genres. The syncretism of a wide range of musical genres has become a common and innovative feature in the trajectory of contemporary popular music (Shim 2006), some of which may "not sound Korean but strange" (Lie 2012). Also, it is common to see the linguistic hybridization, inserting English titles and phrases "sometimes sprinkled with semi-nonsense English lyrics" (*Guardian* 2011) and easily switching between Korean and English, which may enable wider audiences around the world to sing along without knowing the Korean language and without having a sense of the depth of Korean culture. It is precisely because there is not very much Korean in K-pop that it can become such an easy sell to consumers abroad (Lie 2012). This tendency may also be

18 Youna Kim

related to the ambivalent desires of global audiences who multifariously reconstruct, re-identify and mobilize the mixed cultural practices arising from the inherent nature of the Korean Wave's "*mugukjeok*" which means "lacking in or having no nationality" (Jung 2011).

In the context of hybridization, the very idea of Korean-ness, lesser Korean or un-Korean, is a floating signifier whose meaning is contingent upon the appropriation and negotiation by global forces and people, with intended or unintended consequences. What Korean-ness signifies or what meanings are represented in the Korean Wave, and how far these representations map on to established and dominant cultural formations, have to be decided by the indeterminacy and fluidity of meaning-making by people in various contexts in the processes of global cultural change. The interface between cultural change and globalization today is more complex than it appears in the popular imagination; rather than reinforcing old, historically anchored hegemonies, the forces of globalization are also helping to destabilize them, the interaction has become dynamic and the Korean Wave culture testifies to this dynamic interaction (Isar in this volume). Hybridization of culture can be appropriated by cultural agents, subaltern people or minorities as "new spaces and resources" (Bhabha 1994) through which they construct spaces of identity, reflexive narratives and subcultures, or ironically rediscover the past and the present that they have forgotten or neglected, as much as the future of the "becoming of self in the continuous play of history, culture and power" (Hall 1990) in a de-territorialized, cosmopolitan world of media culture.

Cosmopolitanism: beyond global consumer culture?

The multi-directional flows of the Korean Wave media culture and digitally networked communications give rise to the de-territorialization of culture and identity politics transcending national boundaries and engaging with power, cultural difference and diversity in an unpredictable way. A new dynamic for the production of new kinds of diversity has emerged, and the world's increasingly interconnected media cultural environment is more and more the outcome of messy and complicated interactions, spectacular performance and global consciousness (Isar in this volume). The phenomenon of the Korean Wave is one of imagined cosmopolitanism in the realm of global consumer culture. It is accompanied by consumers' desire to travel to Korea, to learn the Korean language and to dress like Korean entertainers, and such global imaginings are facilitated by media companies as well as by the media policies of national governments (Yin and Liew 2005). At the heart of this process is the intimacy of global capitalism with national hegemonies, especially as they deal with state-sponsored events and media campaigns, functioning as a discursive touchstone for state mobilizations over national identity and regional nationalisms (Kavoori in this volume). The Korean government's policy for the Korean Wave now fits in the increasingly globalized market economy as a form of global consumerism where overseas fandom works as a legitimate source of the Korean national pride and public interest, and overseas fans are endowed with consumerist cultural power (Lee in this volume). Transcultural audiences of Asian pop culture, such as the Korean Wave and Japanese culture, reveal complex cultural identity formation and exercise of "consumer power" (Chua 2012). The worldwide spread of Japanese culture is a manifestation not of Japanese power but of how the notion of state-based power is gradually losing its meaning in an increasingly globalized world by the "power of people" engaged in cultural, religious or educational activities to cultivate a common global awareness, increase creativity and enrich the international community as a whole (Ogoura 2006).

Importantly, the primary site for the development and proliferation of this shared global consciousness is located in the mundane, representational domain of the mass media and information and communication technologies, intersected with global interdependencies of transnational migration and digital diaspora today. The everyday domestic cultures that have developed in many neighborhoods of Britain, London in particular, are closer to the vernacular cosmopolitanism signaling the increasingly hybrid, lived transformations which are the outcome of diasporic cultural mixing and indeterminacy (Nava 2007). Younger generations in the U.S. are becoming "pop cosmopolitans," consuming the coolness they now associate with other parts of the world, seeking to escape the constraints of their local culture and carving out a place for themselves in a new imagined world (Jenkins 2006). Pop cosmopolitans' embrace of the global popular media and of cultural difference represents an escape route out of the parochialism and the gravitational pull of their local communities in order to enter a broader sphere of cultural experience. Younger generations distinguish themselves from their parents' culture through their consumption of Asian popular culture to express generational differences or to articulate fantasies of social, political and cultural transformation. American popular culture dominates worldwide markets, but the growing proportion of the popular culture that Americans consume comes from elsewhere, especially Asia. The cosmopolitanism of the commercial and entertainment spheres has historically allowed Western women, as shoppers, readers and spectators, to appropriate the narratives about cultural and racial difference for themselves. Some women in Britain, for example, had feelings of attraction for and identification with otherness represented in the distinctive imageries of heterogeneous "other" origin at a particular historical moment (Nava 2007).

Cosmopolitanism is part of the structure of feeling associated with modernity at a global level. Young women in modern Asia – especially those in subordinate and marginalized positions, discontented with the gendered socio-economic and cultural conditions of society and persisting constraints of life politics within the established dominant order – are likely to imagine alternative lifestyles and desire to move out of the national and local forms of life and to seek a more open, more inclusive, alternative life experience elsewhere (Kim 2011a).

20   Youna Kim

Globalization, as a mediated cultural force, routinely presents an imaginary of consumer cosmopolitanism that can be commonly shared in the images of something better, seemingly progressive and emancipatory lifestyles. People's mediated experience as a global consumer in everyday life is locally situated but globally connected by imagined cosmopolitanism. Media consumers, especially of middle classes and upper classes in modern urban centres, come to embrace the new and imagine themselves as cosmopolitan participants in global commodity culture. Global cultures, both desires and anxieties, become part of the everyday local experiences, leading to banal cosmopolitanism or cosmopolitanization, a dialectic process in which the universal and the particular, the similar and the dissimilar, the global and the local are to be conceived as an interconnected and reciprocally interpenetrating principle (Beck 2006).

However, this cosmopolitanism does not always signal a positive engagement with difference or a happier post-national world, but also presents limitations and paradoxes. Does cosmopolitanism move beyond global consumer culture? Does the de-contextualized consumption of cultural products necessarily lead to a greater understanding of largely marginalized ethnic populations, or between different cultures? Does the ability to dance to the Other's music lead to any real appreciation of the Other's social condition or political perspective? (Jenkins 2006). Or, ironically, does the Korean Wave ambivalently lead to a new version of Orientalism, which can be a unifying cultural signifier for many, if not all, Asians, despite their attempt to defy and de-centralize Western hegemony?

For example, visual images of Psy in *Gangnam Style*, including the two males dancing wildly, fit with the familiar stereotype of Asian males as "sexually unthreatening and comical" (Jung in this volume). "I want to live in South Korea and be ridiculous" (a viewer response to *Gangnam Style* on YouTube). The unthreatening, and often ambivalent, sexuality is an embodied feature of K-pop stars, such as Rain (*Bi*) whose sexuality is described as "a man's body with a boy's face," "an angelic face and a killer body," "a cute face and a sexy body" (Shin 2009). The "androgynous" look of K-pop boy bands is uniquely appealing to French teenagers (*Le Figaro* 2011), and such characters are imagined to transcend gender boundaries and gender-related cultural power. Girls' Generation (*Sonyosidae*), Wonder Girls and other K-pop female idols, with their visible identities as Asian, inevitably place them within the entanglements of race and sexuality in America's popular imagination of Asian women as being docile, cute and sexy, vulnerable and playful. Such representations of Asian female sexuality are relentlessly rehearsed, reinforced and negotiated by their own management companies that see these representations as a means to gain acceptance in the American pop music market (Jung in this volume).

Although K-pop female idols' bodies are re-sexualized or hyper-sexualized to some extent, there is an emphasis on the cute and innocent. Girls' Generation (*Sonyosidae*), perhaps the best representation of K-pop's coy, sometimes childlike, shiny values, is a marked contrast to American female singers who are often more sexualized than their male counterparts (*New York Times* 2011). "Every K-pop video is as high-quality as any top American act like Lady Gaga or Britney Spears, but the image is a lot cleaner, less sexualization" (*NY Daily News* 2011). "With an exotic touch that makes the difference" (*Le Figaro* 2011), in Europe, K-pop style is seen to be visually stunning, fun and happy with an image of cosmopolitan openness: "so colorful and shameless clean and poppy ... looks like a bizarre utopian future where everyone is pretty and dances" (online talk, after *Guardian* coverage of K-pop entry in Europe, 2011). K-pop fan cover dances around the world open opportunities for more pluralistic engagements and inclusive participation that would bring otherwise under-represented and invisible groups out in public spaces and assert individual differences (Liew in this volume). Yet at the same time, K-pop stars' musical-visual presentations for the Western market often conform to the dominant notions of Asian-ness in their racial and sexual identities and try too hard (Jung in this volume).

The greater visibility of the Korean Wave culture in its multiple ambivalence can unintentionally reinforce the existing unequal relations of power and deep-rooted racial imaginings in representational spaces and everyday practices. The cosmopolitanism of popular media culture is not necessarily about the erosion of racial or national difference. On the contrary, racialization has often been part of cosmopolitanism (Nava 2007). The uneven flow and representation of cultural material across national borders often produces a distorted understanding of racial or national differences rather than a more nuanced account of cultural difference and national specificity, while it also represents a first significant step towards global consciousness (Jenkins 2006).

Critically, not all differences have the same value in the global structure of power and hierarchy. In celebrating the supposedly inclusive cosmopolitan consciousness, cultural difference and human pluralism, some forms of cultural difference are seen as more desirable and more valued than others. The hierarchical emphasis on difference and diversity in Europe generates a growing ethnic consciousness and a contradictory force for the reinforcing of nationalism within the uneven and highly contested transnational social field (Kim 2011a; Kim in this volume). Transnational mobility itself, whether physical or symbolic, is not a sign of the decline of the nation and national identity, or a loosening of national identifications in shaping and directing transnational experiences, both lived and mediated. Moving beyond national boundaries and moving freely into other cultures and societies can reveal a sense of contradictions and limitations. In today's digital world, the abstract and de-contextualized yet sometimes uncritically celebrated form of the cultural cosmopolitan as mediated by global consumption practices, such as the Korean Wave, may not necessarily move beyond the conspicuous, relatively happy and trouble-free consumer agency and consumer power, or cosmopolitan choice as a sign of multicultural eclecticism and imagined empowerment

22 Youna Kim

confined within the global cultural marketplace. Cosmopolitanism in this digital age may be limited within the cosmopolitan world of consumption, particularly the space of global media culture and hyper-connectivity that has nevertheless generated global consciousness and the current phenomenon of intensely mobile lives – physical, symbolic and virtual.

The book in outline

This book is divided into three thematically linked sections. Part I of the book will be concerned with the Korean Wave as a global cultural force and with the social, cultural and political implications in their complexity and paradox within the contexts of global inequalities and uneven power structures. It fits with wider debates on the shifting balance of global power and cultural influence, especially in the wake of the economic difficulties today. While acknowledging the continuing significance of Western media imperialism, chapters in this section will explore the importance of soft power and its appropriation by the Korean Wave in the global digital age, and the macro-micro politics of the Korean Wave at national, regional and global levels. Chapter 1 (Joseph Nye and Youna Kim) will consider the Korean Wave media culture as important resources that can produce soft power, while at the same time recognizing potential limits and tensions with other dimensions. Comparing the Korean Wave with other counterparts in Asia, Chapter 2 (Koichi Iwabuchi) will discuss what is emergent, residual and dominant about the studies of the Korean Wave and highlight the possibility and the limit of inter-Asian referencing – de-Westernized production of knowledge and cross-border dialogue as mundane practice. Chapter 3 (Oliver Boyd-Barrett) will consider the Korean Wave as evidence of the multiple centers of media production and influence around the world, often linked to national projects of state-subsidized "soft power" initiative; but will emphasize that these should be viewed within a broader context of hierarchical international relations, dynamics with the major centers of power such as the U.S., and Korea's place within the U.S.-dominated neoliberal order.

Part II of the volume will specifically examine the social, cultural and political meanings of the Korean Wave media culture, including TV drama, K-pop music, cinema, online games and digital cosmopolitan culture. Based on case studies in specific localities, chapters in this section will address the emerging consequences at multiple levels, considering both macro structures and micro processes that influence media production, circulation, representation and consumption. The Korean Wave can be understood as a key cultural mechanism creating the emergence of new and complex identity politics. Based on ongoing ethnographic/media studies in global sites, Chapter 4 (Youna Kim) will discuss five related arguments on the popularity of Korean TV drama: (1) A-ha! emotion, (2) everyday reflexivity, (3) precarious indivi-dualization, (4) pop nationalism, (5) diasporic nationalism and the Internet, while questioning the general assumptions of cosmopolitanism in the seemingly interconnected digital era. Perhaps the most surprising member to join the ever-increasing fandom of the Korean Wave happens to be North Koreans, who, according to testimonials of defectors, particularly enjoy Korean TV drama through the smuggled VCDs via mainland China, or through the Internet today. Chapter 5 (Suk-Young Kim) will address why the Korean Wave drama, known for championing mindless consumerism and hedonistic cultivation of bodily beauty, is allegedly a huge success in a country which still astringently upholds the utopian ideals of a classless nation. K-pop music has recently gained attention in the West increasingly due to the production and circulation of content on the Internet and the social media. Chapter 6 (Eun-Young Jung) will explore the representation of K-pop female idols within the politics of race and sexuality in the popular imagination of the West. Transnational (im)migrant youths play a pivotal role in the transnational flows of popular media culture. Chapter 7 (Jung-Sun Park) will consider how Korean American youths engage with the Korean Wave popular culture and how their engagement is linked to the negotiation of identity and power in the U.S. In an era of digitization, new, independent yet unpredictable patterns of identification are produced and circulated through online cultures across national borders. Chapter 8 (Sang-Yeon Sung) will demonstrate that digital technologies enable East Asian immigrants in Europe to engage with the Korean Wave culture that evokes so-called "Asian values" outside Asia. The popularity of Korean cinema and online gaming as part of the Korean Wave has been identified with the notion of hybridity, emphasizing power to challenge the dominant cultures of the West and power to sustain local/national identities. Chapter 9 (Dal Yong Jin) will critically examine whether hybridity has generated alternative cultures that are free from Western dominance and whether the Korean Wave has developed its own unique space of identity within the contexts of global inequalities. With the advent of the social media and video-sharing websites, the production, consumption and imagination of the digital Korean Wave has undergone reconfigurations in a consumerist cosmopolitan Asia. Chapter 10 (Liew Kai Khiun) will explore the socio-cultural meanings of K-pop dance culture as intersected with race, gender and body discourses that are produced and consumed at an unprecedented level through the social media today.

To reflect the wider implications of the Korean Wave media culture, the final part of the book will further address the Korean Wave's profound significance from various inside/outside perspectives. Despite its relatively short and recent history, the development of the Korean Wave has attracted substantial debates about cultural policy in neoliberal globalization, unresolved questions and critical dialogues. Chapters in this part will discuss the ongoing policy of the Korean Wave in its complexity and paradox within the nation-state and outside, the emerging role of the Korean Wave as a non-Western cultural flow, and its potential in working towards a more equitable world and

24 Youna Kim

cultural diversity in an increasingly interconnected, yet uneven, digital world of power. Chapter 11 (Hye-Kyung Lee) will discuss the Korean Wave's significant impact on cultural policy and social legitimacy of culture in Korea, by highlighting how the Korean Wave has quickly replaced the old frameworks of national policy with the new, neoliberal discourses of global market success and transnational consumerism. Chapter 12 (Kent A. Ono and Jungmin Kwon) will suggest that, in the process of actively consuming the Korean Wave culture, transnational consumers or fans may feel closer to Korean cultural diversity and continue to participate in creating diverse meanings, re-imagining and restructuring existing systems of domination and traditional colonial relations, while simultaneously re-identifying residual imperial culture. Chapter 13 (Anandam Kavoori) will further highlight that at the heart of this process is the articulation of identity politics which is reflexively engaged within the associated realms of technology, performance and cross-cultural transference. New repertoires of cultural expression are emerging, increasingly in a spirit of intercultural fusion. Chapter 14 (Yudhishthir Raj Isar) will suggest that the increasingly complex and trans-border circulations of popular media culture, including the Korean Wave, in the emergence of a mosaic of cultural production centers may require us to recognize and contribute towards the elaboration of a true "Culture of cultures" – as a phenomenon both profoundly mixed and essentially plural, and as a way of changing the whole world for the better.

References

BBC News (2011) "The Dark Side of South Korean Pop Music," June 14.

Beck, U. (2006) *The Cosmopolitan Vision*, Cambridge: Polity.

Berry, C., Liscutin, N. and Mackintosh, J. (2009) *Cultural Studies and Cultural Industries in Northeast Asia: What a Difference a Region Makes*, Hong Kong: Hong Kong University Press.

Bhabha, H. (1994) *The Location of Culture*, London: Routledge.

Chang, K. (2010) *South Korea Under Compressed Modernity: Familial Political Economy in Transition*, London: Routledge.

Chen, K. (2010) *Asia as Method: Toward Deimperialization*, Durham: Duke University Press.

Cho, H. (2005) "Reading the Korean Wave as a Sign of Global Shift," *Korea Journal*, 45(4): 147–82.

Cho, Y. (2011) "Desperately Seeking East Asia amidst the Popularity of South Korean Pop Culture in Asia," *Cultural Studies*, 25(3): 383–404.

Chua, B. (2000) *Consumption in Asia: Lifestyles and Identities*, London: Routledge.

——(2012) *Structure, Audience, and Soft Power: East Asian Pop Culture*, Hong Kong: Hong Kong University Press.

Chua, B. and Iwabuchi, K. (2008) *East Asian Pop Culture: Analysing the Korean Wave*, Hong Kong: Hong Kong University Press.

CNN World (2010) "Korean Wave of Pop Culture Sweeps across Asia," December 31.

Daily NK (2011) "South Korean Media Making a Difference," July 26.

Dator, J. and Seo, Y. (2004) "Korea as the Wave of a Future: The Emerging Dream Society of Icons and Aesthetic Experience," *Journal of Futures Studies*, 9(1): 31–44.

Fiske, J. (1992) "The Cultural Economy of Fandom," in L. Lewis (ed.) *Adoring Audience: Fan Culture and Popular Media*, London: Routledge.

Francezone (2011) "Korea-France Related: Korean Drama Entry in France, Too Early," September 8.

Gray, J., Sandvoss, C. and Harrington, L. (2007) *Fandom: Identities and Communities in a Mediated World*, New York: New York University Press.

Guardian (2011) "Bored by Cowell Pop? Try K-pop," December 15.

Hall, S. (1990) "Cultural Identity and Diaspora," in J. Rutherford (ed.) *Community, Culture, Difference*, London: Lawrence & Wishart.

Hannerz, U. (1997) "Notes on the Global Ecumene," in A. Sreberny-Mohammadi *et al.* (eds) *Media in Global Context: A Reader*, London: Arnold.

Hills, M. (2002) *Fan Cultures*, London: Routledge.

Hu, B. (2010) "Korean TV Serials in the English-language Diaspora: Translating Difference Online and Making it Racial," *The Velvet Light Trap*, 66 (Fall): 36–49.

Independent (2011) "Korean Wave Starts Lapping on Europe's Shores," August 7.

Iwabuchi, K. (2002) *Recentering Globalization: Popular Culture and Japanese Transnationalism*, Durham: Duke University Press.

——(2009) "Reconsidering East Asian Connectivity and the Usefulness of Media and Cultural Studies," in C. Berry *et al.* (eds) *Cultural Studies and Cultural Industries in Northeast Asia: What a Difference a Region Makes*, Hong Kong: Hong Kong University Press.

Jakarta Post (2011) "Korean Wave Casts a Spell in Indonesia," July 18.

Jenkins, H. (2006) *Fans, Bloggers, and Gamers: Exploring Participatory Culture*, New York: New York University Press.

Jin, D. (2006) "Cultural Politics in Korea's Contemporary Films under Neoliberal Globalization," *Media, Culture & Society*, 28(1): 5–23.

——(2007) "Reinterpretation of Cultural Imperialism: Emerging Domestic Market vs. Continuing US Dominance," *Media, Culture & Society*, 29(5): 753–71.

Jung, E. (2009) "Transnational Korea: A Critical Assessment of the Korean Wave in Asia and the United States," *Southeast Review of Asian Studies*, 31: 69–80.

Jung, S. (2011) *Korean Masculinities and Transcultural Consumption: Yonsama, Rain, Oldboy, K-pop Idols*, Hong Kong: Hong Kong University Press.

Kavoori, A. (2007) "Thinking Through Contra-flows: Perspectives from Postcolonial and Transnational Cultural Studies," in D. Thussu (ed.) *Media on the Move: Global Flow and Contra-flow*, London: Routledge.

KBS World (2012) "Export of Korean Pop Culture," August 8.

Kim, K. (2011) *Virtual Hallyu: Korean Cinema of the Global Era*, Durham: Duke University Press.

Kim, Y. (2005) *Women, Television and Everyday Life in Korea: Journeys of Hope*, London: Routledge.

——(2007) "The Rising East Asian Wave: Korean Media Go Global," in D. Thussu (ed.) *Media on the Move: Global Flow and Contra-flow*, London: Routledge.

——(2008) *Media Consumption and Everyday Life in Asia*, London: Routledge.

——(2011a) *Transnational Migration, Media and Identity of Asian Women: Diasporic Daughters*, London: Routledge.

——(2011b) "Globalization of Korean Media: Meanings and Significance," in D. Kim and M. Kim (eds) *Hallyu: Influence of Korean Popular Culture in Asia and Beyond*, Seoul: Seoul National University Press.

Korean Ministry of Culture, Sports and Tourism (2013) News Releases, Research and Statistics, http://www.mcst.go.kr/english/index.jsp

Korea Times (2005) "Is Hallyu a One-way Street?," April 22.

Le Figaro (2011) "La Vague Coréenne Déferle Sur le Zénith," June 9.

Le Monde (2011) "La Vague Pop Coréenne Gagne l'Europe," June 10.

Lee, W. and Seo, J. (2012) "Cultural Population from the South?," in K. Park and S. Snyder (eds) *North Korea in Transition: Politics, Economy and Society*, Lanham: Rowman & Littlefield.

Leung, L. (2004) "An Asian Formula? Comparative Reading of Japanese and Korean TV Dramas," JAMCO Online International Symposium, February–March.

Lie, J. (2012) "What is the K in K-pop? South Korean Popular Music, the Culture Industry, and National Identity," *Korea Observer*, 43(3): 339–63.

Lin, A. and Tong, A. (2008) "Re-Imagining a Cosmopolitan 'Asian Us': Korean Media Flows and Imaginaries of Asian Modern Femininities," in B. Chua and K. Iwabuchi (eds) *East Asian Pop Culture: Analyzing the Korean Wave*, Hong Kong: Hong Kong University Press.

Nava, M. (2007) *Visceral Cosmopolitanism: Gender, Culture and the Normalization of Difference*, Oxford: Berg.

New York Times (2005) "Roll Over, Godzilla: Korea Rules," June 28.

——(2011) "Korean Pop Machine, Running on Innocence and Hair Gel," October 24.

Nilan, P. (2008) "Muslim Media and Youth in Globalizing Southeast Asia," in Y. Kim (ed.) *Media Consumption and Everyday Life in Asia*, London: Routledge.

NY Daily News (2011) "The Korean Invasion: New Yorkers are Screaming for the New Wave of Pop Stars," October 23.

Ogoura, K. (2006) "The Limits of Soft Power," *Japan Echo*, 33(5).

Otmazgin, N. (2011) "Commodifying Asian-ness: Entrepreneurship and the Making of East Asian Popular Culture," *Media, Culture & Society*, 33(2): 259–74.

Paquet, D. (2010) *New Korean Cinema: Breaking the Waves*, New York: Wallflower Press.

Ravina, M. (2009) "Introduction: Conceptualizing the Korean Wave," *Southeast Review of Asian Studies*, 31: 3–9.

Russell, M. (2008) *Pop Goes Korea: Behind the Revolution in Movies, Music and Internet Culture*, Berkeley: Stone Bridge Press.

Shim, D. (2006) "Hybridity and the Rise of Korean Popular Culture in Asia," *Media, Culture & Society*, 28(1): 25–44.

Shin, H. (2009) "Have You Ever Seen the *Rain*? And Who'll Stop the *Rain*?: The Globalizing Project of Korean Pop (K-pop)," *Inter-Asia Cultural Studies*, 10(4): 507–23.

Shohat, E. and Stam, R. (1994) *Unthinking Eurocentrism: Multiculturalism and the Media*, London: Routledge.

Stringer, J. (2012) "Understanding the Role of the South Korean Cinema Industry's Dolby Consultants," *Transnational Cinemas*, 3(1): 41–52.

Tan, S. (2011) "Global Hollywood, Narrative Transparency, and Chinese Media Poachers: Narrating Cross-cultural Negotiations of *Friends* in South China," *Television & New Media*, 12(3): 207–27.

Tomlinson, J. (1997) "Internationalism, Globalization and Cultural Imperialism," in K. Thompson (ed.) *Media and Cultural Regulation*, London: Sage.

Thussu, D. (2007) *Media on the Move: Global Flow and Contra-flow*, London: Routledge.

Wall Street Journal (2005) "Korea's Hip Makeover Changes Face of Asia," October 20.

——(2012) "Behind K-pop's Pop: The Work of Fans," November 4.

Yecies, B. and Shim, A. (2011) "Contemporary Korean Cinema: Challenges and the Transformation of Planet Hallyuwood," *Acta Koreana*, 14(1): 1–15.

Yin, K. and Liew, K. (2005) "Hallyu in Singapore: Korean Cosmopolitanism or the Consumption of Chineseness?," *Korea Journal*, Winter: 206–32.

Yonhap News (2013) "Survey Shows 41% of Hallyu Fans in U.S. Learning Korean Language," January 1.

Part I

Power and politics of the global

Chapter 1

Soft power and the Korean Wave

Joseph Nye and Youna Kim

Why South Korea should go soft

In a recent survey of G-20 nations published in *The Chosun Ilbo*, the Hansun Foundation ranked South Korea as 13th in the world in terms of national power, the ability to obtain what a country wants in international affairs. South Korea ranked 9th in hard power resources defined in terms of military and economic capabilities, but performed more poorly in soft power, ranking 12th. In the words of the paper:

> State of the art factories, high-tech weapons, advanced information communications infrastructure are the key components that a country must have for a stronger international competitiveness. However, for these "hard power" ingredients to become true engines to propel the country's growth and prosperity, they must be backed by more sophisticated and highly efficient "soft power" that runs the hardware. Unfortunately, South Korea is relatively weak in soft power.

The "Wisemen Roundtable on Soft Power in Northeast Asia" convened by the Korea Foundation, the East Asia Institute and *Joongang Ilbo* in February 2008 reached a similar conclusion. In short, South Korea needs to pay more attention to soft power if it is to play a larger role and command more attention in international affairs.

Power is the ability to make others act in a way that advances the outcomes you want. One can affect behavior in three main ways: threats of coercion ("sticks"), inducements or payments ("carrots") and attraction that makes others want what you want ("soft power"). Soft power co-opts people rather than coerces them: If I can get you to want to do what I want, then I do not have to force you to do what I want. Soft power is not the same as influence, though it is one source of it. Influence can also rest on the hard power of threats or payments. And soft power is more than just persuasion or the ability to move people by argument, though that is an important part of it. It is also the ability to entice and attract (Nye 2004).

In behavioral terms, soft power is attractive power. In terms of resources, soft power resources are the assets that produce such attraction. Some resources can produce both hard and soft power. For example, a strong economy can produce carrots for paying others, as well as a model of success that attracts others. In international politics, the resources that produce soft power arise in large part from the values an organization or country expresses in its culture, in the examples it sets and in the way it deals with others. It was a former French foreign minister, Hubert Vedrine (1997–2002), who observed that America is powerful because it can inspire the dreams and desires of others. The U.S. is master of global images through film and television; this, in part, draws large numbers of overseas students, who either stay or bring their experience back home with them.

The soft power of any country rests primarily on three resources: (1) the attractiveness of its culture, (2) its political values, when it lives up to them at home and abroad, and (3) its foreign policies, when they are seen as legitimate and having moral authority. Sometimes, these dimensions can conflict with each other. For example, the attractiveness of the United States declined markedly after the invasion of Iraq, which was seen as illegitimate in the eyes of many nations. In contrast, after the United States used its navy to assist in Tsunami relief in 2005, polls showed an impressive increase in its standing in Indonesia, the largest Muslim country in the world. In China, former President Hu Jintao told the 17th party congress that China needed to invest more in soft power to increase its standing in the world, and Chinese soft power benefited from the successful staging of the 2008 Beijing Olympics, but recent polls show that China's human rights policies and censorship of free speech has limited the growth of its soft power.

A soft power strategy for South Korea

South Korea, with its population of about 50 million people, is not big enough to be one of the world's great powers. But many small and medium-sized countries wield outsized influence because of their adept use of soft power. Canada, the Netherlands and the Scandinavian states, for example, have political clout that is greater than their military and economic weight, because they have incorporated attractive causes such as economic aid or peacemaking into their definitions of their national interest. South Korea should seek to follow these examples.

Seoul has impressive potential for soft power. In addition to its stunning economic success, it has developed a truly democratic political system, characterized by human rights, free elections and the transfer of power between different political parties. Of course, South Korean democracy is not exactly tidy; bribery scandals are all too common and parliamentary fistfights are not unknown. Even so, the fact that Korea fights it out, sometimes literally, in the open is a point in its favor.

Finally, there is the attractiveness of South Korean culture. The traditions of Korean art, crafts and cuisine have already spread around the world. The impressive success of the Korean diaspora in the United States has enhanced the attractiveness of the culture and country from which they came. Many Korean-Americans have risen to important positions, and this has created a positive view about their country of origin. Korean popular culture has proved attractive across borders, in particular among younger people in neighboring Asian countries and beyond.

What can Korea do?

1. Attracting more foreign students to South Korean universities would be one way to reinforce the country's role in this transnational youth culture. This would involve more emphasis on English as well as Korean language instruction, as well as scholarships for students from other countries.
2. Korea can increase its overseas development assistance to raise its profile on other continents besides Asia. Many African countries that are seeing increases in Chinese aid but worry about Chinese domination, would welcome the diversification that Korean aid could provide.
3. Korea could sponsor more exhibits, visiting speakers and broadcasting to convey the story of Korea's success to other countries. In 1960, Korea and Ghana had the same per capita income. Today Korea is not only a member of the OECD, but has become a democratic success story. The Korean government can help convey this story, but its credibility would be enhanced if Korean companies, universities and non-profit organizations also conveyed the message.
4. Korea can host major international conferences and events that draw attention to its successes. The fact that the G-20 met in Seoul in 2010 is a good example, but an active program of sponsorship of non-governmental events would help as well. Topics like health, development and climate change are issues that would draw attention to Korea's efforts.

Korea has a message for the rest of the world, and it needs to see itself as more than a regional actor and think of the ways in which it can contribute to global public goods that are well received throughout the world. This will enhance Korea's standing and create an enabling environment for the pursuit of Korea's foreign policy interests. In short, South Korea has the resources to produce soft power, and its soft power is not prisoner to its geographical or demographic limitations.

Korean Wave popular culture as resources

Since its release in July 2012, Psy's music video *Gangnam Style* (1.5 billion views on YouTube, as of April 2013) has prompted more people around the world to seek information on South Korea, due to the sudden attractiveness

34 Joseph Nye and Youna Kim

or sarcastic humor of an actor's culture. The emergence of Korean popular culture, as exemplified by Psy's *Gangnam Style*, is a ready-made export that is enhancing the country's soft power (British Council 2012; *Daily Mail* 2012; *Forbes* 2012). Under conditions of globalizing market forces in a digital age, *Gangnam Style* has become a "cool" cultural brand promoting Korean exports ranging from mobile phones to cosmetics to consumer electronics. The nation can be reinvented as a more favorable and lasting brand by the government's cultural policy that global circulations of media cultural products promote the construction of soft power, an attractive image of the nation as a whole.

Earlier in 2005, for the first time in the Middle East, Korean popular culture began spreading the non-economic side of its soft power to the political sphere, when the Korean TV drama *Winter Sonata* hit airwaves in Iraq (Kim 2007). The South Korean government (Defense Ministry) reported that the drama signed a broadcast agreement with Kurdistan Satellite Channel, a broadcaster operated by the Kurdistan government. The goal was to generate positive feelings in the Arab world towards the 3,200 South Korean soldiers stationed in northern Iraq. Originally, the Defense Ministry considered providing Korean movies in Iraq, but this was repealed due to concerns that a flock of moviegoers might lead to possible accidents or terrorist attacks. So the final decision was made to broadcast the TV drama *Winter Sonata* which had already proven popular worldwide. The drama was aired with Kurdish subtitles, every Thursday at 5:00 p.m. with reruns every 8 hours. Furthermore, the South Korean government purchased the rights to provide Korean TV dramas for free to broadcasting stations in more Arab countries in an effort to create a favorable image of the nation.

The South Korean government (Overseas Information Service) also gave the popular drama *Winter Sonata* to Egyptian television in 2004, paying for Arabic subtitles (Kim 2007). The broadcast was part of the government's efforts to improve the image of South Korea in the Middle East, where there is little understanding and exposure towards Korean culture. The state-run broadcaster ERTU (Egypt Radio Television Union) aired the drama daily except Fridays on its satellite channel. This led to thousands of fan letters to the Korean Embassy in Egypt, indicating a warm reception by Egyptian audiences. A flood of e-mails and phone calls were received at the Embassy when another Korean drama *Autumn in the Heart* was broadcast in 2004. Many of them called for inviting the leading actors of the drama to Egypt. One of the e-mails was from a professor at a University of Cairo saying that he had watched the drama every night with his wife and two children. A female fan asked the Embassy to broadcast the drama again and to introduce more Korean dramas. Egyptian viewers have launched a Korean drama fan club and website, expressing a newly found interest on the Internet: "I wish I could visit Korea some day" (an Egyptian fan, quoted in *KBS Global Marketing* 2005). The expression of these thoughts indicates that the Korean Wave popular drama is understood in the Arabic cultural sphere. Now, the Korean

Wave popular culture helps young people in the Middle East to raise interest in Korean studies and the Korean language (Korean Ministry of Culture, Sports and Tourism 2013).

These cases signify the Korean Wave popular culture's potentiality as soft power resources that may have a significant and complex impact on cultural diplomacy as well as on trade, tourism, the academy and other national interests across various contexts. Popular culture has become a potentially important resource for soft power diplomacy, transcultural collaborations, dialogues and struggles to win hearts and minds of people. Such a potentiality is evident in the region of East Asia which is still haunted by colonization and violence (Chua 2012). Culture – particularly, popular, media and consumer culture – transcends borders with such frequency and intensity as to constitute an irrevocable and irresistible force that regionalizes and possibly transforms identity (Berry *et al.* 2009). It is this power that governments seek to promote through the articulation and legislation of cultural policy and the promotion of cultural industries, with a renewed focus on identity, culture and nation branding as an essential component of foreign policy thinking.

South Korea is now among the world's 13 largest economies but still does not have its own unique brand or unique cultural identity, partly because for the past 50 years it has focused on building the country, not marketing it (BBC News 2012). The G-20 summit held in Seoul in 2010 increased awareness of South Korea by almost 17%, making it one of the country's most successful marketing events. In Europe, people still associate South Korea mainly with the Korean War or North Korea, sometimes with mobile phones or cars, more than with its culture. South Korea brings its culture to Paris with "Korea Week," an event which aims to enhance the country's international standing and change the image of its economic hard power far outweighing its soft power in the eyes of the global community (*France 24* 2011).

The South Korean government, along with the private sector and the academy, has been working on the recreation of its national image and cultural identity for multiple effects of soft power by integrating the Korean Wave popular culture since the late 1990s. The Kim Young Sam government (1993–98) and the official globalization policy (*segyehwa*) started to respond to neoliberalism and regulatory practices imposed by the U.S. and other Western countries. In 1999, the Kim Dae Jung government (1998–2003) provided the financial support of $148.5 million to the culture industry. Focusing on the so-called three Cs – Content, Creativity and Culture – the government encouraged colleges to open culture industry departments, providing equipment and scholarships. The number of such departments rose from almost none to more than 300 by 2004.

The Roh Moo Hyun government (2003–8) advocated "cultural diversity" and vitality as well as creativity. The Lee Myung Bak government (2008–13) sought to promote "Brand Korea" to enhance the nation's image and soft power through popular culture in a wide range of areas from K-pop music to

Korean food. Various organizations including the Ministry of Culture, Sports and Tourism (MCST) and the Korea Trade-Investment Promotion Agency (KOTRA) set aside budget for programs to promote the national image. To a great extent, the global circulation of Korean popular culture for the creation of soft power is the consequence of Korean national policies.

The Ministry of Culture, Tourism and Sports has been intensely promoting Korea through "Visit Korea" campaigns with the marketing slogan "Korea, Sparkling" and the official tourism website (Korea Sparkling) that provides information about popular TV dramas and movies including storylines, filming locations and leading actors and actresses. The government has also appointed the Korean Wave stars as tourism ambassadors, while hosting events for overseas fan clubs of the Korean Wave. For instance, fans of *Jewel in the Palace* can visit the historical drama's shooting site, Jeju Folk Village, and experience traditional culture such as *hanbok* (traditional clothes), *hanok* (traditional house) and *hansik* (traditional food).

Scenery, as a marker of foreignness, constitutes a mode of visual tourism. Avid fans of Korean TV dramas can become so enamored by the sceneries that the locations become "must see" places and storytelling of the mobile self (Kim 2007 and 2011). "You know, there's this scene where they went up by cable car and got caught in a snowstorm? We went up, too. I even went to the restaurant where the two of them sat" (a Singaporean fan of *Winter Sonata*, quoted in *Straits Times* 2003). As picturesque romance dramas like *Winter Sonata* and *Autumn in the Heart* have dominated TV screens, the snow slope and the beach where the memorable scenes were filmed have become a popular destination for overseas fans.

About 11 million foreign tourists visited Korea in 2012 (Korean Ministry of Culture, Sports and Tourism 2013). In past decades, Korean TV stations and drama producers were often accused of putting too much focus on dramas and unrealistic escapism at the expense of more educational programming, but now they are honored for bringing home foreign currency. Furthermore, the engagement with the Korean drama *Winter Sonata* has created a new aware-ness among the Japanese, and the number of private language schools that teach Korean has increased in Japan: "Watching the drama, I just wished I could understand what he was saying in Korean" (a female fan, quoted in *Yomiuri Shimbun* 2004). Language learning is often about a desire to reinvent oneself in transnational spaces and that desire is crucially influenced by media discourses (Piller and Takahashi 2010).

More than 100,000 international students come to Korea each year, and about 41% of American fans of the Korean Wave popular culture are learning the Korean language (*Yonhap News* 2013). A recent survey in Singapore, for example, shows that the initial motivation for many university students to learn the Korean language is "to gain greater exposure to the Korean Wave popular culture" (Chan and Chi 2011). In Singapore, there is some demand for Korean studies and Korean language instruction, driven by both economics and the Korean Wave, although these demands are small in scale and are being satisfied outside the schools and tertiary institutions (Steinberg 2010). This also implies that such a motivation and demand may prove to be a transient interest which may wane once the hype trend generated by the Korean Wave has subsided.

In a digital age, South Korea can appropriate this opportunity to make its language, culture and society more attractive to wider international audiences and open possibilities for soft power of the Korean Wave popular culture. Today's rapid media globalization and the widespread use of information and communication technologies present new opportunities as well as unprecedented challenges to nation-states. Information is power, and modern information technology is spreading information more widely than ever before in history, which adds the reasons why soft power is becoming more important than in the past (Nye 2004).

The Korean Wave is finally making its way into isolated North Korea despite tight controls set by the regime's authority (Kim 2007 and 2011). In recent years, cases of defections have continued to occur, while the means of access to the Korean Wave popular culture has expanded through the use of the Internet and cellular phones in North Korea (*Daily NK* 2011b). North Koreans caught watching the South Korean media face up to two years in a labor re-education camp, or up to five years in a prison camp for more serious cases.

The 33 North Korean defectors interviewed in a recent study revealed that they had illegally consumed the South Korean media "every day" (34%) or "once or twice a month" (41%) before they fled to the South (*Daily NK* 2011c). "Listening to South Korean songs just makes me feel good. I hum a song without realizing it. Our songs are all about political ideas" (a North Korean defector, quoted in *Daily NK* 2011c). North Korean young people dance to South Korean music (K-pop), sometimes with the lyrics erased, because they want to dance freely and the lyric-less songs would not compel the regime's authority (Young Red Guards) to stop their dance (*Daily NK* 2011a).

These illegal activities may be part of the process of imagining about, and reflecting on, social transformation and other structures of identity, while attempting liberation of desire from established structures. The Korean Wave popular culture in North Korea may provide a new framework for making sense of the world, with a possibility of a multitude of meanings to emerge and circulate in everyday life (Kim 2007 and 2011). Despite the higher risk of execution for consuming the South Korean popular culture, many North Koreans get a taste of freedom, modernity and the free-market fantasies spun by the illegal, smuggled dramas and movies, and now through the Internet.

Driven by globalization and interdependence, Korean Wave popular culture is building a bridge between cultural connectivity and South Korea's strongest form of soft power – the attraction and acquiescence of people without the use of military or economic force. However, given the nature of soft power being uncontrollable and unpredictable, as being shaped by many complex factors including the geopolitics and strategic interests of nations (Fan 2008), the Korean Wave soft power may play a limited role, albeit significant historically.

Korean Wave soft power and its limits

Soft power has been an extremely productive concept but also remains an elusive concept partly because its measurement is a formidable challenge. It is not sufficiently clear how soft power actually works in specific international relationships, and using poll data as an empirical ground of soft power requires much caution, calling for qualitative and ethnographic methods of measuring it (Lee and Melissen 2011). To some extent, Korean Wave popular culture has heightened South Korea's visibility around the world and captured the imagination of a new generation. It has possibly changed foreign perceptions of South Korea, which predominantly has been viewed as an industrial powerhouse and whose achievements have been overshadowed by North Korea, or often ignored at the expense of more attention being paid to the neighboring countries, China and Japan.

Thanks to the Korean Wave popular culture, the awareness and image of South Korea have perhaps changed in the popular mind abroad, for example in Southeast Asia since 2005. Yet, that awareness does not necessarily translate into "better policy" either by or towards South Korea (Steinberg 2010). It is remarkable that leading intellectuals and policy-makers in Southeast Asia, Europe or elsewhere may find it extremely difficult to identify nationals in their own countries who can be considered specialists or knowledgeable about Korea in any depth. The European public remain largely unaware of Korean culture including traditional arts, even though K-pop music has successfully entered the continent since 2011.

Does South Korea want to be remembered and identified overseas mainly by its pop culture? The recent success of Psy and K-pop idol groups has created a cool national image, soft power, in raising its international stature. Yet at the same time, this can create a very partial and distorted picture of South Korea now associated with "a pudgy comic singer and long-legged beauties" (*Korea Times* 2012). A country's image, as a source of soft power, can be both very powerful and very constraining. The global audiences may expect certain conformity with the very partial, or extremely polished, image in the popular cultural forms of K-pop music, dramas and films, without further developing an ability to understand the country's actual conditions and socio-political issues.

The concept of soft power has also been used to represent the power of Japanese popular culture overseas, also known as "Japanese cool." It may well be desirable for the sort of cultural content embodied in "Japanese cool," such

Soft power and the Korean Wave   39

as manga, anime or fashion, to spread naturally around the world through global market forces or people's efforts. Yet, this will not necessarily lead to an increase in understanding of Japan in any depth (Ogoura 2006). Those on the receiving end of contemporary cultural activities either from or related to Japan are not necessarily aware of any Japanese connection and actual conditions there.

The relatively happy, fun, trouble-free, cosmopolitan consumption of popular cultural forms, or the consumers' "hearts and minds," do not always lead to any in-depth understanding of the history, culture and society within which the popular cultural forms are embedded and produced. What is consumed here are meanings and symbolic values which are not used up through the production of culture as commodity, but which continue to circulate in ever increasing and expanding circuits of communication in the emergence of the cultural economy in a new digital age (Chua 2012).

The Korean Wave, with the active role of the nation-state, is a pronounced example of the crossover of culture and economy, and the commercialization of culture through nation branding, taking a neoliberal capitalist approach in the era of globalization. Recent policy discussions in Korea continue to utilize culture as transnational commodity and capital. The Korean Wave idols are often chosen as commodity representatives of Korean brands, helping Korean trademarks to become more fashionable, cool image products through constant product placement and idol promotion (Huang 2011). In the widest possible sense, the Korean culture industry is seen to commodify the nation, exporting its popular culture as a cool national brand.

This dependency on the Korean Wave popular culture to create soft power and develop new markets, such as South America, Southeast Asia and the Middle East, is particularly significant at a time when the world economy shows signs of slowing down (Korea Trade-Investment Promotion Agency 2013). Korea's soft power is likely to be an extension of its economic influence, which is a core component of hard power. With their accustomed nationalism, East Asian countries would like to invest in soft power to expand their existing economic influence and acquire more sophisticated politico-cultural leverage (Lee and Melissen 2011). Popular culture has emerged as a core component of a nation's economic competitiveness which extends to interests in cultural influence and cultural diplomacy.

In cultural diplomacy, however, a greater emphasis should be placed on reciprocal cultural flows and mutual understandings, rather than asymmetrically presenting a nation's own culture, or cultural nationalism, based on the market-driven cultural economy. This unequal condition is most pronounced in East Asia. It has been overwhelmingly Korean and Japanese popular cultures such as TV dramas that enter Taiwan, Hong Kong, Singapore and urban China, yet there is very little flow in the reverse direction (Chua 2012).

The Korean Wave, as a state-subsidized "soft power" initiative, has emerged as a new player for the production and circulation of transnational culture,

40 Joseph Nye and Youna Kim

while consolidating a relatively more growing position in the regional market based on geopolitics and similar historical experiences. The postcolonial periphery is fast becoming a major center for the production of transnational culture, not just a sinkhole for its transnational consumption (Watson 1997). There is a lingering anti-colonial sentiment lurking in the hearts of people in many Asian countries; however, the Korean Wave appears to benefit from the sense of solidarity, sympathy more than resentment, which people have towards the country that shared a similar colonial past and continues to struggle in a current postcolonial situation.

Korea with the sentiment of "*han*" (deep suffering) is seen to be a less problematic source of power and ideological threat than some other countries in Asia, for example "Japanese odour" (Iwabuchi 2002) that Japanese cultural producers try to remove from their products in order not to induce resistance from regional audiences. On the other hand, the aspirations behind the national government's efforts to use popular culture, and the impact of the asymmetrical cultural flows, are limited by the fragmented nature of global audiences who respond differently, by the audience reception as a contested site of negotiation, and even by the possibility of resistance and subversion. This limitation is evident in anti-Korean Wave movements in Japan, Taiwan, China, Singapore, Thailand and so on. It is usually confronted with larger non-consumer communities reinforcing nationalist discourses with the complicity of local media productions and the state (Chua 2008).

For instance, Japanese nationalist groups have held regular demonstrations against Fuji Television, demanding that the television company stop excessively broadcasting Korean TV dramas and other Korean entertainment (*JoongAng Daily* 2011). In Taiwan, too, Korean dramas have faced negative sentiments for the excessive airing of Korean shows in the evening time, between 6:00 p. m. and midnight. In 2010, Taiwanese TV stations aired 162 Korean dramas, or an average of 13 Korean dramas per month (*Dong-A Ilbo* 2012). Initially, Korean dramas were considered as cheap alternatives to their Japanese counterparts. In 2000, at the early stage of the Korean Wave, Taiwan's Gala TV paid $1,000 for one hour of a Korean drama, compared with $15,000 to $20,000 for a Japanese one. After only five years, however, a Korean drama commanded $7,000 to $15,000, and a Japanese one $6,000 to $12,000 (*New York Times* 2005).

The heightened visibility of Korean popular culture has been criticized by the mass media and the public overseas as a cultural invasion of the Korean Wave. Regionalism may be a response or a challenge to globalization, but also one component of globalization that is a complex, conflicting and indeterminate process (Berry *et al.* 2009). While the Korean Wave fosters connectivity within East Asian cultural geography, the diversity of its fandom also demonstrates that the cultural identity of East Asia is neither monolithic nor reified, but envisaged as a variable and asymmetric space of both integration and contestation (Cho 2011).

Soft power and the Korean Wave   41

Linking culture to the nation-state carries a high risk of impeding, rather than promoting, the spread of cultural activities around the world (Ogoura 2006). With the active involvement of the government, the Korean Wave has been largely constructed within nationalistic discourses and policies, and imagined with cultural nationalism – a form of hegemony masked in soft power. Nationalism has been central to the globalization of media cultural products; paradoxically, the question of how global such media are is to ask how nationalistic they are (Chan 2005). This Korean version of nationalistic and expansionistic cultural policy has a tendency to develop into another form of hegemonic cultural imperialism in the region. The Korean Wave popular culture, as resources for soft power for the postcolonial periphery, can ironically generate a new version of cultural imperialism that is deeply embedded in cultural nationalism and its ideological position going against cultural diversity and soft power of attraction.

References

BBC News (2012) "Selling South Korea: No 'Sparkling' Brand Image," January 31.
Berry, C., Liscutin, N. and Mackintosh, J. (2009) *Cultural Studies and Cultural Industries in Northeast Asia: What a Difference a Region Makes*, Hong Kong: Hong Kong University Press.
British Council (2012) "British Council Welcomes 'Soft Power' Survey Results," November 19.
Chan, J. (2005) "Global Media and the Dialectics of the Global," *Global Media and Communication*, 1: 24–8.
Chan, W. and Chi, S. (2011) "Popular Media as a Motivational Factor for Foreign Language Learning: The Example of the Korean Waver," in W. Chan *et al.* (eds) *Media in Foreign Language Teaching and Learning*, Boston: Walter de Gruyter.
Cho, Y. (2011) "Desperately Seeking East Asia amidst the Popularity of South Korean Pop Culture in Asia," *Cultural Studies*, 25(3): 383–404.
Chua, B. (2008) "East Asian Pop Culture: Layers of Communities," in Y. Kim (ed.) *Media Consumption and Everyday Life in Asia*, London: Routledge.
——(2012) *Structure, Audience, and Soft Power: East Asian Pop Culture*, Hong Kong: Hong Kong University Press.
Daily Mail (2012) "Britain Ousts the US as World's Most Influential Nation: Country Tops Rankings for Soft Power," November 18.
Daily NK (2011a) "Young People Surfing the Korean Wave," June 21.
——(2011b) "South Korean Media Making a Difference," July 26.
——(2011c) "The Mighty Power of Pop Culture," September 22.
Dong-A Ilbo (2012) "Korean Wave Backlash in Taiwan," January 2.
Fan, Y. (2008) "Soft Power: Power of Attraction or Confusion?," *Place Branding and Public Diplomacy*, 4(2): 147–58.
Forbes (2012) "The Empire Strikes Back: U.K. Beats U.S. in 'Soft Power', Survey Says," November 18.
France 24 (2011) "Paris to Celebrate South Korea's Culture with Korea Week," November 21.
Huang, S. (2011) "Nation-branding and Transnational Consumption: Japan-mania and the Korean Wave in Taiwan," *Media, Culture & Society*, 33(1): 3–18.

Iwabuchi, K. (2002) *Recentering Globalization: Popular Culture and Japanese Transnationalism*, Durham: Duke University Press.

JoongAng Daily (2011) "Hallyu's Popularity Breeds New Wave of Protests in Japan," November 7.

KBS Global Marketing (2005) "*Autumn in the Heart* Syndrome in Egypt."

Kim, Y. (2007) "The Rising East Asian Wave: Korean Media Go Global," in D. Thussu (ed.) *Media on the Move: Global Flow and Contra-flow*, London: Routledge.

——(2011) "Globalization of Korean Media: Meanings and Significance," in D. Kim and M. Kim (eds) *Hallyu: Influence of Korean Popular Culture in Asia and Beyond*, Seoul: Seoul National University Press.

Korea Times (2012) "Korea's 'Soft Power' Quest," December 5.

Korea Trade-Investment Promotion Agency (2013) KOTRA News http://english.kotra.or.kr/

Korean Ministry of Culture, Sports and Tourism (2013) News Releases, Research and Statistics, http://www.mcst.go.kr/english/index.jsp

Lee, S. and Melissen, J. (2011) *Public Diplomacy and Soft Power in East Asia*, New York: Palgrave Macmillan.

New York Times (2005) "Roll Over, Godzilla: Korea Rules," June 28.

Nye, J. (2004) *Soft Power: The Means to Success in World Politics*, New York: PublicAffairs.

Ogoura, K. (2006) "The Limits of Soft Power," *Japan Echo*, 33(5).

Piller, I. and Takahashi, K. (2010) "At the Intersection of Gender, Language and Transnationalism," in N. Coupland (ed.) *The Handbook of Language and Globalization*, Malden: Blackwell.

Steinberg, D. (2010) *Korea's Changing Roles in Southeast Asia: Expanding Influence and Relations*, Singapore: Institute of Southeast Asian Studies Publishing.

Straits Times (2003) "K-mania Still Rules, Ok?," January 4.

Watson, J. (1997) "McDonald's in Hong Kong: Consumerism, Dietary Change and the Rise of a Children's Culture," in J. Watson (ed.) *Golden Arches East: McDonald's in East Asia*, Stanford: Stanford University Press.

Yomiuri Shimbun (2004) "TV Dramas Melt Hearts, Thaw Japan-Korea Relations," December 7.

Yonhap News (2013) "Survey Shows 41% of Hallyu Fans in U.S. Learning Korean Language," January 1.

Chapter 2

Korean Wave and inter-Asian referencing

Koichi Iwabuchi

East Asia has become a key location in which new digital media such as mobile phones, digital video games, and the Internet discussion site and social networking service flourish among the youth. Production capacity of media cultures such as TV, films and popular music has also been considerably developed. Many researches have examined the distinctive features of East Asian media cultures in terms of the modes of textuality, production and consumption. Among them, Korean media cultures currently sweep over Asian markets. Films, TV dramas and K-pop – various media cultures have been trend-setting in East Asia and accordingly many researches have been conducted about the Korean Wave. In this chapter, I will consider the significance of studying the Korean Wave by putting it in a wider framework of the studies of East Asian media culture connections. Following the recent call for the advancement of inter-Asian referencing and the establishment of East Asian media culture studies (Chua 2010 and 2011; Cho 2011), I will consider how the comparison of the Korean Wave with other counterparts such as Japanese media culture would elucidate what is emergent, residual and dominant about some key issues such as translocal hybridization processes and non-Western articulation of cultural modernities. Such investigation will highlight the possibility of de-Westernized production of knowledge and, no less importantly, urge us to keep on questioning seriously whether and how East Asia as a cultural geography matters. It will also be suggested that the pursuit of the potential of inter-Asian referencing to the full requires making inter-Asian referencing not just a matter of academic research but also of the advancement of people's cross-border dialogue as mundane practice.

Inter-Asian referencing and the studies of East Asian pop culture

Long-standing advocacy of de-Westernizing academic production of knowledge has entered a new stage as the drastic development of the production of media cultures and their transnational circulation in non-Western regions has posed a serious question about the supremacy of American media cultures and the credence of Euro-American cultural dominion in the world.[1] East Asia is one of the most prominent regions in which various kinds of cultural expression and mixing were intensified and intra-regional consumption was set in motion. Examining socio-historically specific experiences that intersected East Asia as a region, many researches seriously examined cultural dynamics of production, circulation and consumption of media cultures in East Asia under globalization processes.[2] Such studies offer new perspectives that go beyond a mere replication of theories derived from Western experiences and give nuanced accounts of specific East Asian experiences.

This has surely advanced the de-Westernized production of knowledge, though a firm binary of Western theory and non-Western derivative experience dies hard (Shome 2009; Thussu 2009). To go beyond this predicament, there have recently been more conscious attempts and practices among media and cultural studies researchers working in and on Asia. A key term is inter-Asian referencing. This is shown by a recent trend that the notion of "Asia as method," which was advocated by a Japanese thinker, Takeuchi Yoshimi in the early 1960s,[3] has attracted renewed attention. In reworking Takeuchi's project, Chen (2010: xv) offers a succinct recapitulation of his idea: "using Asia as an imaginary anchoring point can allow societies in Asia to become one another's reference points, so that the understanding of the self can be transformed, and subjectivity rebuilt" and this will lead to the construction of "an alternative horizon, perspective, or method for posing a different set of questions about world history." Hitherto under-explored intra-regional or inter-Asian comparison is considered highly meaningful for understanding modern trajectories of Asian countries in a new critical light, as it is based on shared experiences of "forced" modernization and less hierarchical relationships than a prevailing West–Asia comparison that is based on assumed temporal distance between them. This is not to conceive of Asian modern experiences in an essentialist term in contrast to and/or separate from Western experiences. "Re-embracing" deep-seated Western inflections on Asian experiences, an inspired inter-Asian comparison and referencing aims to refreshingly elucidate specific processes in which the experiences of Asian modernizations have been formulated, whereby the production of knowledge derived from Asian experiences leads to the articulation of universal visions and values for transmuting Asian societies, the West and the world as a whole. As such, the idea of Asia as method and inter-Asian referencing is not exclusive of academic researchers working outside Asia. It is a self-critical strategic call to activate dialogues among hitherto internationally unattended scholarly works of Asian regions – though still mostly limited to English language works.

Echoing Chen's argument, Chua (2010) suggests the advancement of "East Asian Pop Culture studies." Acknowledging the development of a research community of East Asian pop culture, Chua (2011) further proposes that cultural studies scholars working on Asia should make conscious efforts to advance inter-Asian referencing in a more organized manner. He contends that localized (re)conceptualization in Asian contexts with refined uses of local terminologies and concepts rather than straightforwardly using English concepts is much required in the first place and inter-Asian comparison would be of great help for this purpose. At the same time, Chua argues, more active inter-Asian referencing of localized conceptualization and researchers among scholars working in Asia would be a required next step if we are to make conceptualization and theoretical discussion derived from particular local contexts of Asia translocally and universally relevant. This will evolve in tandem with the establishment of a reference body of publications on East Asian media culture and the formation of an internationally recognized "East Asian pop culture research community" (Chua 2010).

If we are to take this path, however, we need to historically scrutinize whether and how East Asian media culture production, circulation and consumption have been substantially materializing a cultural geography of East Asia and how they have been studied. Taking the studies of the Korean Wave as a case in point, Cho (2011) argues that the historicization of East Asian pop culture in terms of colonial connections as well as the rise (and the fall) of Hong Kong and Japanese media culture in the last 30 to 40 years is necessary to fully comprehend the rise of Korean media culture.[4] It is to take the Korean Wave among other kinds of East Asian media cultures "as the iteration of East Asian pop culture." The notion of iteration, which is repetition with a difference, is employed in relation to the study of Asia by Spivak (2008) that "different histories, languages, and idioms 'that come forth' each time we try to add an 's' to the wish for a unified originary name". Cho also argues that the idea of iteration is important to radically de-essentialize and pluralize the conception of "East Asian pop culture." Cho's reference to iteration is more analogous to Gilroy's notion of "changing same." It urges us to conceptualize East Asia as a cultural geography, in which the rise of Korean media culture is made sense of not as a uniquely Korean phenomenon but in terms of "the historicity as well as the multiplicity of East Asian pop culture" (Cho 2011: 388).

Korean Wave in the East Asian process of cultural hybridization

Indeed, while it is not very common to seriously discuss previous works on Japanese and Hong Kong media cultures in the studies of the Korean Wave, the specificity of the Korean Wave would be better highlighted by rigorous examination of spatiotemporal similarities to, differences from and interrelations with other East Asian media cultures. One issue that such inter-Asian referencing elucidates is cultural hybridization in terms of two associated processes: Asian media culture's negotiation with Euro-American counterparts and the interchange between Asian media cultures. Many studies have discussed how East Asian media cultures have subtly hybridized American media cultures in terms of production techniques, representational genres and comparative consumption (Iwabuchi 2002; Shim 2006). This approach aims to evade both an essentialist view of Asian values and traditions and a simplified view of American cultural domination. It shows how American culture is translated and appropriated in East Asian contexts as well as how cultures and values in East Asia are re-contextualized in popular media texts. It is useful to consider at once the operation of global power configuration in which Euro-American culture has played a central role and the active cultural translation practices in the non-West (Iwabuchi 2002 and 2004). While these issues have been analyzed respectively, not much comparison of East Asian experience of hybridization in negotiation with American cultural hegemony has been done. Still we are repeatedly reminded that Korean media cultures "translate Western or American culture to fit Asian tastes" (Ryoo 2009: 145). However, the time is ripe for more laborious inter-Asian referencing to go beyond such a recurring statement. Comparative analysis would explicate how they are similar and different in terms of the continuum of hybridization processes in East Asia, ranging from creative translation that produces something new, selective appropriation of Western cultures, subtle reformulation of local cultures, eventual replication based on global mass culture formats, re-essentialization of cultural difference between the West and Asia, and the nationalist discourse of the excellence of cultural hybridization (Iwabuchi 2002; Cho 2011).

Hybridization perspective is also significant as it is closely related to the articulation of cultural modernity in various places within East Asia. Various media cultures in East Asia show a different mode of "compressed arrival of modernity" (Cho 2011: 397). This is another intriguing object of rigorous examination through inter-Asian referencing. Representation of family relationship, affective communication, gender relations and material lifestyles in urban settings shows similarities and differences in terms of cultural modernities in East Asia, which have been socio-historically formulated under the trajectory of Western and Japanese domination in the region. Ryoo (2009) argues, for example, that a mode of cultural modernity represented in Korean media cultures is rather different from the Japanese counterparts. The Korean one holds an "in-between stance" which is "neither too advanced nor too behind" in contrast to the Japanese one which is "too post-industrial, too Westernized, and too individualistic to the extent that they seem incomprehensible, incommensurable or for some, simply weird" (ibid.: 146). This is an important point, but still lacks a substantial analysis to verify it. Rather than dealing with Korean or Japanese media culture in general, more text-based examination of specific cases would be required to comprehend varieties of compressed-ness.

No less intriguing is to examine cultural hybridization among East Asian media cultures. This is significant given that media culture markets in East Asia have become synchronized and producers, directors, actors as well as capital from around the region have been working across national borders. Trans-Asian promotion and co-production of media cultures have become commonplace by the collaboration and partnerships among media and cultural industries. While subtle and innovative ways of hybridization of American cultural influences constitute media culture production in East Asia, intra-Asian cultural mixing has also come to be actively generated. Dynamic processes of trans-Asian cultural fusion and inter-textual reworking cannot be fully comprehended by the theories of hybridization that commonly consider non-Western appropriation of American media cultures. However, since the explicit frame of reference is still mostly America (and the West), hybridization analyses, while aiming to capture dynamic processes of the formation of East Asian modernities, tend to lend credence to the centrality of Euro-American modernity. East Asian media cultures have long dexterously hybridized in local elements while absorbing American cultural influences, but cultural fusion has been actively generated among East Asian cultures and producers as well. Remaking of successful TV dramas and films of other parts of East Asia has become unexceptional especially between Japanese, Korean, Hong Kong and Taiwanese media texts, and Japanese comic series are often adapted for TV dramas and films outside Japan.[5] A prominent example is *Meteor Garden* (*Liuxing Huayuan*), a Taiwanese TV drama series that adapts a Japanese comic series. It became very popular in East and Southeast Asia, and Japanese and Korean versions were later produced. Most recently an unofficial Chinese version was also produced. By comparing mutual influences and appropriation, the idea of the original is put into serious question, instead of highlighting the dynamic process of inter-Asian cultural adaptation, which freshly shows both commonality and difference in the constitution and representation of "East Asian modernity" (Le 2009).

Inter-Asian referencing as cross-border dialogue

Modernities and hybridities are not just a matter of cultural representation but of East Asian media culture consumption, of which inter-Asian referencing has become an integral part. Many studies have examined such practices, as is shown by, for example, the examination of how Korean TV dramas or Korean pop music is consumed in different locations by various people in East Asia (Chua and Iwabuchi 2008) or the conceptualization of how feelings such as "nostalgia" are evoked in various contexts (Iwabuchi 2002, 2008). Cho (2011) proposes a more systematic collation of the studies of inter-Asian

48 Koichi Iwabuchi

mediated connections by theorizing "East Asian sensibilities." Being cautious that it should not be considered static or evenly shared but marked by "its asymmetric but synchronous spatialities and its uneven but simultaneous temporalities" (Cho 2011: 394), Cho urges us to clarify emerging "identities, consciousnesses, and mentalities within its cultural geography" in a way akin to Raymond Williams' idea of "structure of feeling" (ibid.: 393). Indeed much more needs to be done to theorize various patterns of people's shared experiences of mediated inter-Asian referencing; for example, in terms of femininity and masculinity (e.g., Jung 2011). However, what is also at stake is, I would suggest, how cross-border dialogue has been facilitated via inter-Asian referencing in East Asia.

An unprecedented extent of circulation and mutual consumption of media cultures produced in East Asia drastically promotes people's mutual understanding and self-reflexive dialogue in a transnational scope. Ordinarily watching TV dramas and listening to popular music from other parts of the region, people have now wider repertoires for reflecting on their own lives and socio-historical issues such as gender relations, the lives of young people and justice of their own societies through the perception of spatiotemporal distance and closeness of other East Asian modernities (Iwabuchi 2004 and 2008). People in Asian countries have long tended to face the West to interpret their own modern experiences in terms of the (Orientalist) conception of cultural difference and developmental temporal lag from a Western point of view. The mediated encounter with other Asian modernities makes many people in East Asia mutually realize how common experiences of modernization, urbanization, Westernization and globalization are similarly and differently represented in other East Asian contexts and that they now inhabit the same temporality. While media culture from other Asian countries occasionally evokes a perception of nostalgia of an Orientalist kind, nostalgia also productively induces a self-reflexive thinking as is clearly shown by the way the consumption of Hong Kong and Korean media cultures in Japan undermines a historically constituted idea of Japan's superiority over the rest of Asia (Iwabuchi 2002 and 2008). Furthermore, everyday practice of media consumption engenders actual cross-border contact. Many people eventually visit other Asian cities, meet people there, start learning local languages, join transnational cyber fan communities, and even relearn the history of Japan's colonialism (in the case of Japanese audiences). Thus inter-Asian referencing via East Asian media cultures has significantly brought about cross-border dialogue as it encourages people to critically and self-reflexively reconsider their own life, society and culture as well as socio-historically constituted relations and perceptions of others.

This emerging landscape in East Asia, I would suggest, echoes relatively unnoticed Takeuchi Yoshimi's sense of pleasurable surprise that he perceived when he first visited China, a sense that triggered the formulation of the idea of Asia as method. Unlike when he visited Euro-American countries, he was then very much impressed by his observation that people's thinking, feeling and experiences in China looked very familiar (and different) to those in Japan as both shared a catch-up positioning and mentality of developmental temporality vis-à-vis Western counterparts. This sense of pleasant surprise has also pushed the development of academic research on media cultures in East Asia in the last 20 years. However, this time, that sensibility is not just derived from researchers' self-critical observation of other Asian societies. Rather, researchers, including myself, have witnessed how media culture connections prompt many people in the region to perceive something similar and different in the composition of modernities of other Asian societies. The development of East Asian media culture connections thus does not display the possibility of inter-Asian referencing just as a method to produce alternative academic knowledge but as a historic opportunity of engendering people's cross-border dialogue as mundane practices, which inspired researchers avidly document, interpret and problematize.

Cultural internationalism and the politics of unshared-ness

The call for the advancement of the studies of East Asian media culture is indeed pressing. Institutionalizing such studies that facilitates inter-Asian comparison of the mode of hybridization, representation of cultural modernities and mutual consumption would have the great merit of innovatively furthering our understanding of the complicated dynamics of cultural globalization in East Asian contexts. At the same time, it is no less important to systematically examine insensibilities and disconnections that have been generated by East Asian media culture connectivity. To further trans-Asian connections, we need to look at their limits as well. Most fundamentally, the disparity in the material accessibility to media culture is still serious.[6] We also need to ask what kinds of mutual understanding are primarily promoted and what are not. A pertinent question here is whose voices and concerns are not represented or included in the East Asian cultural connections as the marketization of media cultures is moving forward. East Asian media culture connection has brought about not just cross-boundary dialogues but also cross-boundary disparity, divisions, antagonism and marginalization in various overlapping ways.

This does not just mean how vast numbers of people in the region remain indifferent to other East Asian media cultures or how many people uncritically consume East Asian media cultures merely for fun. How political issues such as territorial disputes have cast a shadow over the circulation of East Asian media cultures and how East Asian media culture circulation has activated the vicious circle of (cyber) nationalism, especially between Korea, China and Japan, is an urgent object of analysis (Liscutin 2009).

50 Koichi Iwabuchi

Furthermore, any studies of East Asian media culture should bear in mind that the rise of East Asian media cultures does not fundamentally challenge West-centered power configurations but has been formulated under and incorporated into imbalanced globalization processes. This is evident not just in how Western cultural influences are always and already deeply inscribed in the specific formation of media cultures in East Asia but also in how globally configured power relations surpass a West–Asia binary and permeate both. While we have tended to be fascinated with the new ways in which media culture engendered self-reflexive dialogues, we now need to turn our attention more to the issue of marginalization and non-sharing that is accompanied and even engendered by the promotion of inter-Asian mediated referencing in a particular manner. This is required as the Korean Wave – even more so than in the Japanese and Hong Kong cases in the late twentieth century – has been occurring in a context in which global power configuration has come to exercise more control over cross-border cultural connections.

Elsewhere I argue that the global governance of media culture connectivity and diversity have been generated through three interrelated forces of marketization, state policy of national branding and cultural internationalism (Iwabuchi 2010). Their interplay works to deter and limit cross-border dialogic connections in East Asia as it promotes market-oriented international diversity and connections while suppressing other kinds. As the advancement of market-oriented industrial partnership has facilitated the formation of inter-Asian pop culture networks, the kinds of media texts that are promoted to circulate are chiefly commercially and ideologically hegemonic ones in each country, which tend not to well represent socio-culturally marginalized voices within the nation (except those of tokenized multicultural commodities). Although the digital communication technologies have diversified grassroots cultural expressions and mediated cross-border connections including those among marginalized people and activists working for them, we still need to ask what kinds of mutual understanding are predominantly promoted through which media texts and whose voices and which issues are *not* included and/or shared in the emerging inter-Asian cultural public sphere. This predisposition is also pushed by states' promotion of "brand nationalism," which aims to opportunistically administer media culture for the enhancement of national interests in the international arena. It keenly promotes the international circulation of "national culture" while discounting imperative questions of cultural diversity that are not justly recognized within the nation as well as international political economy issues such as hierarchical structuring of affective labor and copyright monopoly by media giants (Iwabuchi 2012).

Together with the two forces has been engendered the rise of cultural internationalism. It is much argued that the growth of transnational connections does not displace the significance of the national but encourages its

Korean Wave and inter-Asian referencing   51

reworking (Hannerz 1996). A case in point is that the national has come to be taken for granted as the unit of global cultural encounter and national cultures are mutually consumed in various internationalized cultural occurrences. Since the 1990s, we have witnessed the substantial increase in global media spaces through satellite and cable broadcasting and the Internet sites as well as global media events and gathering opportunities of sport events, film festivals, TV format trades, food showcases and tourism, in which cultures from many parts of the world are exhibited, compete with each other and are mutually recognized as national brands in the international arena (Urry 2003). In this context, the rise of East Asian media culture connection functions as a significant instance of such international branding showcases. Inter-Asian mediated connections tend to enhance a particular kind of internationalized cultural diversity and encounter in a way to exclusively highlight national cultural boundaries and subdue intra-regional and intra-national issues of socio-cultural marginalization.

An increase in internationalized encounters with people, cultures and images from many parts of the world, in which people enjoy participating in the event by displaying a particular national emblem, has operated as mundane occasions in which banality of national belonging is further promoted (Billig 1995) through the permeation of banal internationalism, which comprehends cross-cultural encounters as those among mutually exclusive national cultures. Banal internationalism forwards a predisposition that when one discusses international mobility, encounter and connectivity, one is apt to implicitly assume the cardinal existence of the delimited national cultural boundaries to come across. The multicultural situation is, for example, interpreted and represented by the media in an international framework in which cultural differences are recognized as those of the nation (Iwabuchi 2005). In relation to the rise of East Asian media culture connection, the internationalized version of multiculturalism tends to overpower or even suppress local multicultural politics. This is displayed by the ambivalence regarding the empowerment of diasporas and migrants by the rise of the economy and culture of the "home" country. A critical researcher of Asian–Australian studies stated about the persisting stereotypical images of Chinese diasporas in Australia: "As we become more dependent on the dollars from the economies of Asia, I would hope that the vestige of 19th century orientalism will fade away" (Kwok *et al.* 2004). It might be the case that the rise of the Chinese economy improves international images of China and enhances social recognition of those diasporas/migrants who identify themselves and are identified as "Chinese" in the host society. However, there is a thin line between the empowerment of diasporas by their association with the images of the home country and the confusion of their identities and differences with those living in the home country.[7]

This is the case with the popularity of Korean media cultures in Japan.[8] Positive reception of Korean media cultures in Japan has not just facilitated self-reflexive views of self–other relations among audiences but also improved the images of resident Koreans who have long been suffering from discrimination as ethnic minorities in Japan. However, while the advance of media culture connection between the two countries draws attention to the demarcation of Japan–Korea national cultural borders to be traversed in an affirmative manner, it tends to overlook the complication of the in-betweenness that resident Koreans have experienced and struggled with in Japanese society. An approving consumption of Korean media cultures tends to make the existence and difference of resident Koreans effortlessly muddled up with and understood through culture and people of the present Korea, making them perceived and represented as "Korean nationals living in Japan." The recognition of Korean residents as fellow citizen living together "here" is subsumed by the recognition of them as those belonging to another nation "over there," showing that the historically constituted discrimination and identity distress that many resident Koreans have been experiencing in Japan has not been well comprehended. This highlights the difficulty and necessity to go beyond the nation-centered framework, as international governance of media culture connections is implicated in the multicultural and postcolonial questions in a way to hamper the politics of inclusion of the ethnic minorities within the nation and to hamper dialogic potentials of East Asian media culture connection.

These considerations raise a question about the analytical unit of inter-Asian referencing. Cho (2011) argues that cautious uses of the term "national culture" would be necessary to the theorization of East Asian pop culture. I agree with Cho that nation is not necessarily "suppressive or even fascist enforcement that erases the diversity and multiplicity of different locales" (ibid.: 390). The nation-state is still a significant unit of analysis as it exerts a considerable institutional and affective power in the articulation of East Asian media culture connections. However, the cost of even a cautious deployment of "methodological nationalism" should be taken seriously as well. A nation-based inter-Asian comparison is useful as long as we fundamentally problematize the supposition of national culture as a unit of cultural connection and diversity. We need to be watchful of whether and how a nation-centered analysis of iteration and East Asian sensibilities might lose sight of the highlighting of "national-territorial" similarities, differences and interactions and be organized in ways to dampen our attention to socio-cultural marginalization within and across the nation. The idea of iteration does not necessarily presuppose national culture as a unit, but theorization of East Asian media culture connections would not be satisfactory if it does not pay a critical attention to how they *interrelatedly* generate inequality and marginalization within a region and nation in terms of class, gender, sexuality, race, ethnicity, sub-region, migration/diasporas and discourage cross-border dialogue. This is reminiscent of the lacuna in the studies of inter-Asian media culture connections, which tend not to critically attend to the politics of

Korean Wave and inter-Asian referencing   53

representation. For example, when I conducted audience research on the Korean TV drama *Winter Sonata* in Japan, or the Japanese TV drama *Tokyo Love Story* in Taiwan, more attention was paid to how audiences positively interpret the gender relations and love romances that are represented in the TV dramas from other Asian societies and self-critically reflecting on their own lives and societies (Iwabuchi 2002 and 2008). This is still a relevant research question in the studies of inter-Asian media culture connections, but what is missing in this investigation is the critical analysis of what kinds of representation of gender relations, for example, are traversing the boundaries in East Asia, and what are not. While the critical studies of queer cultures, ethnic minorities and migrants in the media representation have been much conducted in the national context, these are not yet well explored in the studies of inter-Asian media culture connections. More analyses will need to be done to examine whether and how transnationally consumed texts in East Asia do justice to the cultural differences, inequality and marginalization of each nation. The discussion of de-Westernization tends to overlook intra-regional and intra-national disconnection and disparity (Shome 2009) and the same trap might be laid with the studies of East Asia media culture.

Concluding remarks

Transnational circulation and intersection of various flows of capital, media culture and people interconnects East Asia both spatially and temporally, materially and imaginatively, and dialogically and antagonistically in ways to highlight historically constituted relationships and regionally and globally shared emergent issues. The rise of East Asian media cultures and regional connections has undoubtedly become a significant field of academic analysis, which merits further development, since it contributes well to enriching our comprehension of complicated processes of cultural globalization that theories derived from Euro-American experiences could not solely capture. However, as the phenomenon is no longer "emergent" but has been more and more incorporated into the "dominant" structure of global power configuration, we need to rethink why "East Asia pop culture" matters and for what purpose and for whom "inter-Asian referencing" can be a useful method. Media culture connection in East Asia significantly plays an initial role in the enhancement of cross-border dialogue – affectively, communicatively and participatorily. Yet, there is no guarantee that mutual listening and dialogue is enhanced by itself in the world where issues and voices apart are "sharable but not necessarily or inevitably shared" (Silverstone 2006: 91).

To be engaged with the politics of (non)-shared-ness, researchers' role is first and foremost to offer critical interpretations and analyses of complex processes of mediated shared-ness and non-shared-ness in an intangible

54 Koichi Iwabuchi

manner. At the same time, let us be reminded that "'Asia as method' ceases to look at Asia as object of analysis" (Chen 2005: 141). Method in "Asia as method" suggests less a pure academic methodology than a means by which to engender alternative modes of knowledge production that enable us to tackle with and transform the existing unequal composition of the world. We researchers are urged to consider how to conjointly advance two kinds of inter-Asian referencing in the studies of East Asian media culture connections – academic production of knowledge and the promotion of people's mediated dialogue. The Korean Wave is currently a valuable investigative "method" for progressing this rather ambitious project.

Acknowledgment

An earlier version appears as "Korean Wave as method: Advancing the studies of East Asian media culture connections", in John Lie (ed.) *Hallyu (The Korean Wave)*, Routledge, 2014.

Notes

1 E.g. James Curran and Myung-Jin Park (eds) *De-Westernizing Media Studies*, London: Routledge, 2000; John Nguyet Erni and Siew Keng Chua (eds) *Asian Media Studies*, Oxford: Blackwell, 2005; Daya Thussu (ed.) *Internationalizing Media Studies*, London: Routledge, 2009.

2 For example, in the English language academy, on regional cultural flows and connectivities: Chris Berry, Jonathan D. Mackintosh and Nicola Liscutin (eds) *Cultural Industries and Cultural Studies in Northeast Asia: What a Difference a Region Makes*, Hong Kong: Hong Kong University Press, 2009; Youna Kim (ed.) *Media Consumption and Everyday Life in Asia*, New York: Routledge, 2008. On Korean Wave phenomena: Chua Beng Huat and Koichi Iwabuchi (eds) *East Asian Pop Culture: Analyzing the Korean Wave*, Hong Kong: Hong Kong University Press, 2008; Hae-Joang Cho, "Reading the 'Korean Wave' as a Sign of Global Shift," *Korea Journal*, 45(4), 2005, 147–82; on the popularity of Japanese media cultures: Koichi Iwabuchi, *Recentering Globalization: Popular Culture and Japanese Transnationalism*, Durham: Duke University Press, 2002; Koichi Iwabuchi (ed.) *Feeling Asian Modernities: Transnational Consumption of Japanese TV Dramas*, Hong Kong: Hong Kong University Press, 2004; Anne Allison, *Millennial Monsters: Japanese Toys and the Global Imagination,* Berkeley: University of California Press, 2006; Joseph Tobin (ed.) *Pikachu's Global Adventure: The Rise and Fall of Pokémon*, Durham: Duke University Press, 2004; on the rise of Chinese media cultures and markets: Michael Curtin, *Playing to the World's Biggest Audience: The Globalization of Chinese Film and TV*, Berkeley: University of California Press, 2007; Yuezhi Zhao, *Communication in China: Political Economy, Power, and Conflict.* Lanham: Rowman & Littlefield, 2008.

3 For an English translation, see Takeuchi (2005).

4 Colonial history matters in the inter-Asian circulation and consumption of media culture. It can be argued that if Japan's colonial history often causes the reluctance to accept its culture in other parts of Asia, Korean media culture is free from this sort of

historical burden, which might give Korean media culture a further credence of textual appeal.

5 Regarding the media co-production in East Asia, see Jin Dal Yong and Lee Dong-hoo, "The Birth of East Asia: Cultural Regionalization Through Coproduction Strategies," paper presented at the annual meeting of the International Communication Association, San Francisco, 2007; Albert Moran and Michael Keane (eds), *Television Across Asia: Television Industries, Programme Formats and Globalisation*, London: RoutledgeCurzon, 2004.

6 See *Key Indicators for Asia and the Pacific 2009*, which was issued by the Asian Development Bank, showing that just 10 Asian countries have an Internet usage rate of more than 20%.

7 Regarding Hollywood's recent representation of East Asia, it can be argued, those who are most offended by the continuing Orientalist representations in Japan-related Hollywood films such as *Memoirs of a Geisha* and *Lost in Translation* are less people in Japan than ethnic minorities of Japanese/Asian descent in the Western countries such as Asian-Americans. See Koichi Iwabuchi, "Lost in TransNation: Tokyo and the Urban Imaginary in the Era of Globalization," *Inter-Asia Cultural Studies*, 9(4), 2008, 543–56.

8 For a detailed analysis of the following, see Iwabuchi, 2008.

References

Allison, A. (2006) *Millennial Monsters: Japanese Toys and the Global Imagination*, Berkeley: University of California Press.

Berry, C., Mackintosh, J. and Liscutin, N. (eds) (2009) *Cultural Industries and Cultural Studies in Northeast Asia: What a Difference a Region Makes*, Hong Kong: Hong Kong University Press.

Billig, M. (1995) *Banal Nationalism*, London: Sage.

Chen, K. (2005) "Asia as Method," *Taiwan: A Radical Quarterly in Social Studies*, 57: 139–218 (in Chinese with English abstract).

——(2010) *Asia as Method: Toward Deimperialization*, Durham: Duke University Press.

Cho, H.-J. (2005) "Reading the 'Korean Wave' as a Sign of Global Shift," *Korea Journal*, 45(4): 147–82.

Cho, Y. (2011) "Desperately Seeking East Asia amidst the Popularity of South Korean Pop Culture in Asia," *Cultural Studies*, 25(3): 383–404.

Chua, B. (2010) "Engendering an East Asia Pop Culture Research Community," *Inter-Asia Cultural Studies*, 11(2): 202–6.

——(2011) "Conceptualization and Inter-referencing," paper presented at ELLAK (English Language and Literature Association of Korea) International Conference, December 18, Onyang, Korea.

Chua, B. and Iwabuchi, K. (eds) (2008) *East Asian Pop Culture: Analyzing the Korean Wave*, Hong Kong: Hong Kong University Press.

Curran, J. and Park, M. (eds) (2000) *De-Westernizing Media Studies*, London: Routledge.

Curtin, M. (2007) *Playing to the World's Biggest Audience: The Globalization of Chinese Film and TV*, Berkeley: University of California Press.

Erni, J. and Chua, S. (eds) (2005) *Asian Media Studies*, Oxford: Blackwell.

Hannerz, U. (1996) *Transnational Connections: Culture, People, Places*, London: Routledge.

Iwabuchi, K. (2002) *Recentering Globalization: Popular Culture and Japanese Transnationalism*, Durham: Duke University Press.

——(2004) *Feeling Asian Modernities: Transnational Consumption of Japanese TV Dramas*, Hong Kong: Hong Kong University Press.

——(2005) "Multinationalizing the Multicultural: The Commodification of 'Ordinary Foreigners' in a Japanese TV Talk Show," *Japanese Studies*, 25(2): 103–18.

——(2008) "When Korean Wave Meets Resident Koreans in Japan," in B. Chua and K. Iwabuchi (eds) *East Asian Pop Culture: Analyzing the Korean Wave*, Hong Kong: Hong Kong University Press.

——(2010) "De-Westernization and the Governance of Global Cultural Connectivity: A Dialogic Approach to East Asian Media Cultures," *Postcolonial Studies*, 13(4): 403–19.

——(2012) "Uses of Media Culture, Usefulness of Media Culture Studies: Beyond Brand Nationalism, Into Public Dialogue," in M. Morris and M. Hjort (eds) *Creativity and Academic Activism*, Hong Kong: Hong Kong University Press.

Jin, D. and Lee, D. (2007) "The Birth of East Asia: Cultural Regionalization Through Coproduction Strategies," paper presented at the annual meeting of the International Communication Association, San Francisco, May 23.

Jung, S. (2011) *Korean Masculinities and Transcultural Consumption*. Hong Kong: Hong Kong University Press.

Kim, Y. (ed.) (2008) *Media Consumption and Everyday Life in Asia*, New York: Routledge.

Kwok, J., Khoo, T. and Ling, C. (2004) "Chinese Voices: Tseen Khoo, Jen Tsen Kwok and Chek Ling Reflect on the Political Culture of the Asian-Australian Community," *Meanjin*, 63(2): 149–60.

Le, L. X. (2009) *Imaginaries of the Asian Modern Text and Context at the Juncture of Nation and Region*. A M.A. thesis submitted to the Program in Comparative Media Studies for the Degree of Masters of Science in Comparative Media Studies, Massachusetts Institute of Technology.

Liscutin, N. (2009) "Surfing the Neo-Nationalist Wave: A Case Study of Manga Kenkan-ryu," in C. Berry, J. Mackintosh and N. Liscutin (eds) *Cultural Studies and Cultural Industries in Northeast Asia: What a Difference a Region Makes*, Hong Kong: Hong Kong University Press.

Ryoo, W. (2009) "Globalization, or the Logic of Cultural Hybridization: The Case of the Korean Wave," *Asian Journal of Communication*, 19(2): 137–51.

Shim, D. (2006) "Hybridity and the Rise of Korean Popular Culture in Asia," *Media, Culture & Society*, 28(1): 25–44.

Shome, R. (2009) "Post-colonial Reflections on the 'Internationalization' of Cultural Studies," *Cultural Studies*, 23(5–6): 694–719.

Silverstone, R. (2006) "Media and Communication in a Globalized World," in C. Barnette, J. Robinson and G. Rose (eds) *A Demanding World*, Milton Keynes: Open University Press.

Spivak, G. (2008) *Other Asias*, Oxford: Blackwell.

Takeuchi, Y. (2005) "Asia as Method," in R. Calichman (ed. and trans.) *What Is Modernity? Writings of Takeuchi Yoshimi*, New York: Columbia University Press.

Thussu, D. (ed.) (2009) *Internationalizing Media Studies*, London: Routledge.

Tobin, J. (ed.) (2004) *Pikachu's Global Adventure: The Rise and Fall of Pokémon*, Durham: Duke University Press.

Urry, J. (2003) *Global Complexity*, Cambridge: Polity.

Zhao, Y. (2008) *Communication in China: Political Economy, Power, and Conflict*, Lanham: Rowman & Littlefield.

Chapter 3

Reconfiguring media and empire

Oliver Boyd-Barrett

Writing his classic *The Media are American* close to 40 years ago, Jeremy Tunstall (1977) modified the thrust of his own argument by drawing attention to the importance of regional centers of media production. When he revisited his argument in 2007 with *The Media were American* it appeared as though the profusion of both national and regional centers of production throughout the world had significantly eclipsed older traces of empire. The Korean Wave is a good example of precisely the phenomenon that led the later Tunstall to reverse his argument: the development of a robust national economy, with strong local media production activity across most of the old and some of the "new" media forms, together with substantial export activity to other areas of East Asia and beyond.

My purpose in this chapter is not to examine the Korean Wave in detail, since that is the principal contribution of other authors to this volume, but rather to challenge the basic premise of those who wish to leverage the example of the Korean Wave as primary evidence against media imperialism theory. I shall argue that this line of attack is mistaken, first of all because it is ahistorical. It asks us to ascribe particular significance to present trends at the expense of the past even though what has occurred in the past may be fundamental to our understanding of the present. It also has a narrow conception of media imperialism, in the first instance because it tends to focus principally on the phenomenon of U.S. media imperialism, as though other forms of media imperialism, whether past (stretching back to ancient civilizations) or present – including that of South Korea itself – are unimportant. It is also narrow because it tends to focus, as did the approach of Jeremy Tunstall, on media economics and, in particular, on international trade in media products rather than focusing on aspects of corporate concentration within and control over media markets and their interrelationships with the agendas of political, corporate and other elites, local and global. We can say this is narrow because among other considerations it would invite the conclusion that so long as a media market is not controlled by foreign media then no media imperialism has taken place. I will argue that such a view unreasonably ascribes to the nation-state the status of a fundamental building block in the development of media theory; it fails to take into account the always fluid and porous character of national and other forms of territorial boundary, especially when considered in relation to the twin pressures of globalization and digitization. This view is also complacent in the face of domestic corporate imperialism within national or domestic markets. From here we can proceed to the third major limitation of the argument of those (as in the works of John Sinclair and Stuart Cunningham) who would point to phenomena similar to those of the Korean Wave as undermining classic media imperialism theory. This has to do with the greatly varying levels of power and the hierarchical relations between nation-states. To make sense of global media activity, I argue, one has to look at the broader context of international relations with reference to which our understanding of the nature and significance of nation-states, whether as single entities or in clusters, may be interpreted in terms of the extent to which they owe allegiance to or are allied with any given superpower (whether there be one, two or more of these at any given point in time) or with any given power or power-alliance within a geopolitical or geo-cultural zone of influence. This in turn leads to my fourth and perhaps overriding critique of a tendency to use the Korean Wave as a counter-argument to media imperialism theory. Those who are determined to celebrate a world of media pluralism tend to avoid sustained attention to political coverage and other forms of media representation of the events that, within any given era, are open to interpretation as imperialism, neo-imperialism or neoliberal imperialism. If it is to mean anything, the expression "media imperialism" and its derivatives has to embrace phenomena of media support for, antagonism to, or relationships with the acts or agents of imperialism and imperialistic aggression.

While never disappearing from the research literature, the media imperialism tradition fell out of favor among those who criticized it for being either over-simplistic or out of date (e.g. Straubhaar 1991). The actual phenomenon of media imperialism, on the other hand, has never disappeared or stopped being important. I shall propose that the tradition is sustainable, has evolved, and has never been more relevant than in the current, so-called digital age. It is central to considerations of media and power, and although questions of power do not by any means exhaust the questions we may have about the media, there is a critical urgency for issues of power to be returned to center place in the field. In outlining my reasons for the reinstallation of a concern for media imperialism, I prefer the term "media" to "cultural" imperialism. Although there are clearly many important and dialectical interrelationships between media and culture, I use the idea of "media imperialism" to focus attention on the political economy of the communications industries which is where I believe the analysis of media and power should begin.

Some critics of the early media imperialism thesis have misunderstood it. Both critics of the theory and even some of those who align themselves with it have obsessed about manifest media content. This is usually not in any sophisticated way that might provide a platform for dissection of such things as ideology, confluence with state foreign policies, corporate interest or things of that sort. Rather, content tends to be judged by such considerations as whether or to what extent it is locally produced or imported and its generic status, usually in the context of fears of cultural homogenization. This is to the exclusion of other vitally important variables including transnational transfers of media-related capital, ownership, advertising, expertise, technology, patents, formats and royalties. Some of the original models of media imperialism (e.g. Schiller 1969; Boyd-Barrett 1977) actually did specifically emphasize components of media imperialism that went beyond manifest content. Many scholars (e.g. McChesney and Schiller 2003; Boyd-Barrett 2006) argue the need to broaden our understanding of what constitutes media in the era of technology convergence by embracing not just traditional and "new" media, but also consumer electronics, telephony and computing industries. These media are important both in and of themselves but also because, increasingly, electronic access to "old media" forms is determined by electronic hardware gatekeepers that include cable, satellite and telephony, wired or cellular wireless, and electronic software gatekeepers that include operating systems, Internet service providers, browsers and applications.

Misleadingly, some critics have conflated ideas of media imperialism with the historically specific, still enduring but inevitably finite phenomenon of U.S. global hegemony (notice of whose death, nonetheless, has been much exaggerated). Again, some of the earlier literature (e.g. Boyd-Barrett 1977 and 1982; Tunstall 1977) specifically identified different and competing centers of media production, insisting that media imperialism is exercised by media, corporate and political powers of many different nation-states, not only the biggest, across different time-periods. More recent literature (e.g. Boyd-Barrett 1998b) argues that media imperialism should be understood not only as a transnational but also as an intra-national phenomenon. This extension is supported by a voluminous literature on media concentration and conglomeration at local, national, regional and transnational levels, involving as it does the commandeering of available communications space by small numbers of giant, highly commercialized, media conglomerates (e.g. Arsenault and Castells 2008; Noam 2009). In the context of reorienting the tradition away from earlier presumptions as to who were the proactive forces of media imperialism, recent research (Thussu 2008; Curtin and Shah 2010) focuses on the formation of strong production and export activity from the countries of China and India, some of it commercial, some of it in the form of state-subsidized "soft power" initiatives (for example in the case of China's Xinhua, and CNC World). Other categories include (a) lesser centers of media production as in Beirut, Cairo, Caracas, Dubai, Qatar, São Paulo, that achieve either or both regional (e.g. Telesur) and global reach (e.g. Al Jazeera), (b) centers for the manufacture of pan-Asian or pan-Chinese media product (Seoul for the Korean Wave television dramas and movies widely exported throughout East and Southeast Asia; Hong Kong for informational and entertainment television and movies widely exported throughout Asia; as well as mainland Chinese centers in Beijing and Shanghai for China and the Chinese diaspora) and (c) niche centers of production (e.g. Lagos for video dramas – "Nollywood" – distributed throughout continental Africa and its diaspora; Brazil and Mexico for telenovelas, distributed throughout the world; Moscow for print and broadcast media distributed throughout the former Soviet Union).

In considering newer models of imperialism, finally, we need to take into account that alongside the position of globally or regionally hegemonic or merely locally influential nation-states is the still evolving formation under U.S. leadership of a neoliberal world economic order (NLWEO or the "Empire" – I find Hardt and Negri's 2001 formulation helpful here) that we may think of as a form of pure capitalistic, corporate-driven network of interests (not free of internal conflict), more intensely present in and reflective of some territories, groups and cultures than others, closely allied to plutocracies almost everywhere, and working in uneven partnership with nation-states (and the global regulatory organizations through which these negotiate) some of which we may consider to have been entirely co-opted by the NLWEO. While "Empire" does indeed appear and has become to some extent supra-territorial it has been engineered in significant measure by the aggressive, missionary embrace of Chicago School ("Friedmanesque" or "monetarist") economics of both the Reagan (U.S.) and the Thatcher (Britain) regimes of the 1980s (see Klein 2008). Recent manifestations of the evolution of the NLWEO, involving the unfettered opening up to international capital of national markets hitherto principally manipulated or shuttered for the benefit of local plutocracies, ethnic groups or military, include the U.S. invasions and occupations of Afghanistan and Iraq, the consequent destabilization of Pakistan and adjacent areas of Central Asia and, 2010–12, the so-called "Arab Spring," involving Tunisia, Egypt, Libya and Syria, and the constant stream over several decades of Western invective against Iran (for chronicles of post-World War 2 US imperialism see Blum 2008; Gonzalez 2001; Johnson 2004; Kinzer 2007). These considerations call for a reaffirmation of the relationship between media imperialism and the broader historical process of imperialism as a form of subordination of smaller or weaker nations to the will of larger or stronger nations (Boyd-Barrett, Herrera and Bauman 2010).

Media, information and communications industries interrelate with the NLWEO and processes of globalization in a variety of important ways: (1) they provide the enabling physical infrastructure for global communications (e.g. overland and undersea cables, satellites and satellite delivery systems, and wireless stations for wired and wireless communication, including Internet and telephony); (2) media and communication hardware and software industries are themselves significant domains for international capital accumulation, generally in the form of large multi-media conglomerates operating internationally, and as such are full-blooded corporate members of the NLWEO; (3) they provide vehicles for the advertising of goods and services produced by

62 Oliver Boyd-Barrett

member states and corporations of this order, most of whom are signatories to the World Trade Organization; (4) through their content and the representations of lifestyles in their content, they trigger a "demonstration" effect that stimulates continuing demand for goods and services and that is generally positive for consumerism; (5) many of these media (including Bloomberg, Dow Jones – now owned by News Corporation – and Thomson Reuters) also service the global financial and commercial order through the provision of an economic informational infrastructure, one that is increasingly essential to the operation of modern capitalism, that comprises sophisticated, interactive instruments for the interrogation of massive financial, commercial and corporate databases; in some instances such media also provide electronic marketplaces for trading activity; (6) media also police the ideological boundaries of tolerable expression at national and international levels – promoting content that increasingly serves the interests of neoliberalism (mainly having to do with the progressive abolition of national restrictions on trade in goods and services), marginalizing, suppressing or excluding content that does not and (7) these industries provide critical support to the development of the "surveillance society" or, in other words, to the centralized collection of more and more detailed, instantly accessible intelligence (to those few who control or pay for it), to a degree unparalleled in human history and in a manner that is also increasingly and literally "weaponized," in the form of drone and other forms of robotic warfare.

Despite significant historical change since the 1960s and 1970s, classic examples of unidirectional, power-inflected media imperialism persisted into the 2000s and have in some respects been accentuated, in parallel with evidence of considerable concentration of domestic media industries in most if not all countries. In the business of wholesale global news-gathering and distribution, for example, media around the world continue to be highly dependent on a small number of enterprises for general, video and financial news. The market in all three of these areas is strongly dominated by Associated Press and its video news subsidiary APTN; and Thomson Reuters and its television subsidiary Reuters Television. With the notable exception of Agence France Presse (and its video subsidiary AFPTV), based in Paris, the bedrock of international news reporting by the news agencies is principally headquartered in North America (Associated Press, Bloomberg, News Corporation – which owns Dow Jones news wires and the Wall Street Journal – and Thomson Reuters), seconded by London which is home to the major video newsrooms of APTN and Thomson Reuters (Boyd-Barrett 2010). CNN, as a wholesaler and retailer for television and online news, generally frames international news in ways that are friendly to the U.S. (Thussu 2008; Boyd-Barrett and Thussu forthcoming). While the British BBC World enjoys a reputation for more comprehensive and critical coverage than CNN and its international arm CNNI (CNN International), its coverage is invariably framed within default perspectives that represent Western interests and Western foreign policies as benign. Even Al Jazeera (often celebrated or derided for providing a perspective on the world that privileges the Middle East and Islamic worlds) is directly linked with the interests of one (small) state, Qatar, a monarchical form of "progressive authoritarianism" whose foreign policies appear increasingly to be aligned with those of the U.S. and its allies in ways that arguably have impacted its news coverage (Boyd-Barrett and Boyd-Barrett 2010). Many other international television news operations such as those of China, Russia, Germany or France, for example, may be considered classic examples of state-supported "soft power" initiatives.

In terms of revenues the international movie industry continues to be dominated by the six principal studios of Hollywood and the multinational conglomerates that own them (News Corporation's Twentieth Century Fox, Viacom's Paramount, Sony's Sony Pictures, GE and Comcast's NBC/Universal, Walt Disney, Time Warner's Warner Bros), even as other centers of global production such as Mumbai (Bollywood) in India, and Lagos (Nollywood) make more movies and even reach larger audiences. Almost 40% of revenue for global movie production and distribution (worth $86.7 billion in 2012) is generated from North American audiences, followed by Europe with 23.5% (IbisWorld 2012). While MPAA studios and studio subsidiaries accounted for a modest number, 141, of films released in 2011, most filmmakers need to work with these giants for assistance in finance and/or distribution. Of the top 25 films in terms of 2011 box office, 24 came from the big six studios. In the U.S./Canada, where 607 movies were rated by the Classification and Ratings Administration (CARA) for release in theaters in 2011 (758 were rated altogether, including non-theatrical movies), this market accounted for approximately one-third ($10.2 billion) of the global box office ($32.6 billion), consuming U.S. product primarily, many billions ahead of the next largest national markets, Japan ($2.3 billion), China ($2 billion) and France ($2 billion), and a few decimal points behind the whole of Europe, Middle East and Africa ($10.8 billion) and ahead of the whole of the Asia/Pacific region ($9 billion) (MPAA 2012).

The international music recording industry is dominated by three players: Sony BMG, Time Warner's Warner Music Group and Vivendi's Universal Music Group (a fourth player, EMI, was sold off to Sony and UMG in 2011). The U.S. is the top national market, accounting for $4.37 billion in 2011, ahead of Japan ($4.09 billion) and Germany ($1.47 billion) (International Federation of the Phonographic Industry, IFPI 2012). Despite significant growth of their respective industries in India and particularly China, global computing hardware industries continue to be dominated by U.S.-based corporations such as AMD, Apple, Cisco, Dell, Hewlett-Packard, IBM, Intel and Oracle – which now owns Sun Microsystems and Java – and U.S.-based corporations remain exceptionally strong in computer software and Internet services (including Amazon, eBay – which owns PayPal, Facebook, Google, Microsoft, Twitter), nurtured as many of these are by the concentration of talent and capital in San Jose's Silicon valley, California (Boyd-Barrett 2006). Apple's 2012 $155 billion annual revenues and Microsoft's $74 billion place these two companies alone close to the pinnacle of media capital generators worldwide (compare with Samsung which in 2011 earned $143bn; AT&T's $127bn in 2012; Sony's $78bn in 2012; China Telecom's $50bn in 2011; Comcast's $55bn in 2011; Disney's $43bn in 2012; NewsCorp's $33bn in 2012). Top Internet Service Providers (ISPs) globally are U.S. corporations Comcast Cable (7.15%), Road Runner (4.58%), AT+T (2.5%) and Verizon FiOS (2.15%). Global desktop browser markets are dominated by Microsoft's Internet Explorer (55% of the market in 2012), Mozilla's Firefox – affiliated with Time Warner's Netscape (21%), Google's Chrome (17%) and Apple's Safari (5%) (Netmarketshare 2012).

Microsoft has long enjoyed over 90% control of the global desktop operating system market for PCs (91.5% in 2012), followed by Apple Mac (7.3%) and Linux (1.25%) (Netmarketshare 2012). In the mobile/tablet market, dominant operating systems are Apple's iOS with 61%, followed by Google's Android (28%) and Oracle's Java ME (7%). Google has a global share of over 84% of the desktop search engine market, followed by Yahoo (8%) and Microsoft's Bing (5%). Google's lead is even stronger in the mobile/tablet search engine market at 91%, followed by Yahoo (6%) and Bing (2%). In the more diverse world of mobile telephony market share, Finland's Nokia, South Korea's Samsung and LG Electronics, and Apple dominated in 2012, and similarly in smart phone manufacture where the dominant names were Nokia, Apple, RIM (Canadian) and HTC (Taiwanese). Of the top 10 global mobile operators, 5 were Asian and 4 were U.S./West European. But the mobile phone operating systems were dominated by Android (72%), Apple (14%) and Nokia's Symbian (3%) (mobithinking.com, 2013).

In a single illustration of the enormous field to which media imperialism is addressed and which so many critics and supporters have managed to miss, Millien (2010) notes that due "to the lack of legal reporting requirements in the United States (and in most other countries), there are currently no reliable national or international figures that can adequately report the size of the IP marketplace," but reports International Monetary Fund (IMF) statistics showing that the global intellectual property marketplace was worth U.S. $173.4 billion in 2009 and, in the U.S., $84.4 billion – nearly half of the global total. Millien also refers to an October 22, 2005 *Economist* article entitled "A Market for Ideas," which stated that: "In America alone, technology licensing revenue accounts for an estimated $45 billion annually; worldwide, the figure is around $100 billion and growing fast." Millien quotes Ocean Tomo (2010) estimates that in 2009, nearly 81% of the value of the companies comprising the S&p 500® stock index came from intangible assets – the largest component of which was IP.

But this is far from being the whole story. In a reminder of the importance of looking beyond annual trading activity (or income) to accumulated value (wealth), IMF figures suggest that the overall value of U.S. intellectual property in 2005 was $5.5 trillion, more than the nominal gross domestic product of any other country, and that intellectual property trade accounted for 60% of U.S. exports (totaling $900 billion in 2007) in a country whose GDP was approaching $14 trillion. This compares quite comfortably to the total value of global trade in information and communication technology (ICT) of $4 trillion in 2008 (Slater 2011). The total U.S. revenue for publishing, film and sound recording, telecommunications and Internet industries in 2009 was a little over one trillion. Of this, telecommunications accounted for almost half ($494 billion); publishing accounted for a quarter ($264 billion), Internet service, web services and data processing for less than a tenth ($103 billion), broadcasting for about the same ($99 billion) and motion pictures and sound recording a little less ($91 billion), with the remainder accounted for by the categories of Internet publishing and broadcasting ($20 billion) and "other" ($7 billion) (U.S. Census Bureau, Statistical Abstract of the United States 2012: 710).

The National Science Board (2012) calculates that global value-added by ICT industries (semiconductors, communications equipment, computers, communications, computer programming and data processing) more than doubled from $1.2 trillion in 1995 to $2.8 trillion in 2010 and today the ICT industry accounts for 6% of global GDP. Of total GDP the U.S. alone accounted for 26%. Asia – as a whole, including Japan, China and the "Asia 8" – accounted for 33%, and Europe 22%. From the same source we find that the United States has the highest ICT share of fixed capital investment (26%) of large OECD economies, with the United Kingdom a close second. The United States is the leader in ICT business infrastructure among the larger developed economies with an index score substantially higher than those of France, Germany, the United Kingdom, Japan and South Korea. All of this falls within the broader context of what the same source describes as "knowledge and technology-intensive" industries (KTI) whose global value added totaled $18.2 trillion in 2010, representing 30% of estimated world gross domestic product (GDP).

Even were it sensible to claim that media imperialism theory was mainly about television content and its consumption, which of course it is not, then in the 1960s and 1970s it was certainly correct to point to the dominance of the U.S. as a source for television imports throughout many countries of the world, and to the impact of such imports on prime-time programming (Nordenstreng and Varis 1974). The significance was all the greater in as much as viewers in many countries had only one or two sources of television supply (also keeping in mind that in many of these countries, especially in the developing world, radio was the most consumed medium). In the succeeding 40 years or so a great deal had changed: considerably more television outlets; much higher consumption of television; production technology costs have fallen; considerable increase in local productions – which are preferred by

66 Oliver Boyd-Barrett

consumers, other things being equal, particularly in primetime hours. So a simple argument of U.S.-based media imperialism founded on a criterion of the proportion of local programming imported from the United States for prime time viewing no longer has much meaning for most countries. It is still quite high when all viewing of motion picture entertainment is factored in, regardless of source, whether terrestrial television, satellite or cable, recorded programming, computer or mobile downloaded. We may also wonder about the significance of the fact that the U.S., which continues to export so much, imports relatively little. And we should note that of total revenues represented by the global television market (from advertising, subscription and public funding), North America had the largest share in 2009, accounting for 39% of almost 270 billion euros, followed by Europe (31%), Asia Pacific (21%), Latin America (8%), Africa and the Middle East (2%) (International Television Expert Group 2010).

Contrary to conventional thinking we can protest that there has been a considerable intensification of U.S.-based media imperialism. In most countries, including countries that either were Communist (e.g. Former Soviet Union) and countries that still are Communist (including China, but not, in this context, North Korea or Cuba) together with countries, like Britain or France, that we may describe as social democracies – where mainstream television was either highly propagandized or guided by state-regulated and sometimes state-governed principles of public service broadcasting – there has been a rapid proliferation of television outlets, most of them advertising-driven or, increasingly, driven by subscription revenue for multi-channel cable or satellite delivery (expected by ITVE 2010 to exceed television advertising worldwide by 2013), and intense commercialization, impacting even those channels that are still ostensibly governed by a logic of public service yet must demonstrate ability to compete for large audiences so as to justify the state subsidies or state-sanctioned license fees on which they depend. What this amounts to, in effect, is the global extension of a model of broadcast regulation that was developed in the United States and ratified by Congressional legislation in the 1930s, and whose primary characteristic was the free distribution of publicly owned airwaves to the capitalist enterprises that could best show means and intent to exploit them for profit through the sale of advertising. By common consent this model has tended to produce cheap television that is entertainment driven or, when dealing with news and real world events, seeks to entertain more than inform (infotainment). It is formulaic, undemanding, repetitive and easily manipulated for state and capital propaganda. Its primary purpose was and continues to be to capture audience attention for as long as possible and, in effect, to sell that attention to advertisers. Its contents have long been dominated by themes of sex, celebrity, sport and violence, infused with values favorable to corporate capitalism, consumption and individualism, while being strikingly under-representative and/or misrepresentative of large groups of the population – particularly the working class – exhibiting behaviors, attitudes and values prejudicial to women, racial minorities, gays and lesbians.

The global extension of this model, therefore, is hardly a matter of mere academic interest. Broadcasting has been the single most important source of popular information throughout most of this period, yet the substance and quality of that information in terms of its suitability as a basis for considered action – as would be required in a properly functioning democracy – is abysmal by almost any standard. By 2010 the subscription-driven paid television market, primarily cable and satellite, had begun to level with that of the advertising-based market. But this too was a form of television that originated mainly from the United States and was driven by U.S. telecommunications and television industry interests, including big corporate names such as AT&T, Comcast and Time Warner.

Critics of media imperialism routinely take earlier proponents of media imperialism to task for their apparently simplistic fears of a monolithic U.S. dominance of television worldwide. Yet that is precisely what has happened, even if not in the expected form of television products imported from the U.S. – although by far the strongest leaders of television program format sales worldwide are the UK and U.S., followed some way behind by the Netherlands (ITVE 2010). Much more significant is global adoption of an approach to television that was invented by U.S. media corporations and that in many countries looks rather like U.S. television – soap operas, celebrity features, reality shows, game shows, U.S. news formatting, heavy presence of advertised global brands and so on.

We should not overlook how, since it began, global space and time have contracted, largely because of U.S. and Western-dominated systems of communications hardware and software, and that the officially enshrined values of the largest economies of the world (principally the U.S., followed by Europe, former Soviet Union, India, China, Brazil, Indonesia) look every day more similar, and more compatible with the philosophy of neoliberalism, long advocated by U.S. elites: a philosophy of the "free" market executed through unregulated monopolistic or oligopolistic capitalist production and exchange, consumerism and individualism. It is not that these values make any sense on even the most fundamental of criteria – sustainability. On the contrary, it is increasingly evident that with ever accelerating speed they are destroying the planet through global warming, exhaustion and pollution of world resources including its earth, forests, rivers and oceans, and the annihilation of a substantial proportion of all living species. We need pay little heed to the hypocrisy with which these values are celebrated by capitalists who prefer monopoly and oligopoly to competition, whose own scandals, criminality and incompetence (as in the crisis of the global financial and banking system that erupted in 2008 and continued unabated, or even intensified, into 2012) are assuaged by the egregious state generosity of a system of socialism-for-the-rich that they control, who preach free capital flow yet resist freedom of

68 Oliver Boyd-Barrett

international movement for labor, who apply intense pressure on smaller nations to open up their markets while protecting their own domestic producers in agriculture and other favored domains. What is most important and significant here is that every day more, the lords of the major economies of the world, who dance to the music of "freedom" while subjecting their populations to more and more surveillance and control, converge upon an ideology of the "free" market while indulging their same gross hypocrisies in practice.

Some critics of media imperialism seem oblivious to the original connections – identified by Innis (1950), McLuhan (1967), Schiller (1969), Boyd-Barrett (1998b), Thussu (2006) – between the rise of new media forms and the emergence, shaping and consolidation of empires. Schiller (1969) was among the first to integrate the analysis of media hardware (including satellite) and software (both infotainment content and advertising) with the various economic and political needs of the United States for industrial growth at home, penetration of foreign markets and consolidation of superpower status. Many scholars have continued to explore these connections in the context of convergence between media representations of the world and the foreign policies of their respective home governments. Others have looked at global media such as the international news agencies or international 24-hour television news channels, or national media that also enjoy considerable international following, where these are found to serve as conduits of propaganda on behalf of their home governments specifically or of a generalized neoliberal commercial, corporate and financial world order. Theories of agenda-setting (Weaver, McCombs and Shaw 1997), framing (Entman 2003), indexing (Bennett, Regina, Lawrence and Livingsone 2008) and of the "propaganda model" (Herman and Chomsky 2002) significantly converge in their relevance here. When dealing with many international events over the past decade or so, from the disintegration of the former Soviet Union and subsequent wars of secession (e.g. Chechnya), the disintegration of Yugoslavia and the emergence of new states such as Croatia, Serbia and Kosovo, through to 9/11 and its immediate segue to the American and allied invasion and occupation of Afghanistan in 2001 (in its twelfth year, as I write), various stripes of U.S.-supported (or incited?) "orange revolutions" in the former Soviet Union and Central Asia, the struggle between Russia and the U.S. over Georgia and South Ossetia in 2008, the American and allied invasion and occupation of Iraq in 2003 (in its tenth year as I write, despite an equivocal US "withdrawal"), Western destabilization strategies in Bolivia (ongoing), Congo (ongoing), Mali (ongoing), Haiti (2004), Honduras (2009) and Venezuela (ongoing) as well as in various manifestations or episodes of the "Arab Spring" of 2011 – most egregiously in Libya 2011 and Syria 2012 – or the persistent U.S. and Israeli propaganda war against Iran, media scholars are confronted with the challenge of unpicking the ways in which mainstream and alternative media, across all modes or platforms, "frame" stories to align with particular interests. Much of this activity justifiably falls within the context of discourses of imperialism, especially in countries or regions, as in Central and South America, Iraq, Iran, Libya, North Africa, Pakistan or Palestine, that have long been subject to the depredations, intimidations and manipulations of hegemonic power and imperial ambition.

Even as some scholars working in the areas of international and intercultural communication and related fields articulated their differences from more traditional models of media and cultural imperialism, they directly or indirectly contributed to the evolution and sophistication of the very same models they attempted to discard. While several scholars have concentrated on ways of thinking about cross-cultural media flows that do not seem so much dependent on relations of power – to include, for example, variables of geographical, cultural and linguistic proximity and cultural discount (see Sinclair, Jacka and Cunningham 1996) – ultimately these confirm the vitality of regional and local centers of media influence yet without undermining the continued exertion of media influence on local or regional centers from imperial or ex-imperial powers – indeed, South Korea, which largely owes its foundation and maintenance to the U.S., is a case in point. Relating to Castells' (2000) proposition of a new world order that is definable in terms of networks, Straubhaar's (2007) research has contributed helpful sophistication to our understanding of media flows, acknowledging the co-existence of several different kinds of flow, including the classic unidirectional flows from more powerful to less powerful countries.

The passion for social justice that inspired the original theories of media and cultural imperialism has been enveloped by a newer generation of critical postcolonial assessment of so-called processes of globalization. Some contributions deepen our appreciation of ideas of culture in relation, particularly, to formal ideologies of the nation-state, ethnicity and identity (Appadurai 1992); they have helped expose the complexity of relations between the global, national and local (sometimes prematurely understating or even "disappearing" the nation state – see Sparks 2007) and through the use of concepts such as glocalization (Robertson 1992) and inter-localization (Szalvai 2008) they demonstrate both the fluidity of cultural change in interaction with media flows and the hybrid character of products, flows, audiences and individual identities. Recent literature on ideas of hybridity (e.g. Kraidy 2005; Chan and Fung 2011) advises against losing sight of the power relations that structure hybrid formations. Certain interests have greater influence than others over how, where, by whom, with what capital and other resources products will be made, whose "cultures" precisely will be represented and how far these representations map onto known cultural formations that exist outside of media space.

Conclusion

My basic intention in this chapter has been to urge that studies of the Korean Wave, as of comparable phenomena elsewhere, take full account of historical,

70 Oliver Boyd-Barrett

cultural and intellectual context. A fully contextualized approach, therefore, will foreground the complex relations of interdependency between South Korea and the United States. It will move beyond a binary dialectic between local Asian media production and Western media imperialism towards a more complex analysis of relations between media (hardware, software, infrastructure) industries and the establishment, maintenance and decline of hierarchical relations among nations and between nations and other power formations. Even in the case of complex hybrid formations it will preserve an unflinching focus on the play of power.

The globe is confronted with an interrelated array of crises that are of staggering significance, including: climate change; environmental degradation and pollution of air, land and water; massive loss of species on land and in water; seemingly uncontrollable corporate and financier greed; worsening inequalities between the 1% and the rest; corporatization of supposedly democratic systems; aggressive neocolonial wars in Afghanistan, the Congo, Iraq, Iran, Libya, Syria and elsewhere. Singly and collectively these crises invoke the need for a much more comprehensive understanding of "imperialism" in its contemporary manifestations, and of the role of media at the service of empires and "Empire."

References

Appadurai, A. (1992) *Modernity at Large: Cultural Dimension of Globalization*, Minneapolis: University of Minnesota Press.

Arsenault, A. and Castells, M. (2008) "The Structure and Dynamics of Global Multi-media Business Networks," *International Journal of Communication*, 2: 707–48.

Bennett, L., Regina, G., Lawrence, R. and Livingstone, S. (2008) *When the Press Fails: Political Power and the News Media from Iraq to Katrina*, Chicago: University of Chicago Press.

Blum, W. (2008) *Killing Hope: U.S. Military and C.I.A. Interventions since World War II*, Monroe: Common Courage Press.

Boyd-Barrett, C. and Boyd-Barrett, O. (2010) "24/7 News as Counter-hegemonic Soft Power in Latin America," in S. Cushion and J. Lewis (eds) *The Rise of 24-Hour News Television*, New York: Peter Lang.

Boyd-Barrett, O. (1977) "Media Imperialism: Towards an International Framework for the Analysis of Media Systems," in M. Gurevitch, J. Curran and J. Woollacott (eds) *Mass Communication and Society*, London: Arnold.

——(1982) "Cultural Dependence and Mass Media," in M. Gurevitch, J. Curran and J. Woollacott (eds) *Culture, Society and the Media*, London: Macmillan.

——(1998a) "The Globalization of News," in O. Boyd-Barrett and T. Rantanen (eds) *The Globalization of News*, London: Sage.

——(1998b) "Media Imperialism Reformulated," in D.K.Thussu (ed.) *Electronic Empires*, London: Arnold.

——(2006) "Cyberspace, Globalization and Empire," *Global Media and Communication*, 2 (1): 21–42.

——(2010) *News Agencies in the Turbulent Era of the Internet*, Barcelona: Generalitat de Catalunya: Col-leccio Lexikon.

Boyd-Barrett, O., Herrera, D. and Bauman, J. (2010) *Hollywood and the CIA*, London: Routledge.

Boyd-Barrett, O. and Thussu, D. (forthcoming) *Media Imperialism*, London: Sage.

Castells, M. (2000) *The Rise of the Network Society*, New York: Wiley-Blackwell.

Chan, J. and Fung, A. (2011) "Structural Hybridization in Film and Television Production," *Visual Anthropology*, 24 (January–April): 1–2.

Curtin, M. and Shah, H. (2010) *Reorienting Global Communication: Indian and Chinese Media beyond Borders*, Chicago: University of Illinois Press.

Entman, R. (2003) *Projections of Power: Framing News, Public Opinion, and U.S. Foreign Policy*, Chicago: University of Chicago Press.

Gonzalez, J. (2001) *Harvest of Empire: A History of Latinos in America*, New York: Penguin.

Hardt, M. and Negri, A. (2001) *Empire*, Boston: Harvard University Press.

Herman, E. and Chomsky, N. (2002) *Manufacturing Consent: The Political Economy of the Mass Media*, New York: Pantheon.

IbisWorld (2012) Industry Report Q Press8711-GL, *Global Movie Production and Distribution*, clients1.ibisworld.com

IFPI (2012) *Recording Industry in Numbers*, London: IFPI.

Innis, H. (2007, original 1950) *Empire and Communication*, Toronto: Dundurn Press.

International Television Expert Group (2010) *Global TV 2010 – Markets, Trends, Facts and Figures* (2008–13) http://www.international-television.org/tv_market_data/world-tv-market-2010.html, retrieved December 10, 2012.

ITVE (International Television Export Group) (2010) *Global TV 2010 – Markets, Trends, Facts & Figures (2008–2013)*, http://www.international-television.org/tv_market_data/world-tv-market-2010.html. Accessed August 28, 2013.

Johnson, C. (2004) *Blowback: The Costs and Consequences of American Empire*, New York: Holt Paperbacks.

Kinzer, S. (2007) *Overthrow: America's Century of Regime Change from Hawaii to Iraq*, New York: Times Books.

Klein, N. (2008) *Shock Doctrine*, New York: Picador.

Kraidy, M. (2005) *Hybridity: The Cultural Logic of Globalization*, Philadelphia: Temple University Press.

McChesney, R. and Schiller, D. (2003) *The Political Economy of International Communications: Foundations for the Emerging Global Debate about Media Ownership and Regulation*, Programme Area: Technology and Society, United Nations Research Institute for Social Development. Paper No. 11.

McLuhan, M. (1967) *The Medium is the Message: An Inventory of Effects* with Quentin Fiore, produced by Jerome Agel, 1st edn, Random House.

Millien, R. (2010, Dec. 16) "The US$173.4B Global Intellectual Property Marketplace?" http://dcipattorney.com/2010/12/the-us173–74b-global-intellectual-property-market place/ retrieved August 20, 2012.

MPAA (Motion Pictures Association of America) (2012) *Theatrical Market Statistics*, http://www.mpaa.org/Resources/3037b7a4-58a2-4109-8012-58fca3abdf1b.pdf. Accessed August 28, 2013.

Mobithinking (2013) Global mobile statistics. Mobithinking.com/mobile-marketing-tools/latest-mobile-stats/a#subscribers, retrieved May 17, 2013

National Science Board (2012) Science and Engineering Indicators 2012, Chapter 6: Industry, Technology, and the Global Marketplace, Washington, D.C.: National Science Board.

Netmarketshare (2012) *Market Share Statistics for Internet Technologies*, www.netmarketshare.com, retrieved Dec. 4, 2012.

72 Oliver Boyd-Barrett

Noam, E. (2009) *Media Ownership and Concentration in America*, New York: Oxford University Press.

Nordenstreng, K. and Varis, T. (1974) "Television Traffic – A One-way Street? A Survey and Analysis of the International Flow of Television Programme Material," *Reports and Papers on Mass Communication*, No. 70, Paris: UNESCO.

Ocean Tomo, LLC (2010) http://www.oceantomo.com/productsandservices/investments/intangible-market-value (last visited November 15, 2010).

Robertson, R. (1992) *Globalization: Social Theory and Global Culture*, London: Sage.

Schiller, H. (1992, original 1969) *Mass Communications and American Empire*. 2nd edition, Boulder: Westview Press.

Sinclair, J. (1999) *Latin American Television: A Global View*, New York: Oxford University Press.

Sinclair, J., Jacka, E. and Cunningham, S. (1996) *New Patterns in Global Television: Peripheral Vision*, New York: Oxford University Press.

Slater, G. (2011) *The Value of Expanding the Information Technology Agreement: An Industry Standpoint*, World Trade Organization. www.wto.org/english/tratop_e/inftec…/speaker 12slater.pdf, retrieved August 20, 2012

Sparks, C. (2007) *Globalization, Development and the Mass Media*, London: Sage.

Straubhaar, J. (1991) "Beyond Media Imperialism: Asymmetrical Interdependence and Cultural Proximity," *Critical Studies in Mass Communication*, 8: 39–59.

——(2007) *World Television: From Global to Local*, Thousand Oaks: Sage.

Szalvai, E. (2008) "Emerging Forms of Globalization Dialectics: Interlocalization as a New Praxis of Power and Culture in Commercial Media and Development Communication," doctoral thesis published on OhioLink, August 2008.

Thussu, D. (2006) *International Communication: A Textbook*, London: Sage.

——(2008) *News as Entertainment: Rise of Global Infotainment*, London: Sage.

Tunstall, J. (1977) *The Media are American*, London: Constable.

——(2007) *The Media were American: U.S. Mass Media in Decline*, New York: Oxford University Press.

U.S. Census Bureau (2012) *Statistical Abstract of the United States*. 2012.

US International Trade Commission (1999) *Recent Trends in US Services Trade*, 1999 Annual Report, Washington: US Government.

Weaver, D., McCombs, M. and Shaw, D. (1997) *Communication and Democracy: Exploring the Intellectual Frontiers in Agenda-setting Theory*, New York: Routledge.

Part II

Popular media and digital mobile culture

Chapter 4

Korean Wave pop culture in the global Internet age

Why popular? Why now?

Youna Kim

This chapter considers the Korean Wave pop culture in the global Internet age and addresses the socio-cultural and political implications in their complexity and paradox within the context of global inequalities and uneven power structures. Why popular? Why now? Specifically, it discusses five related arguments: (1) A-ha! emotion, (2) everyday reflexivity, (3) precarious individualization, (4) pop nationalism, (5) diasporic nationalism and the Internet, while questioning the general assumptions of cosmopolitanism in the seemingly interconnected digital era. This discussion is based on my ongoing ethnographic/media studies in global sites (2005, 2008, 2011, 2012), as well as my previous work concerning the Korean Wave (2007).

A-ha! Emotion: pop culture as a site of emotional talk

> Here I am just talking about TV (drama), but I come to know more about myself! Is this a psychotherapy session?
>
> (Korean middle-class woman in her 20s, quoted in Kim 2005)

Popular TV drama provides topical material for everyday talk and functions as an emotional, revelatory, self-reflexive and shared cultural resource, almost like a ritual social event – as demonstrated in my ethnographic research, *Women, Television and Everyday Life in Korea: Journeys of Hope* (2005). One of the key pleasures that women find in drama is the validation of their own kind of talk. This validation works well because drama tends to use the same forms of talk that women use among themselves in everyday language, and also because its discourse provides common knowledge of the characteristically female patterns of social interaction and interest – the personal, intimate, emotional and familial relationships. What is subtly implicated in women's talk about drama is the discursive power of everyday life and everyday practices. Talking is crucial to aspects of power and regulation. Korean TV drama evokes tremendous pleasure among both working-class and middle-class women, as its familiar and recognizable form meets the socio-psychological needs and desires of the women viewers struggling to make sense of human conditions in modern life.

Popular pleasure is first and foremost a pleasure of recognition that is deeply rooted in the women's everyday common sense and closely relevant to their everyday reality. Through deep engagement with the meaning of TV drama and its integration into the everyday, women viewers can find the means to understand their social roles, their relations to others and the possibilities for social action. I argue this viewing quality in terms of what I call "A-ha! Emotion," an emotional resolution and closure in the experience of the relevant and recognizable forms of popular culture. A-ha! emotion is a magical re-affirmation of the sense of rational order over the meanings of relational human conditions. Surprisingly triggering and stimulating thinking, A-ha! emotion becomes a point of immediate recognition of popular drama that is particularly relevant to women's lived experience.

There is a significant manifestation of interest in the way in which women viewers recall the details of episodes and dialogues of their favorite drama and further relate those details to their own life circumstances and experiences – generating an unintended methodological consequence, a therapy situation, or "a psychotherapy session," as one woman explicitly stated while discovering a fitting interpretation, A-ha! It usually happens that women's talk about the ritualized viewing of their favorite drama surprisingly digresses towards a reflexive articulation of their intimate personal lives – e.g. their life conditions, formerly private complaints and discontents – surprisingly reaching knowledge not prefigured in one's starting paradigm. I argue, here lies the potentiality of TV talk as a method to be considered for an understanding of women's everyday life. The banality of the most ritualized talk often takes place over the most serious occasions of daily life as the only way of saying the unsayable. It is important to recognize that the outpouring of emotions is possible in the (research) context of talking about TV, drama in particular. This is not to suggest that TV drama can be a therapy genre, but that there is a certain therapeutic quality in the emotional way in which women talk about characters and circumstances in drama with particular relevance to the conditions of their own lives and experiences. This emotional expression, which is kept unsaid or repressed in a relatively restrictive culture, is seen to be a fragmented, partial, expressive mark of self. It may be the case that Korean/Asian women operate with such emotional categories of experience, conveying internal states of feeling, but they take them seriously "in a way that Europeans do not," and their notion of personhood and emotional structure is "quite different from the European autonomous ego" (Marcus and Fischer 1986: 47). Popular TV drama – or the research interview on popular TV drama – has the capacity to create a rare, sometimes therapeutic, space where women's emotions could be voiced in available language codes as a process of self-discovery (for details, see Kim 2005).

The extent of the Korean Wave overseas, including popular TV drama, has left observers in a state of surprise and puzzlement, searching for answers to explain the sudden interest in Korean popular culture. However, the first common response in various transnational locations is that Korean TV dramas are emotionally powerful. "The unique intensity of Korean emotion plays well to the more restrained cultures around the region" (Taiwan's Gala TV vice president, quoted in *Korea Herald* 2005). One feature the Chinese particularly like about Korean dramas is the way they can "express their emotions freely, that it is a democracy" (*Financial Times* 2005). Japanese women feel that the hero of Korean drama *Winter Sonata* is not only handsome, intelligent and successful, but also sensitive, caring and understanding towards women. The depth of fans' adulation is striking: "If there was ever such a man in Japan, then I wouldn't be suffering like this" (*Japan Times* 2004). To Western eyes, this kind of Korean drama seems "old-fashioned" and the hero of *Winter Sonata* "might be written off as a wimp in a Western drama" (*Financial Times* 2004). Contrary to Western popular culture, particularly American drama, with its strong emphasis on sex appeal, the Korean drama depicts "love in its purest form without any nude or lustful contents to mitigate the essence of true love" (*Asia Cable* 2005).

Korean TV dramas are seen to be capable of dealing with love relationships in a more tender, significant and emotional rather than sensual way. It is interesting to recognize that the emotional purity or the raw emotion conveyed in Korean dramas, primarily through sensitive "male" characters, is seen as a unique expression of Korea's modernity by viewers around the region (*Wall Street Journal* 2009). This feminization of masculinity, to some extent, employing feminine aesthetics, caring and new masculine identities, may challenge the hitherto clearly defined gendered order in Asia while reflecting an imaginary empowerment of women within Confucian society. This emotional level of investment in human relations and social realities constitutes a major source of popular pleasure that continues to hook the women to Korean drama. It provides some of the most recognizable and relevant material that allows viewers to build a felt sense of the self. Thus, what makes Korean cultural forms popular has to do with a pleasure of recognizable human experience with powerful emotional responses, a felt sense of the texture of life that reaches not only the intimate sphere but also the heart of the reflexive self.

Everyday reflexivity: Reflexive modernity

> Why are we poor?
>> (North Koreans starting to question, after watching South Korean drama)

The notion of reflexivity has, since the mid-1980s, been a crucial issue for social researchers in Western academic debates – notably in critical ethnography and feminist epistemology – emphasizing the necessity of reflecting on the conditions (e.g. power relations) under which knowledge is produced. But what about the reflexivity of ordinary people? What about people in a culture where repression is supposed to be pervasive? What is it about the globally connected media world that provides openings for everyday people to make sense of their lives in critical ways? I consider reflexivity as the major mechanism of grasping a relationship between globalization (e.g. the Korean Wave), as a mediated cultural force, and experience, since I argue it is precisely reflexivity that is at work in the everyday experience of global media culture – as demonstrated in my work, *Media Consumption and Everyday Life in Asia* (2008).

The media are central to everyday reflexivity – the capacity to monitor action and its contexts to keep in touch with the grounds of everyday life, self-confront uncertainties and understand the relationships between cause and effect, yet never quite control the complex dynamics of everyday life. Reflexivity is an everyday practice. It is intrinsic to human activity, since human beings routinely keep in touch with the grounds of what they do, what they think and what they feel as a circular feedback mechanism. But there is a different and significant process in contemporary everyday life, which has changed the very nature of reflexivity by providing conditions for increased capacities for reflexivity "in the light of new information or knowledge" (Giddens 1991: 20). This reflexivity involves the routine incorporation of new information or knowledge into environments of action that are thereby reconstituted or reorganized. This evolving reflexive project is not just a direct cause-and-effect in the speed of social and cultural change but an increasingly insistent and intense process of mediation.

The question, however, is, to what extent and in what ways? Whose reflexivity? This reflexivity is experienced differently by different social subjects in different social locations, defining those societies as distinctive. Reflexivity needs not to be understood as a universal capacity of subjects or a "generalized experience that cuts across social divides," but to be understood in specific life world contexts where it arises unevenly and often ambiguously with competing reflexivities. There is a need to recognize situated reflexivity, specifying the different experiences of reflexivity situated within different social spaces. The degrees of reflexivity and its particular character and content may differ – stronger and weaker, emotional and rational, positive and negative in its implications. It is necessary to recognize the partial nature of reflexivity in relation to the relative openness of the social world and the different restraints on agency.

The difference also consists in the "scale of knowledge and information" made available in a globalizing modern condition under which reflexivity takes place. Especially, the extraordinary range of knowledge and information that today's global Internet makes available constitutes a unique phenomenon, whose importance for understanding present life situations can undermine traditional arrangements and transform traditional forms of social practices. The quantity and quality of reflexivity may be changing, as different kinds of understandings with the use of incoming non-local information through the global media can affect the reflexive monitoring of action in a culture-specific way. Increased flows of the media in the global Internet age can be seen as an important resource for the triggering and operating of everyday reflexivity. The media are not the only contributor to the process of reflexivity, but the degree of the media's contribution depends on what other sources of reflexivity might or might not be available and who can access and utilize them as meaningful resources. It seems important to note that, unlike Euro-American societies where people might draw on expert psychological knowledge in their understanding of the self, such models and sources might not be widely available and used among people elsewhere. When other sources such as psychotherapy and self-help expertise are not readily available in the actual circumstances of day-to-day life, transnational media programming and the Internet, including social networking sites and blogging, can be appropriated for an implicit therapeutic function and self-analysis to deal with the culture of everyday life in today's primarily visual, digital media-dominated environment. It is not just media's ubiquity in everyday life, but its unique and plausibly powerful capacity to affect the meaning making of everyday experience, its capacity to trigger a heightened reflexive awareness of the world, which is arguably a key cultural dynamics and challenge.

It is via the increased exposure to Others and reflexive capacities that people make sense of life conditions which differ from their own and come to question the taken-for-granted social order. Significantly, what is emerging here can be the problematization of society itself, the increasing awareness of its structural rigidity and discontents as well as the interrogatory attitude towards the surrounding world. Ordinary people may not destabilize the whole system, but the border-crossing transnational media can prompt them to critically reflect on the legitimacy of their own social system and imagine new possibilities within the multiple constraints of their social context. Engagement with the transnational media constitutes a heightened awareness vis-à-vis gender, sexuality, class, social mobility and so on. It is possible that the Korean Wave culture, too, has not just become the site where such reflexivity takes place, but actually provides the specific terms and forms of everyday talk and practice in the light of incoming knowledge. Often, when local media productions largely fail to respond to the changing socio-economic status and desire of people – youth and women in particular – in a transitional Asian society, it is transnational media culture that is instead appropriated for making contact with the diverse formations of culture and for making sense of what it means to be a modern self (for details, see Kim 2008).

Korean TV dramas are infused with urban middle-class scenes as representations of modernization, yet affectively portray youthful sentimentality and provide an imaginary for an increasingly regionalized "Asian modernity" (Erni and Chua 2005). Korea acts as a "filter for Western values making them more palatable to Chinese and other Asians" (*New York Times* 2006). In the urban centers of Asia, there are many young viewers whose desires and aspirations overlap with the way Korean TV dramas are presented – the beautiful urban environment, young and single professionals, aestheticized lifestyles and the pure love which is still possible. TV dramas are often seen as a source of aspiration and reflexivity in transitional society, and globalized dramas can serve the function of extending the space for reflexivity (Kim 2005 and 2008). "It was kind of like an awakening. I started to learn about South Korea through the boom, and then I wanted to know more and more" (a female fan, quoted in *Japan Economic Newswire* 2005). "It all started with dramas. I like to ask the teachers about the things I watch on TV. I want to learn the language, too" (a Singaporean fan taking a Korean culture class, quoted in *Straits Times* 2009). Nowadays the urban youth around Kathmandu, Nepal can not only name the cast in their favorite Korean dramas but also talk to each other in the Korean language (*Republica* 2010). There is an emergence of an Asian generation of middle-class youth across urban centers, for whom the identification with Asian-ness is not about essential Asianism but about "pop Asianism" (Siriyuvasak 2008). Asian cultural distinctiveness or the construction of a regional identity has emerged as a consumerist practice, and the pan-Asian identity is possibly constituted in the consumer community and consumerist modernity (Chua 2008).

This is a part of the process of uneven global capitalism and of the social imaginary for a mobilization of self in an increasingly mobile Asia. Young Asians' travel is related to the increasingly mobile patterns of the everyday, taking on a new significance in the construction and narration of individuals' life stories, mobility biographies (Kim 2010). Especially among the youth and women, traveling can be apprehended as a "must see" practice, and part of what traveling means is affirmations of cultural differences acquiring a wider transnational meaning through the recognition and experience of differences in the realm of individual freedom and gender modality. The media are seen to be enabling mobilities at multiple levels, by the symbolic, virtual and imaginary travels through space or actual physical displacement between different places.

Perhaps, it is most important to recognize an intersection between Korean popular culture and the mobilization of inner self and possible social change to emerge within communist North Korea, where real-life situations are felt to be particularly constrained and mobility in a variety of capacities and forms becomes all the more important. Copies of TV dramas, movie videos and music CDs are increasingly smuggled across the border of China into North Korea by those who have been abroad on business. "Once upon a time, one had to come back from an overseas trip with a truckload of cigarettes. Now my North Korean colleagues want me to bring movies, especially tapes of South Korean TV dramas" (a Westerner working in Pyongyang, quoted in

Korea Times 2006b). South Korean dramas have become so widespread across North Korea that since 2004 the regime has launched a sweeping crackdown on university students – the biggest audiences (*Time Asia* 2004; *Korea Herald* 2009). In some parts of North Korea people have good reception of Chinese TV signals and watch South Korean drama directly (*Radio Free Asia* 2007). Now, media technologies and computer-savvy youth make North Korea's isolation more difficult in the light of new images, concepts and lifestyles.

"Why are we poor?" the North Korean people are starting to ask, after watching South Korean drama (*Korea Herald* 2009). This critical reflection emerging from the viewing moment is a sign of coming change. Such change in awareness, knowledge and the interrogatory attitude may not always lead to social transformation in the short run, but new possibilities may arise from this capacity for reflexivity, questioning and rethinking of the givens of prevailing dimensions of social construction. The people's capacity to make sense of the meanings of everyday life, or the grounds of what they do, what they think and what they feel, has become dependent on the unofficial mediation of South Korean popular culture which is increasingly present in the daily exigencies of people now. "North Koreans love the fact that South Korean TV drama is not about politics, but about love and life, the fundamentals of human existence anywhere in this world" (a defector, quoted in *Radio Free Asia* 2007). Such cultural encounter with entertainment can evoke "utopian feelings of possibility" (Dyer 1992) acting as temporary answers to the specific inadequacies of society and showing what solutions "feel like." Increased flows of the media are important resources for the triggering and operating of everyday reflexivity (Kim 2005 and 2008); perhaps even more so in an extremely rigid and repressive society like North Korea where other sources of reflexivity might not be readily available. The significance of media consumption practices can be understood as a creative, dynamic and transformative process, often involving active and intended engagement. Its appeal and plausibly powerful capacity can invite new cultural dynamics, challenge and social change in North Korea.

Family: precarious individualization

> An example of an Asian country that has modernized and retained its traditions.
> (On the Korean Wave drama, *New York Times* 2006)

What does it mean to be a free and independent individual in Asian societies today? To what extent do people, women in particular, have control over their lives? How do the transnational media intersect with imagining different lives for women? The troubling signs of female individualization as intersected with everyday media culture have become a new arena of anxiety – as demonstrated in my recent work, *Women and the Media in Asia: The Precarious Self* (2012). Signs of female individualization have been proliferating as a defining feature of contemporary modes of identity, albeit untenable and ambivalent, within the discursive regime of self – embodied in regulatory practices in society where individualism is not placed at the heart of its family-centered culture. Arguably, the media are central to the signs of emergent cultures of female individualization producing the alternative social, cultural and symbolic relations women wish to live within and define the kind of self they wish to become. Seeming suggestions of individualization are encountered, mediated through popular media imaginaries that are present and often intentionally used as resources for reflexivity and self-imagining. This also provides a condition for an increased awareness of cultural differences and of women's own positions in relation to global Others, new symbolic objects of identification and contestation.

The rise of female individualization in urban Asia, albeit complex and often contradictory, has been reflected in, and enabled by, the gendered socio-economic change – higher levels of educational attainment than ever before, labor market participation, feminization of migration, delayed marriage and non-marriage, declining fertility, increasing divorce rates and family breakdown (for details, see Kim 2012). These indicators of family-at-risk represent visible and provisional, if not permanent, cases of individualization. The social transformations in many parts of contemporary urban Asia appear to engender similar, but not the same, trends and consequences of individualization which is notably linked to Western/European social theory in the processes of second modernity. Individualization is characterized by a growing emphasis on individual autonomy and independence from traditions and social institutions. Women are now released from traditional gender roles, and find themselves forced to build up a "life of their own" by way of the labor market, training and mobility (Beck and Beck-Gernsheim 2002). Confronted with a plurality of choices, individuals' life politics is organized around an increasingly reflexive and calculable mode of thinking to colonize the future with some degree of success (Giddens 1991). At the heart of life politics lie enterprising agents, who strategically plan, avidly self-monitor and manage a life of their own. The individual is becoming the basic unit of social reproduction. Family members form an elective relationship or a permanent do-it-yourself project, shifting from traditional expectations of "being there for others" to contemporary notions of "living one's own life" as a free and independent individual (Beck and Beck-Gernsheim 2002).

However, what it means to be a free and independent individual in Asian societies today is a much more complex and paradoxical issue. Individualization is not an all-encompassing trend or a radically sweeping process that shares different developments in social structures and cultural domains, as well as the levels of agency and reflexivity operating within. Despite high levels of reflexivity and possibilities potentially available for change, agency is not "becoming freed, unleashed or released from structure and its constraints," but instead is regulated by structure, operating within broader systems of constraint. The social and cultural fields are not totally restrictive but dialectically positioned; the complexity neither closes the avenue for change for women nor holds it wide open for any kind of empowerment.

The current growth of singles and delayed marriage in pursuit of higher education and work can be seen as an indicator of precarious individualization, which may challenge the stability of the family but not necessarily hold a privileging logic of self-invention and freedom. What does individualization mean in the context of the family? Traditional external constraints on marriage and family, the hetero-normative expectation of marriage by 30 in East Asia or much earlier in South Asia, have not progressively disappeared. The family, not the individual, is still the basic unit of social reproduction in Asia. Individualization, or family-oriented individualization, encompasses a much more complex and delicate, culture-bound balance between individual and family, whose values and practices differ significantly from the individualizing trend of the West. Often, an imagined future of individualization is simultaneously organized around the modalities of marriage and family. This is evident in the varying degrees to which transnational Asian women remain both autonomous from, and dependent upon, concrete familial relations in their diasporic existence and do not necessarily desire individual autonomy or freedom from the notions of marriage and family, even while continually transgressing national borders and producing new narratives of individual freedom (Kim 2011).

This unresolved identity of individualization serves as an important context within which the role of the media, including the Korean Wave culture, can be understood in its intersection with Asian transformations. Transnational flows of the media have emerged in globalizing Asia with a seeming emphasis on individualization and new heterogeneous choices within a neoliberal capitalist culture of freedom. New media technologies, the Internet in particular, are often uncritically celebrated as a democratic revolution in everyday life, and a seemingly free-floating move towards individualization, a do-it-yourself lifestyle culture that is continually produced and consumed in neoliberal consumer societies of Asia. The media, not only the global cultural force but also the national and local mediation, can be understood as a key cultural mechanism creating the emergence of precarious individualized identities in the region (for details, see Kim 2012).

On one hand, the media's growing emphasis on individualization and lifestyle choices, as well as a process of reflexivity at work, apparently signifies de-traditionalization, individual autonomy and emancipation from oppressive traditional social forms, including the conventional family and gendered self. New ways of conducting life and constructing the self with changing expectations and relations between men and women are playfully signified in the various images, symbols and narratives of popular media culture that appear to weaken the determining influence of gender and represent imagined empowerment through the de-traditionalization of the private and public spheres. The often de-contextualized representation and playful engagement invite individuals to compare experiences, to become free from fixed gender identities and unequal power, and to orientate themselves towards free choices in the consumerist market or further relate to a cosmopolitan outlook transcending national cultural boundaries.

On the other hand, there are also emerging forms of re-traditionalization, new models of cultural continuity and re-integration replacing ongoing rupture, and the symbolic production of regulative forms of social control over the lives of individuals, women in particular. The pulls of regulative traditions still operate in the competing regime of signifiers, of dialectical relations between gender, work, sexuality and family that are being reconstituted in ambiguous and sometimes contradictory ways that simultaneously de-traditionalize and re-traditionalize contemporary female subject formation. Pre-existing social structures, regulative traditions and families, if not overly deterministic, continue to play an integral role in structuring the parameters and workings of con-temporary media culture, while prompting a relational reflexivity, a relationally constructed emotionality and sociality to function as a moral ideal in a wider, complex and uncertain cultural narrative and vision about social change in modernizing Asia (for details, see Kim 2008 and 2012).

What makes Korean TV drama appealing is its dramatization of "Asian sensibilities," including family values and traditional emotive delicacies that are warmly embraced by cross-generational viewers in the Asian countries where full-fledged modernity has yet to arrive (*Korea Now* 2001). "Korean dramas are favored because they are rich in the more traditional Confucian values, which place emphasis on familial relationship, filial piety and sibling love" (*China Daily* 2005). Unlike American dramas, in which the focus is on romance between young lovers and the family has often disappeared, Korean dramas are perceived by the Asian audiences to embrace reality by dealing with diverse relationships in the Confucian familial framework. Increasingly, rich Asians look for new sources of entertainment, or alternative cultures, not necessarily American or European. These responses imply that the Korean Wave is a contemporary manifestation of Asian traditions, a yearning to rediscover cultural links between Asian societies that were interrupted by the Western colonial wave (Kishore 2006).

Paradoxically, however, Korean society itself is a dramatic indicator of the crisis of traditional identity. The Korean divorce rate has rapidly increased from 5.8% in 1980, to 11.1% in 1990, 16.8% in 1995, 33% in 2000, and today almost 50% (KWDI 2009). Korea would have the world's lowest birth rate, 1.15 in 2009, as a growing number of women delay marriage/family life in pursuit of employment and self-actualization. The Korean Wave of popular culture embraces this paradox. On one hand, it reflects women's changing socio-economic status and modern lifestyles, thereby decentralizing traditional male power and creating possibilities for gender negotiations and new subject formations. The imaginary representation of youthful female individualism, both entertaining and empowering, appeals directly to middle-class Asian women in their 20s and 30s. Yet on the other hand, Korean popular drama is deeply embedded in the structure of family and relations with others, stressing the centrality of family values and age-specific normative biographies. While individualism is certainly becoming more and more a part of the way young women nowadays think about themselves and the world, they are not invited to stand out as individuals but are expected to remain in traditional, family and relational networks. Often, younger generations in Asia have a set of competing values and reflexivities – simultaneously modern and traditional – the strong desire to choose individualized lifestyles, but at the same time the respect for elders and the importance of family ties which might clash with their lifestyle choice and individual freedom (Kim 2008). Tradition is reinvented and reinterpreted through the rejuvenation of traditional forms of life pivoting on the family and foundational morality acceptable to the moral capacity of the contemporary self in the transnational flow of popular culture.

Decentralizing contraflow: pop nationalism

> Koreans deserve their place and yes they deserve to be heard here (Europe) too. Why focus on American music? It's good to hear other things.
> (Online talk, after *Le Figaro* coverage of the K-pop concert in Paris, 2011)

Implicitly yet profoundly, Korea's historical colonial victimhood is pointed out as an intriguing reason behind the popularity of today's Korean Wave. As a Korean producer of popular film explains, "For centuries Korea has been occupied by China, Japan or the US. We are not seen as a threat to anybody" (quoted in *Reed Business Information* 2005). The success of Korean popular culture can be understood by global power relations and political sensitivities. "Korea is surrounded by powerful neighbors. Throughout history, we have suffered and endured. Koreans keep hope inside and never give up," commented the producer of *Jewel in the Palace* (*San Francisco Chronicle* 2005). This suggests that the political conflicts and socio-cultural tensions of the divided nation have been used to good effect to create emotionally powerful contents. Korean culture reflects the nation's unique sensibility "*han*" – a Korean word for a deeply felt sense of oppression and deep-seated grief: "Korean dramas express sadness particularly well. The writer of *Autumn in the Heart* would cry when writing his script. The actors, during rehearsals, started crying too" (producer of *Winter Sonata* and *Autumn in the Heart*, quoted in *Time Asia* 2005). Thus, the reason behind the successful phenomenon is a combination of Korea's tragic history, the intensity of Korean emotive culture, and the non-threatening nature of its people. Often, the ambivalent nature of foreignness in imported Western cultural products can be perceived by two extremes – fascination and threat – but the threat is less manifested in the way Korean popular culture is received across Asia and elsewhere.

The rise of the Korean Wave phenomenon is seen as a "long-awaited flowering of post-colonial Asian artistic expression," and a creation of a "regional Asian cultural manifestation against the erstwhile domination of Western culture" (Dator and Seo 2004). The postcolonial periphery has strengthened its national culture industry to compete against the dominant flow of Western media products. This indicates a potential "plurality of actors and media flows" (Chadha and Kavoori 2000), and could be read as a "symptom of the shifting nature of transnational cultural power in a context in which intensified global cultural flows have decentered the power structure" (Iwabuchi 2002). Though the decentering tendency occurs within the context of global inequalities and uneven flows, a current image of global media flows may not be that of settled centers of economic and cultural power, but of a "decentered network, in which the patterns of power distribution are unstable and shifting" (Tomlinson 1997). The transnational mobility of Korean popular culture is a facet of decentralizing multiplicity of global media flows today. The Korean Wave phenomenon can be seen as a conscious, and often intentional, way to counter the threat and insensibility of the Western-dominated media market within the context of global inequalities and uneven power structures.

A key feature of the rise of the Korean Wave is the active role of the nation-state focusing on the creation of "cool" national brands, inevitably reinforcing a commercialized "pop nationalism" that appropriates popular culture to promote political and economic interests. On one hand, Korean popular culture has changed the dynamics of the media landscape in Asia challenging the characterization of globalization as a Western-centric uneven cultural force, and its growing visibility is an example of the decentralizing multiplicity of global media flows, or of the "contra-flow" (Thussu 2007) emerging to service an ever growing geo-cultural market against a one-way flow from the West to the peripheral rest. But at the same time, its increasing volume and velocity have generated a sense of discontent and tension in some local communities of Asia, giving rise to a backlash of anti-Korean sentiment (*Korea Times* 2006a). Especially, the Internet has become an influential medium throughout East Asia, and the case of "Hating the Korean Wave" inside the Japanese blogosphere and online community is a culminated form of the nationalist and even xenophobic sentiment towards the Korean version of nationalism (Sakamoto and Allen 2007).

However, a paradox is that this sign of Korean pop nationalism – newly expressing self-confidence, pride, inner passion and energy through popular culture – is also the very reason why the Korean Wave has powerful appeals across Asia: "I could just feel how Koreans are proud of their tradition and culture. The clothes, food, history, and all those things explored. Korean people still feel so confident about themselves" (a Taiwanese fan of *Jewel in the Palace*, quoted in *Korea Herald* 2008). This is a reflection of Asia's yearning for an independent cultural force, a particular speaking position in the struggle

Korean Wave pop culture in the global Internet age   87

for national cultural identity amidst the threatening presence of the mediated space of the West, now that the borders of the nation are becoming increasingly vulnerable to Western hegemony of globalization (Kim 2008). A future of Asia, of the nation and self-identity, is being re-imagined and relearned through decentralizing alternative cultural flows, including the Korean Wave, and this imagining and reflexivity is not just a sign of a newly found self-confidence but also a sign of anxiety in an increasingly mediated and precarious world of everyday life.

Diasporic nationalism and the Internet: cosmopolitan openness?

> My room is small, the UK television is in my closet. It's just not interesting ... Why try to know them when they don't try to know us?
>
> (Korean middle-class woman in London, quoted in Kim 2011)

> The Internet is super! Every day, the first thing I do is to open the Chinese website (Sohu) and read news.
>
> (Chinese middle-class woman in London, quoted in Kim 2011)

> I stop fighting [racism] because it was my choice to move here, because my English is not good enough. I cannot even express frustration to outsiders as they say, "You live in attractive London!" My friend depressed in Paris hears the same, "You live in Beautiful Paris!"
>
> (Japanese middle-class woman in London, quoted in Kim 2011)

The increasing, multi-directional flows of the ethnic media, information and communication technologies facilitate people's transnational, nomadic, back-and-forth movements creating new and complex conditions for identity formation in diaspora – as demonstrated in my ethnographic research, *Transnational Migration, Media and Identity of Asian Women: Diasporic Daughters* (2011). Since the 1990s, the mediated networks established through the Internet and the transnational ethnic media, such as the Korean Wave culture, have been instrumental in facilitating these changes in contemporary movements, allowing dispersed yet networked migrants to maintain transnationally their home-based relationships and to regulate a dialectical sense of belonging in host countries. The media, mostly taken for granted, go along with diasporic subjects; and the Korean Wave phenomenon can be understood in this context of transnational migration systems and processes. These new kinds of transnational networks, connections and various capacities of mobility are now changing not only the scale and patterns of migration but also the nature of migrant experience and thinking. Importantly, a provisional nomadic sensibility ("willing to go anywhere for a while"), as well as new socio-cultural forms of management of diasporic everyday life, have been facilitated by the mediation of the rapidly evolving media technologies. Today's provisional diaspora with the nomadic symptom may present a profound paradox resulting from the double capacity of the ethnic media use to produce and organize new space of one's own that enables quotidian dwelling "here" and hyper connecting "there." The present wave of migration differs significantly from previous waves in that contemporary trans-border movements have been intensified, diversified and feminized to some extent, and the processes of digital diasporas have created new meanings of diasporic subjectivity and new consequences that are yet to be known and understood in detail.

For example, the following data are from Korean middle-class women (single, aged 26–33), who had been living and studying in London for three to seven years:

> I am suddenly addicted to our Korean media. I rarely watched TV in Korea as my social life was busy, colorful … Through website *Naver* I get all information.

> It's all there! Through the Internet I watch Korean dramas, download movies, music every night. On *Cyworld* I keep in touch with friends, express what I am doing, how I feel, what made me angry today … I cried while watching Korean dramas alone. Perhaps the first time I cried while living abroad, never cried over any hardship. It suddenly evoked a repressed feeling and made me realize home.

> It's like proud B&B culture – people will always come to the city of Buckingham Palace and leave. It signals to foreigners, "If you don't like it, go back to your country." I will never belong.

Displaced subjects can find social ontological security in their own communication channels and become attached or even more ("suddenly addicted") to the inclusive mediated community, while becoming less interested or connected to the host society. The new connection to the ethnic media from the national homeland and its substantial impact can promote disengagement and further distance to the mainstream. New ways of being and feeling at home are created and sustained by means of virtual engagement. Variegated ritualistic links – via the Korean social networking website *Cyworld*, infotainment online portal *Naver*, food, drama, film, music as a constant background – are established in the structure of everyday life. This mediated experience away from home has multiple purposes: a response to the loss of belonging, a self-determined need to seek symbolic inclusion, a desire to connect with significant others back home, and a pleasure to expand the space for self-expression, understanding and articulation in the language of home. The habits and strategies to experience home in the routines of diasporic lives develop into the Internet resources. But what is significant here is not just the sheer availability of the Internet now but the self-determination of users and its consequences. They affirm a sense of continuity, self-esteem and deliberate nationalism that is emotively noticed and powerful.

> Watching TV back home I imagined life here, but living here I become indifferent. Never felt my essential self as Korean so strongly before. I become more Korean, unique while living abroad ... I don't fit quite here or quite there. I can live anywhere in the world if there is a good job and the Internet connection for all Korean stuff.

An evident paradox is that the more physically close, the more they try to remain different, distinct. The search for uniqueness becomes intense and dependent on the ethnic media space where the symbolic construction of internal and external boundaries is regularly sustained. Although some aspect of lifestyle change can make women feel incompatible with lives back home, there is a strong denial of association or influence from the Western host society, finding themselves located neither "quite here" nor "quite there"; indeed, neither place is desirable any longer. To resist a Western influence is a quality that manifests itself in lived relations of difference, often as a reaction to the hegemonic racial order and denigration, as a conscious way of re-claiming status. Ironically, the choice to live in the world does not necessarily lead to an expanded worldview or enlargement of self, but rather a con-strictive one that is an inevitable consequence of the lived experience of social closure.

> I do not say it aloud but continually feel racism, everyday little things that I try to ignore. I say "not aloud" because what we have to say will not matter to them anyway.

> All my friends in London happen to be Asians, who are interested in Korean culture, TV drama and music ... It is a small Asian connection, does not go beyond that.

In European capital cities, such as London and Paris, cultural difference and human pluralism have been revalued as a resource and an opportunity and appropriated into the re-visioning of the cosmopolitan space, yet it can present an exclusive rhetoric, rather than an open-minded interest or an awareness of the existence and equal validity of other cultures. In celebrating the suppo-sedly inclusive cosmopolitan consciousness, which forms of cultural difference are seen as desirable and valued, and which are excluded? Cosmopolitanism as a normative, moral and philosophical ideal means "learning from each other's differences through conversation" (Appiah 2006), or "overcoming national identity as an ideological or naturalized constraint" (Beck 2006) and trans-cending all identities by "a universal identification that does not place love/loyalty of country ahead of universal humanity" (Nussbaum 1997). However,

90 Youna Kim

this overwhelmingly normative ideal of cosmopolitanism can be seen as merely celebrating cultural differences and human diversity, uncritically assuming an inclusiveness and engagement with differences. Much of the motivation and possibility of becoming cosmopolitan subjects depends on the contexts, discursive and communicative encounters and common existential experiences. A world of increasing flows of people and cultural mélange with its allure of cultural diversity and cosmopolitan gloss may appear to be a comfort zone for strangers, but it can also be experienced with a highly implicit stance of racism ("everyday little things"), subtly signaled hostility that can co-exist without manifesting conflicts and come to be internalized. The resulting consequence of everyday banal racism and exclusion, of this actual and repeated experience in everyday diasporic life, can be a self-conscious rejection towards the mainstream host society, or highly selective social interaction within an ethnic enclave.

The consequence of increasing transnational movement is not the emergence of robust cosmopolitan subjects and a loss of distinctive identity, of difference that undermines its own cultural particularity. Rather, to a great extent, lived diasporic experience underlies the nation as a viable project of identity-building and reinforces the securing of national identity defined in ethno-cultural terms, in a world of different visions, hierarchical norms and values. The construction of national identity occurs by a growing ethnic consciousness in the experience of the dialectics of power and the reason of feeling towards an unrepresentative position within the transnational. Nationalism is a conscious micro-political practice of positioning and struggle; feeling beyond nationalism, or cosmopolitanism, should be preconditioned on symmetrical representation and inclusion. Transnational mobility and mediated connection to the Korean Wave culture in the global Internet age does not easily generate a cosmopolitanizing experience of the world, but rather presents concrete manifestations of nationalism and the limits of imagined cosmopolitanism in the motivations to act. Diasporic nationalism becomes particularly potent and perhaps more salient through transnational flows and movement, nationalizing transnational spaces and the Internet's simultaneously dis-embedding and re-embedding capacities in forming partial yet unending connection with home and possibly its long-term viability in the rooted experience of diasporic subjects (for details, see Kim 2011).

References

Appiah, A. (2006) *Cosmopolitanism*, New York: Norton.
Asia Cable (2005) "All You Need is Pure Love," February 18.
Beck, U. (2006) *Cosmopolitan Vision*, Cambridge: Polity.
Beck, U. and Beck-Gernsheim, E. (2002) *Individualization*, London: Sage.
Chadha, K. and Kavoori, A. (2000) "Media Imperialism Revisited," *Media, Culture & Society*, 22: 415–32.

China Daily (2005) "S. Korean Soap Opera Sparks Boom in China," September 30.

Chua, B. (2008) "East Asian Pop Culture: Layers of Communities," in Y. Kim (ed.) *Media Consumption and Everyday Life in Asia*, London: Routledge.

Dator, J. and Seo, Y. (2004) "Korea as the Wave of a Future," *Journal of Futures Studies*, 9: 31–44.

Dyer, R. (1992) *Only Entertainment*, New York: Routledge.

Erni, J. and Chua, S. (2005) *Asian Media Studies: Politics of Subjectivities*, Oxford: Blackwell.

Financial Times (2004) "South Korea's Soppy Soaps Win Hearts Across Asia," December 14.

——(2005) "South Korea's TV Dramas Express Young People's Yearning for Greater Freedom," August 12.

Giddens, A. (1991) *Modernity and Self-identity: Self and Society in the Late Modern Age*, Cambridge: Polity.

Iwabuchi, K. (2002) *Recentering Globalization: Popular Culture and Japanese Transnationalism*, Durham: Duke University Press.

Japan Economic Newswire (2005) "Korean Boom Changing Japanese People's Perceptions," August 16.

Japan Times (2004) "Korean Wave May Help Erode Discrimination," June 27.

Kim, Y. (2005) *Women, Television and Everyday Life in Korea: Journeys of Hope*, London: Routledge.

——(2007) "The Rising East Asian Wave: Korean Media Go Global," in D. Thussu (ed.) *Media on the Move: Global Flow and Contra-flow*, London: Routledge.

——(2008) *Media Consumption and Everyday Life in Asia*, London: Routledge.

——(2010) "Female Individualization?: Transnational Mobility and Media Consumption of Asian Women," *Media, Culture & Society*, 32: 25–43.

——(2011) *Transnational Migration, Media and Identity of Asian Women: Diasporic Daughters*, London: Routledge.

——(2012) *Women and the Media in Asia: The Precarious Self*, Basingstoke: Palgrave Macmillan.

Kishore, M. (2006) "The Korea Enigma," *Korea Foundation Newsletter*, 15(4).

Korea Herald (2005) "Is It All Over Already?," July 11.

——(2008) "The High Tide of the Korean Wave," February 4.

——(2009) "North Koreans Fall in Love with South Korean Dramas," November 3.

Korea Now (2001) "Cultural Ambassadors on the Rise," September 11.

Korea Times (2006a) "Hallyu Phenomenon Faces Backlash in East Asia," January 16.

——(2006b) "Hallyu and Political Change," September 10.

KWDI (2009) Documents and Databases. Seoul: Korean Women's Development Institute.

Le Figaro (2011) "La Vague Coréenne Déferle Sur le Zénith," June 9.

Le Monde (2011) "La Vague Pop Coréenne Gagne l'Europe," June 10.

Marcus, G. and Fischer, M. (1986) *Anthropology as Cultural Critique*, Chicago: University of Chicago Press.

New York Times (2006) "Korea's Pop Culture Spreads through Asia," January 2.

Nussbaum, M. (1997) *Cultivating Humanity*, Cambridge: Harvard University Press.

Radio Free Asia (2007) "North Korea Cracks Down on Korean Wave of Illicit TV," July 17.

Reed Business Information (2005) "Asian Market Finds its Seoul," October 9.

Republica (2010) "Ubiquitous Korean Wave," March 7.

Sakamoto, R. and Allen, M. (2007) "Hating 'The Korean Wave' Comic Books?," *Japan Focus*, 4, October.

San Francisco Chronicle (2005) "South Korea Soap Operas Find Large Audiences," August 28.

Siriyuvasak, U. (2008) "Consuming and Producing (Post)modernity," in Y. Kim (ed.) *Media Consumption and Everyday Life in Asia*, London: Routledge.

Straits Times (2009) "Korean Wave Now a Tsunami," December 13.

Time Asia (2004) "He's Still There," December 6.

——(2005) "South Korea: Talent Show," November 14.

Tomlinson, J. (1997) "Internationalism, Globalization and Cultural Imperialism," in K. Thompson (ed.) *Media and Cultural Regulation*, London: Sage.

Thussu, D. (2007) *Media on the Move: Global Flow and Contra-flow*, London: Routledge.

Wall Street Journal (2009) "Riding the Korean Wave," May 19.

Chapter 5

For the eyes of North Koreans?

Politics of money and class in *Boys Over Flowers*

Suk-Young Kim

"If you stay with me, every day, you will get to enjoy incredible riches beyond your imagination." Whispers of seductive temptation come from a high school boy named Gu Junpyo, the dashing heir to an immense fortune, whose strikingly beautiful countenance fills the TV screen with sheer visual pleasure. Charismatic and eager, he directs his enamored gaze at bewildered Geum Jandi, a high school girl sitting across a cozy table for two. Motley tropical flowers float in a glass bowl of cold water as a fragrant centerpiece, enhancing the aroma of tea and delicate desserts served on fine china. Their feet touch the soft white sand of the South Pacific while the azure horizon sends foamy breezes to caress the fleeting moment. The girl turns breathless and confused. Leading up to this scene, when she was brought to his family's private island by private jet for a weekend getaway, she had been a courageous fighter against the boy's tyranny. She had resisted his proposals to give in to his realm of influences, but now, after so many refusals, she is on the verge of surrendering to his unflinching passion – and even more, to the magnetic power of his wealth manifested in material refinement and physical beauty.

The sensual quality of the scene from a popular South Korean drama, *Boys Over Flowers* (*Kkotboda namja*, aired in South Korea in 2009), stems from the fact that the drama reproduces the desire of a Japanese manga aimed primarily at young female readers who seek instantaneous passion and romance in implausible fantasy stories. Based on the wildly popular Japanese manga *Hana Yori Dango* by Kamio Yoko, which was circulated in installments from 1992 to 2004, the longest serialization in the history of that genre, the dramatic narrative about the improbable courtship among four rich and handsome boys and a lovely but impoverished girl was later adapted into a TV drama in virtually every East Asian nation and enjoyed pan-Asian popularity. TV productions in Taiwan (2001), Japan (2005), South Korea (2009) and the PRC (2010) were all scrutinized by loyal fans and were often given a comparative analysis.[1] In each respective nation, the drama's wild success turned emerging young actors into superstars whose fame quickly spread across East Asia and beyond.

Perhaps the most surprising members to join the ever-increasing fandom of this multinational franchise were North Korean viewers, who, according to

94   Suk-Young Kim

occasional testimonials of defectors, enjoyed the South Korean version of the show through VCDs smuggled in via mainland China. Hiding from the draconian surveillance of the regime and compromising their own security, what did North Korean spectators find in this drama when they secretly watched it? What did they see in the world of beautiful young people whose relations are sutured by excessive contrasts between affluence and poverty?

This chapter explores the reasons *Boys Over Flowers*, known for championing mindless consumerism and hedonistic cultivation of bodily beauty, was allegedly a huge success in a country that still, albeit nominally, opposes the decadent culture of the open market economy while upholding the utopian ideals of classless society. Was it sheer voyeuristic curiosity about the forbidden outside world that fueled its popularity among North Korean viewers? Or was it the seductive visual quality of the show, replete with material affluence, that glued North Korean viewers to the TV, despite the dangers such stealthy activity might pose to them? I investigate why *Boys Over Flowers* gained a following in North Korea through a close reading of the drama's narrative, with a particular focus on its subversive politics of money, class and ideals for equitable society. In the process, I hope to illuminate the ever-increasing transnational friction that North Korean settlers in South Korea, and North Koreans trying to adapt to the increasing presence of open market (*jangmadang*) in that country, endure as volatile subjects caught in between conflicting political and economic logics.

How did the *Boys* land in North Korea?

After the South Korean broadcasting station KBS2 aired 25 episodes of the drama from January to March 2009, fragmented reports started to leak out of North Korea about the drama's popularity through defectors and traders who travel back and forth between China and North Korea. According to their account, the drama was so successful that the young North Koreans emulated the distinctive fashions and hairstyles of the main characters. According to Radio Free Asia's report on September 15, 2011, its contact person in Northern Hamgyeong Province claimed that the drama was enjoying a sensational popularity among school students, and in a reverse interview, this contact person asked the reporter how many episodes there are in total. In the city of Cheongjin, many junior high school students emulated the hairstyles of the two leading male actors and labeled them after the characters' names, such as Gu Junpyo-style or Yun Jihu-style. Even more, a short plaid skirt featured as a part of school uniform in the drama is named after its female protagonist, Geum Jandi, and is a highly sought-after item among young women in the city of Hoeryeong – to the point that it is extremely difficult to find plaid-patterned cloth in the marketplace.[2]

The drama's surprising ability to cross over to the forbidden land caught even the attention of its producers. Jeon Gisang, who directed *Boys Over*

Flowers, shared his insights as to why it crossed the inter-Korean border so easily:

> I heard that [South] Korean dramas are intriguing [to North Korean viewers] partly because the story moves forward very fast. One of the advantages of watching Korean dramas is to enjoy a wide variety of subject matters and to have a peek at a wide range of South Korean people's lives, such as fashion and food. I think that's why it's popular. Since North and South Korea have been divided for a long time, both sides feel a strong sense of cultural alienation from each other. But someday, when Korea becomes reunited, I hope North Koreans won't feel so strange about South Korean culture. I believe this can be done by having North Koreans watch [South] Korean dramas: watching dramas will be akin to receiving an immunization shot for North Koreans, who will get acquainted with South Korean ways of life such as clothing, food, and music.[3]

The interview, meant to explain the drama's astonishing popularity in North Korea, instead reveals an intriguing paradox regarding its ability to account for the consumptive realities of South Korean society. Keep in mind, *Boys Over Flowers* was intended to provide *South* Koreans with an escape from harsh reality by emulating the fantasy world of graphic novels. Characterized by excessive consumptive pleasure, it was designed as a respite from the dire circumstances of soaring unemployment and the collapse of the middle class and social services in the aftermath of the 2008 global financial meltdown. The South Korean media, for this reason, severely criticized the drama's materialism propelled by overwhelming product placement. A newspaper article with the revealing title "*Boys Over Flowers*: Is It a Drama or an Advertisement?" chastises the way producers placed an extraordinary number of products in the drama, to the point that the development of the protagonists' stories was severely interrupted.[4] In another article, poignantly titled "*Boys Over Flowers*' Popularity Stems From Escapism," popular culture critic Yi Heon-eop argues that the drama is the natural product of economic depression, as it opted to focus on fantasies of escape rather than expose sobering reality. In this respect, Yi argues that *Boys Over Flowers* is quite akin to Hollywood's romantic melodramas, such as *The Love Parade* (1929), *Monte Carlo* (1930), *One Hour With You* (1932) and *The Merry Widow* (1934), which were extremely popular during the Great Depression era.[5]

In the interview, the South Korean director, quite contrary to the many criticisms that *Boys Over Flowers* was turning a blind eye to the harsh reality many South Koreans were facing, presents the drama as if it were documentarian evidence of actual material circumstances in South Korea – to the point of predicting that it will be a fine educational tool to introduce South Korean ways of life to people from the North. Such a conviction is based on

96 Suk-Young Kim

the premise that the South and North Korean value systems are so drastically opposed that Koreans of both sides need a cultural introduction to each other before even attempting to integrate.

Quite contrary to the idea that the series presents unique, yet veritable ways of South Korean life distinguished from North Korean life, this chapter proposes that the drama's ability to create a sensation among North Korean youth has deeper roots in cultural and ideological identification. Although the mindless consumerism and material affluence featured in *Boys Over Flowers* might well be the main point of attraction for North Korean viewers, who find themselves in even more dire economic circumstances than their struggling Southern counterparts, I advance the notion that North Korean viewers can also relate to the deeper registers of South Korean life as captured in the drama: the merciless politics of money and insurmountable social hierarchy. Though hidden behind the glittering imagery of excess in emulation of the original graphic novel series, significant issues are raised – the apparent class struggle and the moral imperative as a foundational component of a proper class background. In my view, it is these ideological concerns that profoundly attract North Korean viewers to *Boys Over Flowers* as they provide the pleasure of identification: after all, the value system that North Koreans see beyond the visual pleasure is quite similar to their own.

Welcome to the world of Sinhwa, the empire of myth

No other forces wield more lasting power in the lives of South Koreans than large conglomerates (*chaebol*):[6] from the moment they wake up to the moment they go to bed, it is nearly impossible to escape *chaebol*'s influence in one way or another. From the toothpaste they use in the morning to the public transportation they take to work, *chaebol* has a hand in producing virtually all the items so indispensable for everyday needs. And yet, while wielding so much power and influence in the lives of ordinary citizens, members of *chaebol* live in a privileged universe segregated from the workers of their commercial empire, who are also consumers of their products. Their actual lives are veiled in mystery for the most part, but they have provided a rich terrain for a dramatic imagination. Seasoned with both fascination with the unknown and abhorrence of unlimited power, stories involving *chaebol* abound on Korean TV, especially as the fates of these financial elites become entangled with those of the ordinary citizens (*seomin*)[7] so much so that these programs could even constitute their own genre.[8]

Boys Over Flowers is no exception in this tradition. The drama opens with a stream of news coverage unanimously reporting on the prosperity of the conglomerate. First comes the domestic news coverage of Sinhwa Group's selection as the largest sponsor of the 2012 London Olympics. This impressive news clip soon fades out, giving way to a stream of global news coverage of Sinhwa's success. As a myriad of images capturing a commercial entity fills the screen in a montage sequence, a narrative voice begins to provide a more thorough background to the grand stature of this financial empire:

> Sinhwa Group has always been the number one group since the economy started to take off in South Korea. From electronics, oil refining, and automobile manufacturing to communications and retail, South Koreans can hardly avoid Sinhwa. It may be possible to live in South Korea without knowing the name of the president, but it is impossible to live without knowing the name Sinhwa. It is the largest conglomerate in South Korea, literally a grand kingdom.

This unlimited powerhouse is the family company of the main protagonist, Gu Junpyo. The influence of this large organization even transcends the power of the state itself, closely resembling a mythical kingdom (it is no coincidence that "Sinhwa" translates into "myth" in Korean). In a rapidly moving montage that marks the opening scene, a close-up of a black-and-white photo of the founder of the company (Gu Junpyo's grandfather) and South Korean President Park Chung-hee tellingly exposes the iconic image of the developmental stages South Korea went through in the 1960s and 1970s, when the state and large corporations fed each other's interests under the nationalistic agenda of rapid economic recovery from the devastating aftermath of war.

Though this partnership might have taken place under the banner of the public interest, it generated various side effects, such as the increasing gap between rich and poor and the suppression of democratic measures in governance. Growing economic inequality is sustained by oppression, but the genre of drama possesses all the tools to revamp it with beauty. More specifically, in *Boys Over Flowers*, the ugly face of tyranny is masked by the excessive physical beauty of the *chaebol* characters. The incarnation of Sinhwa Group's future is the heir apparent, Gu Junpyo, played by lanky model-cum-actor Yi Minho. The character enters the drama like a mythical god descending from his chariot. He makes his first appearance with an entourage in the social hall of the exclusive Sinhwa High School, founded by his family company. Collectively known as F4, Gu Junpyo and his three other wealthy, powerful and handsome friends exude an aura of mythic deities – the effect of which is augmented by brilliant spotlights placed behind their backs, illuminating their beautiful faces and slender figures. They are soon surrounded by a mob of worshipers: girls scream at the mere mention of their names and boys drop their jaws in awe of their charisma.

The personality cult is a familiar theme in North Korea, with its long-standing propaganda machinery to mythologize every aspect of the nation's leadership. From birth to death, North Korean leaders' lives are filled with sacrosanct stories that simply go unchallenged. In that sense, the North Korean leaders' influence over their people's lives is akin to the irrefutable power that

98 Suk-Young Kim

Sinhwa Group wields over the lives of characters in the drama. But unlike the omnipotence of the North Korean leadership, the ultimate authority of the Sinhwa Group, as embodied in its future leader, Gu Junpyo, has to endure, albeit temporarily, an unexpected challenge from a "nobody" of the weaker gender who has nothing to lose.

What shatters the materially affluent, but spiritually moribund world of Gu Junpyo is the daring challenge posed by Geum Jandi, who comes from a background very different from his own: her family owns a small dry-cleaning business, and she works many odd jobs to contribute to the family finances. At the outset of the drama, she enters the prestigious Sinhwa High School not as a student, but as a delivery person to hand over a dry-cleaned school uniform to one of the students. There she witnesses the ghastly hazing of one boy, who happens to be the owner of the uniform Jandi has come to deliver. Having challenged the authority of F4, the student is repeatedly tormented by a mob of students who faithfully carry out cruel punishment on behalf of their leaders. Unable to withstand the endless bullying any longer, he decides to commit suicide by jumping off the school building. Jandi dramatically saves him at this critical moment, and she becomes an instantaneous hero whose courage is publicized in the media. This incident ignites public anger against the cruel practices that take place in the most privileged institution in the nation. When demonstrations break out and acerbic criticisms of plutocracy abound, Sinhwa Group decides to admit Jandi to their school on a fellowship to control the damage done to its public image.

There at school, the unruly girl is singled out for her humble background, and she eventually collides with the almighty Junpyo, who expects absolute obedience from everyone around him. Quite contrary to other students who obsequiously follow the directives of Sinhwa's heir, Jandi openly confronts him and thereby becomes another target of collective hazing. Junpyo expects unconditional surrender from exasperated Jandi, but instead, he is met with fiercer resistance. Baffled by the unexpected defiance staged by a girl who owns nothing but pride and courage, he becomes intrigued by her and falls in love. Eventually, Jandi's resistance gives way to reciprocal feelings of love, and despite many challenges, especially Junpyo's mother's multiple attempts to split the two, the drama ends with their happy union. In the final episode, Junpyo emerges as the successful and deserving heir to his family fortune and Jandi ends up studying medicine in a university also established by Sinhwa Group.

In what seems to be a typical Cinderella fairy-tale plot, where a penniless girl with a heart of gold marries a dashing prince who has it all, Jandi's conversion to plutocracy is still worth noting. How did she transform from a valiant fighter against the tyranny of the financial empire to a docile recipient of the wealth she fiercely resisted? What triggered that drastic transformation? Was she putting up a genuine fight at the beginning of the drama, or was it a coy plot to intrigue Junpyo, the bored dandy who feels he has seen it all? Trying to induce a logical explanation for the drama's exaggerated plot, which stages caricatures from the graphic novel, might be futile, but the money-first policy in *Boys Over Flowers* is so pervasive that it sheds light on North Korea's coming of age to capitalism. Analogically, Jandi's transformation could be read as the journey of North Korean viewers themselves. Deviating from the socialist ideals of economic egalitarianism, North Korea in recent years is gradually experiencing various forms of open market, including the thriving black market, which became the arena for *Boys Over Flowers* to circulate. Could North Korean viewers see a parable of their potential future in the uncanny story of Jandi's rise to fortune?

Material dandyism and class struggle

In a significant gesture, the narration at the opening of the drama points to the crucial logic of the developmental state, wherein economic growth overrides equal opportunity for education:

> When the founder of Sinhwa Group visited the president to receive a medal for having reached the 10-billion-dollar mark in total export volume – the first South Korean company to have done so – he asked the president: "Sir, please allow me to build a school where my grandson can attend." Thus the Sinhwa Foundation for Private Education was born. No such school [designed exclusively for the wealthiest] had ever existed in the history of the nation, and the president issued a special law to allow for its creation, since it was a time when economic development was more important than equal opportunity in education. Nowadays, there is even a saying that a family without a Sinhwa alumnus/a cannot speak of family prestige, pointing to the fact that Sinhwa has built its reputation as a place of, for, and by the upper 1 percent.

The open pursuit of aristocratic privileges for students of Sinhwa High School makes the site a microcosm of the brutish division of social hierarchies. Even among the wealthy students, there is a strict ranking based on their parents' social status – with F4 at the summit of the student body. From the opening scene, the drama captures the difference between F4 and the rest: the four protagonists' special classroom is adorned with mahogany desks, thick carpet and crystal name plaques, presenting a huge contrast to the ordinary classrooms for other students. Even within F4, Junpyo is the unchallenged leader by virtue of his family's unrivaled fortune. In this respect, Sinhwa High School is a ground to train young members of high society to dominate the food chain that defines the hierarchy of the real world.

In a way, F4 is the contemporary Korean rendition of dandyism, coated with seductive material abundance: well-fitting high fashion, perfect hairstyles, delicate cuisine and palatial residences of the bored youth, which collectively become the focus of the visual pleasure the drama offers to both South and

North Korean viewers – so much so that the pleasure stemming from the allure of money becomes the matrix where human relationships are formed and dissolved. In the end, the drama presents a paradoxical stance that poignant class struggle can only be resolved by the power of money. Although the unequal distribution of wealth created the conspicuous difference between large conglomerates (*chaebol*) and ordinary citizens (*seomin*), the conflict between them can only be resolved when the former embraces the latter with voluntary generosity.

In preparation for the surprise weekend trip to the South Pacific described in the opening paragraph of this chapter, Junpyo takes Jandi to a department store that his family owns. He presses the emergency button and expels all customers in order to enjoy private shopping time with the girl he loves. Once he succeeds in evacuating the store, he starts to pile up luxury-brand items Jandi needs for the trip, neither asking for her opinion, nor bothering to look at the price tags: suitcases, sunglasses, summer dresses, sandals and hats. When they arrive in his private jet at the island of New Caledonia, also owned by his family as described in the first paragraph, he arranges a helicopter ride over the shallow green marshes, which are shaped like a heart when seen from the sky. This is the moment when Jandi starts to develop special feelings for Junpyo – a first step toward a reconciliation between *chaebol* and *seomin* prompted by the power of money.

Sinhwa Group's heir does not end his excessive materialistic splurging with Jandi alone, but he also tries to win the hearts of her family by sending top-notch appliances and furniture to their modest house, which does not even have space for all the lavish gifts. These incidents of mind-boggling consumption are deployed in the drama to provide decisive motivation for Jandi to open her heart to her former tormentor.

Not only does money resolve and dissolve human relations, but it also provides a profoundly strong analogy for interpreting human action and decision. In the third episode, Seohyun, the wealthy and beautiful girlfriend of Jihu, one of the members of F4, explains to Jandi why she decided to pursue a new chapter in life in France: "I believe that making a decision to do something or not to do something is very similar to shopping overseas. If you want something, you have to reach out right at that moment. You might have regrets if you miss the chance." As the drama presents it, life-altering decisions can be understood and made along the lines of compulsive shopping urges.

In the ensuing episodes, the viewers find that Jandi, who has been putting up an admirable resistance against mammonism as the moral center of the drama, recycles this analogy between consumptive desire and crucial decisions. In Episode 5, when the school students taunt one of their classmates, Minji, for having gone through extensive plastic surgery to alter her looks in order to attract Junpyo, Jandi immediately comes to the victim's defense and gives an impassioned lecture to the mob of students: "You girls buy everything with money that you desire. Minji also bought her looks, at the expense of tremendous pain. How can you claim that her beauty is not hers?" Although Jandi indicates that the price Minji paid for her new body was endurance, she endorses the purchasing power of a consumer who is willing and able to pay for the goods she desires. Little by little, Jandi succumbs to the logic of monetary transaction as the foundational approach to establishing and resolving social relations.

Acceptance of this free market logic and the ensuing economic disparity as a way to articulate human relations and actions become the defining characteristic of people from different generations and walks of life throughout *Boys Over Flowers*. In a disturbing image, Jandi's parents kneel down in front of much younger Junpyo when he visits them for the first time. Whether for love of his status or with sincere wishes for their daughter's happy future with him, Jandi's parents prostrate and look up to Junpyo like worshipers of a benevolent emperor. When Jandi's father is taken away by loan sharks after failing to pay his hefty debt, Jandi's mother pays a visit to Junpyo's mother, the President of Sinhwa Group, and kneels when she asks for money in an effort to save her husband from harm. To enhance the dramatic humiliation of the poor, the scene presents Jandi's mother pouring a bucket of coarse salt on her head as a sign of self-negation while kneeling before the mother of her daughter's boyfriend.

A deceptive moral relief from watching these appalling images of class hierarchy is guaranteed for South Korean viewers – and most likely for North Korean viewers – by the fact that the submission of the underprivileged to the rich and powerful is masked by temporary challenges to plutocracy. Ultimately, economic and social inequality is accepted by both *chaebol* and *seomin* as de facto reality, but the blunt rhetoric of economic disparity at times hides behind the *seomin*'s semblance of defiant resistance against their oppressors, only to revert to the world order as established by the ruling economic forces. What enables North Korean viewers to identify with the moral plight of characters in *Boys Over Flowers* might be such temporary reinvention of the poor and the oppressed into valiant revolutionaries who can stand up against injustice.

During one of the fights between Jandi and Junpyo, she rebukes him for trying to win her heart with endless expensive gifts: "Friendship is not bought by money, it is exchanged between hearts." Junpyo falls silent at this sudden criticism of his aggressive attempts to transform a human relationship into a market transaction. In a similar battle in Episode 12, Jandi faces Gang, the draconian mother of Junpyo and the President of Sinhwa Group, when she visits her office to return the money that her mother received at the expense of self-humiliation. When Gang sees that Jandi is returning the money, she challenges her:

Gang: I heard that your family is struggling financially. Would it not be wise to put aside your pride?
Jandi: It is not a matter of pride. It is our family decision.

Gang: If you think the money is not enough, okay, fine! I see that you have some talent in negotiations. Let's make a deal.

Jandi: Please, I beg you. Do not insult me or my family anymore.

  [...]

Gang: This money is the price of your mother's kneeling down in front of me. Are you going to let it go because of your pride? Wouldn't you regret it? It's quite a sum for some *seomin*'s pride.

Jandi: I did not know that pride came with a price tag. If so, then how much does your pride cost? I hope you can change your opinion that a *seomin*'s pride can be bought and sold at a certain price. By the way, you cannot buy people with money. You do not seem to realize that.

Jandi courageously upholds the dignity of the common people in this scene, but little by little, the viewers see her increasing inclination to embrace the lure of wealth. Soon after this showdown with the most powerful *chaebol* in the country, the viewers see Jandi marveling at the riches of Sinhwa Group's global hotel chain and coveting endless luxury items on display at their premium shopping mall in Macau. She incarnates the ideological purity of the morally untainted class, and yet, by the end of the drama, she emerges with enormous economic gain as a result of her relationship with Junpyo: she takes advantage of the free college education provided by Sinhwa Group, whose president she bravely challenged. Going from rags to riches may be what many North Korean neophytes to the open market dream of; still, on the surface, the drama establishes a credible impression of how the ascendance of a commoner, be it economic or ethical, can only take place in a morally justifiable manner. While trying to emulate the looks of Junpyo and Jandi, North Korean fans might also take illusory satisfaction from the fact that there is a way to have it all for ordinary people – to obtain wealth by moral behavior.

Politics of vision

If we take this South Korean drama as a supreme champion of the logic of the open market, with its endless capacity for product placement and its star actors heavily courted by the advertising industry, its popularity in North Korea speaks doubly for the failure of that society: branded as the losing side of history, communism can no longer provide a viable economic model to sustain North Korea, yet what seems to creep in to replace that failed system is the depressing ideology that social relationships are subject to the power of materialism. But the drama's ability to place a beautiful façade on the ruthlessness of the market system sublimates that inequality into spectacular visual pleasure. With pervasive popular influence and the ability to transform inequality into dreamlike romance, *Boys Over Flowers*, and South Korean TV dramas at large, propagate the rules of the market economy in North Korea –

For the eyes of North Koreans?   103

a nation with an impenetrable ideological front on the surface but gradually turning toward various forms of open market.

The South Korean media are becoming increasingly aware of the growing influence of their products on North Koreans, both within and outside of the country: "New settlers regarded the media as the first means to get acquainted with the South Korean society. According to a 1998 survey conducted by the Korean Broadcasting System, 89 percent of the survey participants responded that television helped them most significantly in settling into South Korean society."[9] At the same time, the South Korean media seem to feign naivety about the lack of critical perception among North Korean settlers, faced with the deluge of South Korean media products. Anxieties fly high about the potential misperceptions these newcomers might have about the drama's ability to capture the realities of life in South Korea:

> New settlers become exposed to commercial media while lacking the ability to critically filter media content. They are prone to developing the desire for an economically affluent society while being surrounded by extreme forms of consumerism. For instance, a teenager who settled in the city of Gwangju after escaping North Korea bought a $10,000 sofa and a $5,000 flat-screen TV when he received settlement funds from the South Korean government. Another North Korean settler, Mr. Hyeon, on the other hand, told the reporter that he was quite surprised to see that the house given to him in South Korea was quite small and rundown compared to the ones he saw in South Korean TV dramas. New settlers feel relative poverty when they compare their own realities with what they see on South Korean television. This is why we need to provide media education for new settlers (before they become integrated into South Korean society).[10]

Indeed, as if responding to the worrisome sentiment regarding North Korean settlers' lack of critical filtering of South Korean media, such "media education" starts quite early nowadays, aiming at not only North Koreans who are now in South Korea, but also those who are in North Korea proper – the imagined consumers of South Korean media and culture at some point in the future. "Open Radio for North Korea," for instance, is a South Korean radio program for North Korean listeners, who possibly watch South Korean TV dramas through bootleg copies smuggled into the country via China. One notable series is called "Demystifying South Korean Society Through Drama," which ran a program on *Boys Over Flowers*:

> What do you listeners think of this drama? Were you curious to find out whether all South Korean high school students enjoyed such luxurious school facilities as you see in the drama? Were you curious to find out whether all South Korean boys are as handsome as Gu Junpyo and Yun

> Jihu while all the girls are as pretty as Geum Jandi? In South Korea, there are high schools founded by the state, and there are also public schools and private schools. Life in Sinhwa High School that you see in the drama is closer to the realities of a South Korean college – the difference is that the students are wearing school uniforms in the drama. And if you watch the drama, all men and women are beautiful. I would say that most South Korean actors and actresses are quite good looking. As for ordinary people, there is quite a bit of diversity: there are beautiful people, there are good-looking people, and there are people with very unique looks. As far as the standard of living is concerned, ordinary Koreans are better off than Jandi's family but worse off than Junpyo's family. It's because Jandi's family struggles and Junpyo comes from a family with a rich conglomerate.[11]

The infantilizing vision of North Korean viewers as lacking any critical faculties ironically points to the South Korean media's own lack of critical perspective on itself. As much as it hopes to claim its difference from its North Korean counterpart, structural similarities abound, which ultimately explains its cultural currency in North Korea: the viewers there can identify with the logic of class struggle and social hierarchy that they see in this South Korean drama.

In place of North Korean ideals for equitable society steps in individual meritocracy in *Boys Over Flowers*. But that meritocracy as a means to advance qualifying individuals must stop at the glass ceiling, where they are at the mercy of those who have the ultimate power to control social mobility. This is quite similar to the North Korean ideals of utopia within limits, where every subject has to stay under the glass ceiling of the almighty leader. In place of struggle between the landed class and landless peasants in North Korea, there is social conflict between those who have it all and the rest. But at the end of the day, the intensified class struggle, which sets the stage for the main crux of narrative force, peters out in the merciful face of the almighty power – be it the heroic leaders of the sacred state or the beyond-rich heir to the multinational conglomeration.

Notes

1 There is plenty of media coverage referencing the similarities among the three productions. See Kwon Gyeongsung, "The Success of *Boys Over Flowers* in Taiwan, Korea, and Japan Lies in the Original Manga," *Mediatoday*, September 14, 2009, http://www.mediatoday.co.kr/news/articleView.html?idxno=82841 (accessed March 6, 2013); http://nownews.seoul.co.kr/news/newsView.php?id=20090115601015 (accessed February 10, 2009); http://sports.donga.com/HTML/News/2009/01/23/2009012350000 0165256/2009012350000016525602020000000.html (accessed February 1, 2009). On the other hand, some private bloggers have compared the three productions' cast to the original manga characters. See http://blog.daum.net/ttoobee/11743296 (accessed February 26, 2013) and http://nuriencorp.tistory.com/101 (accessed February 26, 2013).

2 Mun Seonghui, "North Korea Falls for Drama *Boys Over Flowers*," Radio Free Asia, September 15, 2011, http://www.rfa.org/korean/in_focus/skdrama-09152011130127.html (accessed February 22, 2013).

3 Yi Wonhui, "2011 New Years Special Report: New Waves of Change in North Korea, Part 3, 'South Korean Dramas Are So Interesting,'" Radio Free Asia, January 11, 2011, http://www.rfa.org/korean/temp/new_year_sp-01052011113720.html (accessed February 22, 2013).

4 http://sports.hankooki.com/lpage/entv/200903/sp2009031207180594350.htm (accessed March 16, 2009).

5 Yi Heon-eop, "*Boys Over Flowers*' Popularity Stems From Escapism," http://www.i-bait.com/read.php?cataId=NLC001047&num=2554&tcataId= (accessed March 1, 2013).

6 Large conglomerates whose development was sponsored by the South Korean state in the post-Korean War era. Samsung and Hyundai are the two best-known *chaebol* in South Korea.

7 Directly translated as "plebeian," the word refers to ordinary citizens who belong to the middle and lower-middle class in a colloquial sense.

8 There are simply too many *chaebol* dramas to list them in full detail, but some that enjoyed critical acclaim as well as a broad following are: *Days of Ambition* (KBS2, 1990–91), *Love and Ambition* (MBC, 1987; remade by SBS, 2006), *Whatever Happened in Bali* (SBS, 2004), *East of Eden* (MBC, 2008–9) and *Secret Garden* (SBS, 2010–11).

9 Bak Geunyeong, "Dreaming of Flowery South Korea While Watching *Boys Over Flowers*" [in Korean], SisaInLive, February 28, 2009, http://www.sisainlive.com/news/articleView.html?idxno=3898 (accessed February 22, 2013).

10 Bak Geunyeong, "Dreaming of Flowery South Korea While Watching Boys Over Flowers."

11 Gim Yeongmi, "Demystifying South Korean Society Through Drama, Part 3," Open Radio for North Korea, December 23, 2011, http://www.nkradio.org/paper/news/print.php?newsno=7713 (accessed February 22, 2013).

References

Bak, G. (2009) "Dreaming of Flowery South Korea While Watching *Boys Over Flowers*," [in Korean] SisaInLive, February 28.

Gim, Y. (2011) "Demystifying South Korean Society Through Drama, Part 3," Open Radio for North Korea, December 23.

Kwon, G. (2009) "The Success of *Boys Over Flowers* in Taiwan, Korea, and Japan Lies in the Original Manga," *Mediatoday*, September 14.

Mun, S. (2011) "North Korea Falls for Drama *Boys Over Flowers*." Radio Free Asia, September 15.

Yi, H. (2009) "*Boys Over Flowers*' Popularity Stems From Escapism," *Bait*, March 2.

Yi, W. (2011) "2011 New Years Special Report: New Waves of Change in North Korea, Part 3, 'South Korean Dramas Are So Interesting,'" Radio Free Asia, January 11.

Chapter 6

K-pop female idols in the West
Racial imaginations and erotic fantasies

Eun-Young Jung

Jon Toth, a twenty-nine-year-old white guy, a computer scientist who had driven twelve hours straight from New Mexico [to see the SMTOWN LIVE WORLD TOUR III held in Anaheim, CA on May 20, 2012], "I was definitely not the kind of guy you'd expect to get into a nine-girl Asian group." But before long Toth was studying Korean, in order to understand the lyrics and also Korean TV shows. Then started cooking Korean food. Eventually, he travelled all the way to Seoul, where, for the first time, he was able to see the Girls perform live. It was a life-changing experience. Toth concluded, "I might not know how much I love these girls."

(An interview in "Factory Girls: Cultural Technology
and the Making of K-pop" by John Seabrook,
The New Yorker, October 8, 2012)

The recent worldwide explosion of Korean pop music is a cultural phenomenon as unexpected in Korea itself as in the numerous countries throughout most of the world that now have rapidly growing fan bases for K-pop. This cultural and commercial explosion is celebrated in the Korean mass media and nurtured with pride by the Korean government. This chapter offers a critical look at some of the complexities in the K-pop global phenomenon and focuses on K-pop's problematic relations with the Western market, the U.S. in particular. Psy's record-setting *Gangnam Style* music video, which reached more than a billion YouTube views within six months after its posting (in July 2012), is the latest and undeniably most spectacular instance of the extraordinary international spread of contemporary Korean pop music. Psy would seem to have penetrated even into the U.S. mainstream pop market like a speeding comet, although it is still too early to know to what extent his sudden stardom can last past this one video alone. Recent attempts by some of the biggest Korean pop stars to break into the U.S. pop market have resulted in momentary flashes of wide publicity, but have largely been disappointments, attesting to the complex challenges presented by the U.S. mainstream pop market – challenges that may continue to make it difficult for lasting development of a place for Korean pop music in the U.S.

As a part of the Korean Wave (Hallyu) phenomenon since the late 1990s, the sector of Korean pop music known as K-pop, referring to especially manufactured idol pop by young boys' and girls' bands (and a few solo singers), has become increasingly popular in Asia and has begun to gain adoring young fans worldwide, including in the U.S., in recent years thanks largely to its availability via the ubiquitous Internet and social media. Yet overseas responses to K-pop idols' musical and visual styles have not always been positive. Their failure, especially in the U.S., despite their individual efforts and aggressive promotion and investment by their ambitious management companies, severely damaged their pop star image and in some cases literally ended their singing careers upon their return to Korea. The three solo idol singers BoA, Rain and Se7en and the two girl bands Wonder Girls and Girls' Generation attempted to break into the U.S. pop market between 2008 and 2012, but flopped, despite their enormous success in Korea and throughout Asia. Not only were they attempting to penetrate a market with no prior interest in Korean or other Asian pop music, but their visible identities as Asian inevitably placed them within the entanglements of race and sexuality in America's popular imagination. Ironically, such entanglements may have partially helped Psy to be successful in the U.S., as visual images of Psy and others in the music video, including the two male comedians dancing wildly, fit with the familiar stereotype of Asian males as sexually unthreatening and comical. The focus of this chapter, though, is on Korean female idols, whose image challenges have run headlong into American stereotypes of Asian women as exotic sexual objects.

Popular music, whose appeal relies somewhat less on language than do films or television shows, should traverse national boundaries somewhat more easily, it would seem. Indeed, listeners worldwide often enjoy listening to music whose lyrics are in a language they do not know or understand well, as we have witnessed from the case of Psy's *Gangnam Style*, which is mostly in Korean with the exception of a few English words (e.g. "sexy lady," "baby"). Yet, it is also clear that the transnational flows of popular music have limits, and these limits have less to do with language or musical style than they do with, for lack of a better term, "image." Particularly since the dawn of music television in the early 1980s and the heavy reliance on visual materials ("the video") to promote and market popular music, the physical appearance of the musicians and the reactions to their appearance by the audience of potential customers have been very important commercially and aesthetically. In other words, for contemporary international marketing of popular music – videos, concert tours, DVDs, photo albums, downloads and social media interactions – (physical, visual) image matters. K-pop idol manufacturers seem well aware of the power of image as they focus heavily not only on *perfecting* their idols' physical features but also on actively exploiting the idols' images, racy (and racial) and sexual, in their music videos. Although the lyrics used by K-pop idols in their songs aimed at the U.S. market make no explicit reference to race, the visual contents are usually linked to the entanglements of race and sexuality in the popular imagination – each video playing on the American audience's racialized notions of sexuality and sexualized notions of racial identity.

This chapter focuses on two K-pop female acts – Wonder Girls and Girls' Generation – who attempted to garner their biggest success, between 2009 and 2012, not by offering new musical styles but by negotiating and repackaging their Asian female sexuality in attempts to play to the realities – and fantasies – of the U.S. pop market. A similar approach had been attempted in 2008 by Korea's sensational female idol singer BoA (see Jung 2010). While it should be noted that the attempts by the two male solo singers, Rain and Se7en, in the late 2000s also deserve in-depth analyses as each case bears on distinctive aspects and dynamics of the U.S. pop market environments and America's racial and sexual imaginings, this chapter specifically focuses on the female idols, who have been far more aggressively promoted overseas than the male idols by their management companies, especially with regard to the U.S. market.

Female singers in many cultures around the world have long relied on their abilities to tease and arouse the sexual desires of the male audience, not only in the commodified popular music of the twentieth and twenty-first centuries, but in previous eras as well. In Asia, traditions of the female entertainer as musician/dancer offering sexual favors, or promoting fantasies thereof, include the *geisha* of Japan, the *gisaeng* of Korea and the *taledhek/tandak* of Java, among others. The female entertainer, though of lower social status and physically weaker than men, was routinely able to exert power over men by emphasizing the erotic, even when her "act" was merely an act, playing to fantasies that might not be realized.

As peoples of different racial identities entered each other's imaginaries through the centuries of Western colonial expansion and race-based domination, racial "Otherness" in the realm of sexuality came both to titillate and to repel. Sexual attraction between members of different racial groups has been deemed illicit, dangerous, even unnatural; and resulting sexual union and marriage have sometimes been officially forbidden. At the same time, race itself has been eroticized. More particularly, non-white races have been, and still are, essentialized erotically by whites (who may imagine themselves to be more complex and exempt from essentialized, racialized sexual stereotyping, the images of the virile white male adventurer/conqueror and the virtuous and pure white female notwithstanding): the hyper-masculine black male, the tough and strong black female, the hyper-feminine Asian female (submissive or dominating), the emasculated Asian male (physically weak and comical), the slick gigolo Latino, the hyper-sexual Latina, and so forth. These sexualized racial stereotypes are reinforced incessantly in the entertainment media (Wu 2002; Prasso 2005), although they did not arise there – one only need think of Cho-cho-san in Puccini's *Madame Butterfly* in the realm of performing arts (Head 2003). Not only is this Asian female erotically appealing, but her submissive nature draws her irresistibly to the white male, who is stronger and more desirable than Asian alternatives. The fantasy, then, identifies not only the sexuality of the Asian female, but that Asian female's desire for the Western male. Writ large, a weak, submissive Asia is seduced and falls for the strong West; the West retains power and may (as in *Madame Butterfly*) choose to abandon Asia. In his classic *Orientalism*, Edward Said notes the West's association of the "Orient" with "the freedom of licentious sex," imagining it as "a place where one could look for sexual experience unobtainable in Europe" (1978: 190).[1]

It is in the postcolonial world of the late twentieth and early twenty-first centuries that these conflations of sexual and racial stereotypes have been rehearsed so relentlessly that they become unquestioned, hegemonic truths, unconsciously figuring as reified categories by which the West, still imperiously, understands, makes sense of and controls racial others and imagines the erotic desires of racial others (Lewis 1996; Columpar 2002). My concern in this chapter is with the eroticized images and imagined desires for racially Asian females as held by Westerners and the ways in which Korean female idols and their management companies methodically attempt to produce and market those images, exploiting what they believe to be ingrained stereotypes of Asian females as irresistible seductresses, docile, dominating, or both. As they play to these stereotypes in hopes of financial gain, of course, they also become duplicitous in perpetuating them.

At the same time, this drive for "commercial success" in the West, and particularly in the U.S., is driven not purely by financial aspirations, but by the postcolonial desire for recognition and acceptance by the nation at the absolute peak among world entertainment economies. Though colonized by Japan, and not by any Western country, the overwhelming presence of American military and popular culture in post-World War II South Korea promulgated a power imbalance, as much cultural as military or economic, with American popular culture in a lofty position as the world standard, at first to be emulated, and now to be challenged, even "conquered." It is this drive for soft power (Nye 2004) parity, or triumph, that plays as much to Korean pride as to music industry economics, with the whole Korean nation cheering for the American embrace (even if exoticist) of Psy. Other Korean pop performers have not found the magic key to American acceptance, despite calculated efforts to exploit Orientalist fantasies. Still, one cannot imagine them getting as far as they did (making debuts and appearing on network television) without exploiting such fantasies.

In the first case, the five-girl group known as Wonder Girls presents the conventional China Doll stereotype that they are ready to serve men with their docile, cute, sexy, vulnerable and playful attitudes. These stereotypical representations of Asian female sexuality are reinforced and controlled by their Asian male managers who see these representations as a means to gain acceptance in the U.S. pop music market.[2] In the second case, the nine-girl group known as Girls' Generation presents in their U.S. debut music video a similar combination of the duality: docile feminine ladies in classy dresses and sexy powerful women in shorts or skinny pants. While their female bodily sexuality seems less racialized than BoA's in her infamous videos of *Eat You Up* (Jung 2010), at least in the sense that no interaction with other races is displayed in the music video, the group's U.S. debut appearances on mainstream American TV shows reveal its efforts to negotiate and to accommodate the American audience's racial imaginations and by repackaging themselves as more sexually provocative than in the music video and their usual images.

Wonder Girls

The five-girl group Wonder Girls (early 2007 debut in Korea, 20–24-year-olds) made their U.S. debut in summer 2009 by releasing an English version of their typical idol K-pop, bubblegum pop song *Nobody* (released in 2008 in Korea). By joining the Jonas Brothers (a popular American boy band at that time) on the North American leg of their tour "Jonas Brothers World Tour 2009," Wonder Girls' U.S. debut initially received some measurable coverage by the U.S. pop media (Liu 2009; Wong 2009). Like most K-pop girl groups and boy bands in Korea, Wonder Girls have a carefully managed career and group image prepared and manufactured by their management company JYP Entertainment. Their U.S. promotional photo has them seated together on a Rococo-style bench in matching bob hairstyle wigs, large earrings, heavy eye-makeup, long fake eyelashes and matching tight mini-dresses with colorful stockings (retro-themed), an image that again brings to mind the stereotypical China Doll look, and perhaps even the cliché that all Asians "look alike." In this case, however, the image was conceived by their Korean male manager, Jin-Young Park (hereafter JYP). He has extensive experience in the U.S. pop music market, having produced the male singer Rain's U.S. debut in early 2006 (Jung 2010). Even though one member (Sunmi) was replaced with a new member (Hyelim) soon after their U.S. debut, the same promotional photo featuring the ex-member has continuously been used in the U.S., which reinforces the notion that all Asians "look alike" as each member's individual difference is not recognized by the American pop media. For example, the January 2012 article in the popular American magazine *The Atlantic* "Does Korean Pop Actually Have a Shot at Success in the U.S.?" used the same promotional photo regarding the group's release of the film *The Wonder Girls* through TeenNick and their new marketing strategy, targeting the teenage market in the U.S., as a positive move (Michel 2012).

Unlike BoA's *Eat You Up*, with a different video released in the U.S. than in Korea, the music video of Wonder Girls' song *Nobody* released in the U.S. is the same as the original Korean version released in Korea in 2008, but in English. The music video follows a typical K-pop music video formula, a mini-movie-like style with a complete storyline. It starts with JYP performing his 2006 song *Honey* on the 1960s Motown-style stage with Wonder Girls as his backup singers, dressed alike in girlish white dresses. After the show, JYP is introduced with a new song, *Nobody*, by two music producers, and he practices the song for his next show while Wonder Girls are practicing their chorus and backup dancing, again, all in feminine white dresses (one even with an oddly oversized white bow on her head). Right before the show begins, JYP is using the restroom and soon discovers that there is no toilet paper. JYP desperately calls for help but no one comes to his aid. The show, however, must go on. The onscreen music producers order Wonder Girls to perform *Nobody* instead. The five girls, all in identical tight mini-dresses, successfully finish their performance as JYP arrives on-stage to congratulate them awkwardly. The song continues as scenes of Wonder Girls featured in newspapers and television appearances flash by. As the group seemingly becomes more successful they wear skimpier and flashier dresses on-stage. The music video ends with JYP at a different toilet stall encountering the same problem as he pulls the very last sheet off the dispenser. The music video's light comical tone fits well with Wonder Girls' bubblegum pop style and their playful girlish image.

The lyrics of the song describe a desperate woman who is begging her lover to come back and insisting that he is the only one she wants:

> You know I still love you baby.
> And it will never change. *Saranghae* [meaning "I love you"]
> I want nobody nobody but you
> I want nobody nobody but you
> How can I be with another man
> I don't want any other
> I want nobody nobody nobody nobody

There is nothing terribly provocative or daring in this song. Its catchy refrain "I want nobody nobody but you" with an accompanying dance movement is repeated numerous times. Many online comments talk about how cute and sexy those girls look and at the same time how funny their English accents sound. A viewer on YouTube writes, "ahahahahahahaha I want your body? your body not chu!! I want your body your body not chu!! XD." Another viewer comments, "Absolutely love this, though instead of dubbing it would be better to subtitle." In addition to criticism of their accented English, their singing skills have also been brought into question. In Korea they have been referred to as the "Tuneless Girls" ("Ppiksal Kŏlsŭ") and despite their improvement over the past few years in some degree they are still not considered as talented singers. Nevertheless, their cute, sexy, exotic Asian female images seem enough to cover such perceived shortcomings; their song *Nobody* momentarily broke into the top-100 on the U.S. Billboard Charts on October 22, 2009, reaching No. 76 (Ko 2009).

Nevertheless, Wonder Girls' U.S. career did not show much promise subsequently, and most of their live shows were localized to the large Asian and

Asian-American communities in California, including Los Angeles and San Francisco, where they were assured sufficiently large audiences who could appreciate their cutesy appeal. After the song *2 Different Tears* (released in Korean, English and Chinese in May 2010) was poorly received in the U.S., they returned to Korea and focused on Korean promotion for a while. However, with their career in Korea showing no sign of revival, Wonder Girls briefly returned to the U.S. market with the teenage market in mind and released the semi-documentary film *The Wonder Girls* and a featured song in the film *Like Money* in summer 2012. Despite some positive prediction in the American pop media, their second-round attempt in the U.S. *again* flopped. The music video for the song *Like Money*, featuring the successful Senegalese American singer and producer Akon (who produced Lady Gaga, among others), opens with the girls becoming human from dead/broken robots and then goes on simply to display the girls doing group dancing and singing in black-tone body tights. The song lyrics, co-written by Grammy Award-winning American songwriter Cri$tyle, describe the girls' sexual desire and the man's response:[3]

> [Wonder Girls]
> Love me like money ...
> I'm trying to show you how to touch me
> [Akon]
> Love you like money
> Love you like cars
> Love you baby love you babe wherever you are

The suggestive song lyrics are degrading to the girls as they want to be treated as "money" and "cars" in the song portraying them as the stereotypical Asian women who are eager to be treated as vulnerable and unintelligent sexual objects. Also, the visual aspects are at once futuristic yet outdated and random by making the girls cyborg-like trans-human characters, which not only remind us of 1970s and 1980s American science fiction films such as *Tron*, but also refer to a stereotypical Asian as an emotionless robot, as one viewer recognized: "I think it was a HUGE ERROR to choose a stereotype as-concept (Asian are robots?) for me the video clip is an epic fail" (online talk on YouTube). Like BoA's *Eat You Up*, Wonder Girls' *Like Money* is mostly an American team production – reflecting the American racial and sexual views on Asian women and the Korean (at least JYP's) desire to be accepted by the mainstream U.S. pop market even if they have to greatly compromise themselves to be racially, sexually and musically acceptable.

The overall production of their second attempt was not coherent but somewhat awkward, and some fans did not welcome the featured black artist Akon, known for his misogynist and sexist expression,[4] being paired with their girls, as evident in their comments on YouTube:

Black n Yellow Black n Yellow Black n Yellow.

Wonder girls are too good to sing with this sell out clown. Let's not forget that akon is the one who appeared in the video. "I Just Had Sex", I mean, jeesus! ... Of all the people, why freaking akon?

JYP's inconsistent production and marketing strategies seem to continuously complicate the group's career development as JYP quickly arranged for the group's Japan debut in fall 2012, not with a new song but with the 2008 song *Nobody*, instead of promoting the song in the U.S. (Han 2012). While Japan has been a big market for K-pop idols since the early 2000s because of their successful localized marketing, Wonder Girls' quick jump on the market turned into an instant fiasco in Japan, placing the group's future career further in question.

Girls' Generation

The nine-girl group Girls' Generation (also known as SNSD, abbreviation for the full Korean name, *Sonyŏ Sidae*, 2007 debut in Korea, 21–23-year-olds) is under the same management as BoA: S.M., the most dominant K-pop idol maker. By implementing the conventional Japanese idol production system in the mid-1990s, S.M. fully systematized the total procedure of young pop idol making and initiated overseas marketing that became K-pop idol business standards. After obtaining a breakthrough by boy band H.O.T. in China (Pease 2006) and moderate success by girl group S.E.S. in Japan (Jung 2009) in the late 1990s and early 2000s, S.M. began to prepare its trainees for international activities (e.g. foreign language training) and to form idol groups with Korean Americans, Korean Japanese or non-Korean foreigners. With BoA's Asia-wide success, making a breakthrough in the U.S. pop market then became one of S.M.'s highest priorities. Despite BoA's flop in the U.S., S.M. has been persistent in trying to make the first breakthrough for K-pop in the U.S. with one of its popular associate acts, Girls' Generation. Although S.M. seems to be taking more careful steps lately, Girls' Generation's initial attempt in the U.S. has employed musical and visual packaging very similar to BoA's, even though it has already proven to be ineffective.

By strategically including two Korean American members (Tiffany and Jessica), Girls' Generation was produced with the U.S. pop market in mind from the beginning. From their initial innocent, cutesy, happy girl images and typical bubblegum pop songs (*Gee, Genie, Oh!*), as they grew more mature, yet *not* overly sexy, feminine images were adapted with newer songs (*Run Devil Run, Hoot*). Their extremely well-manicured physical features (the result of numerous plastic surgeries and strict diet plans), beautiful long legs in particular, and overall visual images are packaged as the perfect "graceful" female fantasy by the Korean media. Indeed, they have come to be known as the nine *goddesses* (called *yŏsin* in Korean).[5] As the group became the most popular K-pop girl group in Korea, while its rival girl group Wonder Girls was, mistakenly, away from the local scene for their U.S. attempts, the next step was to expand to the Japanese market. With S.M.'s firmly established partnerships in Japan, Girls' Generation's Japan debut was an instant success without adding much extra effort besides releasing their hit Korean songs in Japanese.

Signed with Interscope Records (Universal Music Group) in 2011, Girls' Generation made their U.S. debut performances on two major U.S. television talk shows, *Late Show with David Letterman* and *Live! With Kelly*, on January 31 and February 1, 2012. These appearances, of course, earned them instant wide exposure. The group's U.S. debut song, *The Boys*, was co-written and co-produced by Grammy Award-winning singer-songwriter and producer Teddy Riley (famous for his work with Michel Jackson) and S.M.'s in-house producers. It follows the latest conventions of typical idol K-pop songs, dance-oriented, minimalistic lyrics and short catchy refrains. The phrase "bring the boys out" is repeated 21 times! The lyrics portray sexually daring girls who enjoy the male gaze (e.g. "looking at me," "watching me – watching me") and are confident in their ability to attract the boys with their body moves:

> I can tell you're looking at me, I know what you see
> Any closer and you'll feel the heat
> You don't have to pretend that you didn't notice me
> Every look will make it hard to breathe
> B-Bring the boys out (x 5)
> ... Soon as I step on the scene
> I know that they'll be watching me – watching me –
> Get up, I'mma be the hottest in this spot
> ... I wanna dance right now, We can show 'em how the girls get down
> ... All the boys (x2) want my heart, Better know how to rock and don't stop
> Oh Gee, We make you so hot, Girls' Generation we won't stop
> B-Bring the boys out

Again, we witness a shift similar to that of our earlier case of Wonder Girls, from girlish, romantic, happy, falling-in-love songs to aggressive, daring, provocative, erotic, sexual desire-driven songs. The group's most successful K-pop song, *Gee* (2009), for example, tells the story of a first love and how excited and happy she feels as she falls in love at first sight. Yet their U.S. debut song *The Boys* is all about physical attraction and sexual power, and such lyrical content is delivered in a manner different from their usual styles, particularly on the *Late Show with David Letterman* appearance. Also different from the music video, in which they wear long gowns and tiaras, for their appearance on the David Letterman Show the girls dressed more sexily, including fishnet stockings, and their dance moves and facial expressions were much more suggestive and less cutesy than their earlier dancing styles. Responses to the David Letterman Show performance were concentrated on the girls' sexy dance moves, and were lacking in praise for either the song or their singing skills. Many complained about the change from K-pop to American pop and suspected that they were lip-synching. YouTube viewers' comments and Twitter tweets include:[6]

> ... hot chick_ :)

> The asian girls are cute, though_the singing is meh.hope old geezer didn't try to hit on them.[7]

> Um what's this shit girl group! Lip Sync and just some untalented strippers! Girls generation is a joke!

The Letterman clip has barely made a few million views since its release, contrasting sharply with the over 94 million views for their K-pop hit song *Gee*, for example. Many American viewers seemed to be overwhelmed by seeing such a large number of Asian girls and some felt that there were more than nine girls, as expressed on YouTube and Twitter:

> Do we really need like_15 girls singing at the same time? What a bunch of shit, wouldn't be surprised if this hit the top 10 ... sad times we live in.

> The weirdest Asian group is performing on Letterman, there's like 50 of them.

These exaggerations of the numbers clearly indicate the widespread fear of America being invaded by "hordes" of Asians. The infamous racist rant by a former UCLA student, white female, posted on YouTube as "Asians in the library" on March 14, 2011 indicates how such images are widely conceived by many Americans.[8] In her video, in which she self-identified as a "polite, nice American girl," she fumed about the ill-mannered "hordes of Asians" on campus, including in the library and dormitories, complaining about their use of cellphones and derisively mimicking an Asian accent. Even though the original video was taken down and she made a formal apology, numerous response and parody videos, including many song versions, have been circulating widely. Her perception of Asians as foreign hordes threatening, or polluting, the U.S. is similar to the viewers' responses to Girls' Generation's appearance on the popular nationwide television show.

More than the song itself and their performance, a brief interaction after the David Letterman Show performance is also telling. The two main guests, Bill Murray and Regis Philbin, dressed in sports costumes celebrating the upcoming Super Bowl, attentively watched the girls during the performance. After the performance, Philbin approached the group as he was blowing his referee's whistle – a clearly disrespectful and undignified indiscretion, apparently taken as a laughable and acceptable joke by the audience. While the song lyrics and the girls' suggestive body expression could be responsible in part, being objectified in such a ludicrous way by a white male so unproblematically is a clear indication that these Asian girls are not taken seriously as musicians, but instead treated only as something to look at (or to play with) or even as objects of derision.

Girls' Generation's performance on the daytime talk show *Live! With Kelly* on the following day revealed yet another aspect of America's popular racial imagination of Asians as the perpetual foreigners in the U.S. who "can't speak English." After the performance, for which they were dressed more casually than on Letterman, the group was interviewed by the host Kelly Ripa and guest co-host Howie Mandel.[9] As one of the two Korean American members Tiffany took the questions, Mandel complimented her English with "Your English is very good." Surprised by her answer "I was born in America" (with her perfect California accent) and the other girls' giggles, Mandel repeated, "Aaand … YOUR ENGLISH IS VERY GOOD!" Trying to save the rather awkward moment, Tiffany cheerfully responded, "I know, I know, thank you so much, I studied so hard!" with big smiles and everyone laughed. Still, Mandel's startled reaction to Tiffany's English as "good" reveals in no uncertain terms his racialized presumption that anyone looking Asian in the U.S. must be a foreigner, unable to speak fluent and accentless American English.

Girls' Generation did recently succeed in attaining a major American label contract and in having the debut performances on the major American television programs, but they have yet to establish themselves in the U.S. pop market. As many viewers pointed out, beside the mediocre song with simple lyrics, the very concept of a girl group, especially its unusually large size of nine (or more?) members, seems unappealing to Americans as it is not only an outdated concept within the American pop market (harking back to the 1960s) but also rekindles racial unease concerning Asians, in "hordes," invading the U.S.

Conclusion

This chapter has attempted to demonstrate the persistent challenges encountered by Korean idol groups in the face of American racial stereotypes of Asian females and the Korean music industry's often misguided strategies to exploit these stereotypes. This would seem to show a facet of immutable racialized attitudes in the American media and the society. When it comes to the mainstream pop music market in the U.S., the presence of Asian and Asian-American singers remains extremely limited (Wong 2004; Wang 2007; Yang 2008), with only two truly notable exceptions: Far East Movement (Asian-American male hip-hop and electro pop quartet) and Psy. The "forever-foreignness" of Asians and Asian-Americans (Wu 2002) continues to be firmly etched into the mindset of many Americans. Even some of the most successful pop stars from Asia, such as Wonder Girls and Girls' Generation, and Rain and BoA before them, have failed to break into the mainstream U.S. pop music market, despite their high-profile collaborations with leading U.S. record labels and producers and their decisions to sing in English and produce musical sounds and visual images intended to play to American tastes. To some extent, problems with English language pronunciation may be cited as one factor. But more fundamentally it seems that ingrained stereotypes have proven to be remarkably resistant to change as manifest in the responses to Asians by young and old Americans alike. And the choice to present Korean female idols in seeming conformity to these stereotypes not only reinforces the stereotypes, but prevents the idols themselves from being taken seriously as musicians.

In examining the U.S. market-targeted songs and visual images presented by the female Korean singers, it is apparent that their racial and sexual identities are not only manipulated by American labels and producers but also continuously negotiated by their own management teams. As noted *and* criticized by many audiences and viewers, these Korean singers' musical-visual presentations for the U.S. market often merely aim to conform to the Western stereotypical notions of Asian-ness in their racial and sexual identities and try too hard to follow trendy American pop sounds instead of bringing in something new and different. Perhaps, after witnessing Psy's success with his innovative musical-visual creation, K-pop idol singers and groups may develop new material (musical sound and visual presentations) and different strategies in their attempts to break into the U.S. market, but the idol legacy has certainly not been one of great innovation.

At this point one could hardly say that Asian pop musicians have made the commercial breakthrough they have been hoping for in the U.S. pop market, with the possible solitary exception of Psy. Yet, it is clear that there will be more and more attempts to transform racist stereotypes as younger Asian and Asian American artists become more confident of their own racial identities and their presence and image in media culture continue to improve. In the meantime, in order to gain further entry into the U.S. pop market, these Korean singers and groups will need to re-evaluate their outdated and misguided strategies and to be more creative and original – perhaps thereby placing themselves outside the "idol" mode altogether.

Notes

1 *Cf.* Behdad's remarks about French colonial literature, in which one finds identification of Asia ("the Orient") as "le pays d'aventures," [the land of adventure] a domain of lustful sensuality, and an absolutely lawless region where "tout ... est possible" [everything ... is possible] (1990: 46); and Levine's study of British differentiation between "respectable" European and "unrespectable" native women in colonial society (2000: 5–21).

2 Portions of my discussion here of Wonder Girls have previously been published in Jung (2010), an article that also deals at length with BoA's attempt to break into the U.S. market with an overtly sexual song and music video playing on racial stereotypes (*Eat You Up*). On BoA's *Eat You Up*, see also H. Kim (2008).
3 http://www.youtube.com/watch?v=quE6Cq4Q2bs.
4 For example, see YDNIMPORTER's 2009 article "Letter: Please, Yale, Don't Endorse Akon" in *Yaledailynews*. 5 March. http://yaledailynews.com/blog/2009/03/05/letter-please-yale-dont-endorse-akon/.
5 Google search of "Sonyŏsidae Yŏsin" (meaning "Girls Generation Goddess" in Korean) brings more than 13 million results. The group's success with such concepts has inspired many copycats not only in Korea (e.g. Nine Muses, 2010) but also in Japan (e.g. seven-girl group Bikyaku Jidai (meaning Beautiful Legs Generation in Japanese), 2012). For more details on the Japanese version of Girls' Generation, see Yanagi (2012).
6 http://www.youtube.com/watch?v=AO9yFjodDtM.
7 The "old geezer" refers to Regis Philbin whose physical response to the group has been ridiculed by many viewers. For example, see the photo in "SNSD & Regis Philbin for 'Viagra' on 'Late Show With David Letterman'," posted on the Asian entertainment news site, Asian Junkie. http://www.asianjunkie.com/2012/01/snsd-regis-philbin-for-viagra-on-late-show-with-david-letterman/.
8 A retrieved version is available at https://www.youtube.com/watch?v=FNuyDZevKrU.
9 https://www.youtube.com/watch?v=e40urQIYU98.

References

Behdad, A. (1990) "Orientalist Desire, Desire of the Orient," *French Forum*, 15(1): 37–51.

Columpar, C. (2002) "The Gaze As Theoretical Touchstone: The Intersection of Film Studies, Feminist Theory, and Postcolonial Theory," *Women's Studies Quarterly,* 30(1/2): 25–44.

Han, M. (2012) "Wonder Girls' Japan Debut, Predictable Result," *Seoulnews*, May 14.

Head, M. (2003) "Musicology on Safari: Orientalism and the Spectre of Post Colonial Theory," *Music Analysis,* 22(1–2): 211–30.

Jung, E. (2009) "Korean Wave in Japan vs. Japanese Wave in Korea," *Asian Musicology*, 14: 5–40.

——(2010) "Playing the Race and Sexuality Cards in the Transnational Pop Game: Korean Music Videos for the US Market," *Journal of Popular Music Studies,* 22(2): 219–36.

Kim, H. (2008) "BoA Showcasing the U.S. Debut Song *Eat You Up* on 10th," *NewsEn*, September 19.

Ko, C. (2009) "The Wonder Girls Enters the U.S. Billboard," *Asia Economy (Asiae)*, October 28.

Levine, P. (2000) "Orientalist Sociology and the Creation of Colonial Sexualities," *Feminist Review,* 65: 5–21.

Lewis, R. (1996) *Gendering Orientalism: Race, Femininity, and Representation*, New York: Routledge.

Liu, M. (2009) "Asian Superstars Wonder Girls Open for Jonas Brothers," *The Seattle Times*, June 28.

Michel, P. (2012) "Does Korean Pop Actually Have a Shot at Success in the U.S.?," *The Atlantic*, January 30. http://www.theatlantic.com/entertainment/archive/2012/01/does-korean-pop-actually-have-a-shot-at-success-in-the-us/252057/ (accessed January 8, 2013).

Nye, J. (2004) *Soft Power: The Means to Success In World Politics*, New York: PublicAffairs.

Pease, R. (2006) "Internet, Fandom, and K-Wave in China," in K. Howard (ed.) *Korean Pop Music: Riding the Wave*, Kent: Global Oriental.

Prasso, S. (2005) *The Asian Mystique: Dragon Ladies, Geisha Girls, & Our Fantasies of the Exotic Orient*, New York: PublicAffairs.

Said, E. (1978) *Orientalism*, New York: Vintage Books.

Wang, O. (2007) "Rapping and Rapping Asian: Race, Authenticity, and the Asian American MC," in M. Nguyen and T. Tu (eds) *Alien Encounters: Popular Culture in Asian America*, Durham: Duke University Press.

Wong, A. (2009) "5 Things to Know About The Wonder Girls," *The People's Magazine*, October 25.

Wong, D. (2004) *Speak It Louder: Asian Americans Making Music*, New York: Routledge.

Wu, F. (2002) *Yellow: Race in America Beyond Black and White*, New York: Basic Books.

Yanagi, M. (2012) "Bikyuki Jidai Debut Single 'Perfect Imagination'," *Jworldorder*, October 23. http://jworldorder.com/music/news/133-bikyaku-jidai-debut-single (accessed January 6, 2013).

Yang, M. (2008) *California Polyphony: Ethnic Voices, Musical Crossroads*, Urbana: University of Illinois Press.

Chapter 7

Negotiating identity and power in transnational cultural consumption

Korean American youths and the Korean Wave

Jung-Sun Park

In the contemporary globalized world, transnational (im)migrants' lives are imbued with many complexities, largely due to their multiple affiliations and constant border-crossing (Appadurai 1991, 1996; Basch *et al.* 1994; Gupta and Ferguson 1994; Hu-Dehart 1999; Kearney 1995; Ong 1999; Xavier and Rosaldo 2002).[1] Located "in-between," they are "fully encapsulated neither in the host society nor in their native land" but "nonetheless remain active participants in the social settings of both locations" (Glick-Schiller and Fouron 1990: 330).[2] Thus, they often build their niches in the interstices among various social, cultural and political communities. While not enough scholarly attention has been given to the lives of a segment of transnational (im)migrant populations – youths – their experiences can shed light on many critical aspects of global transformation, as they are major consumers of various kinds of popular culture, among the most active voices in cyberspace, and one of the most mobile groups who frequently cross real and virtual borders. Among other groups, Asian-American youths have played a critical role in the transnational circulation of products, information and people. Their interest in and easy access to diverse popular cultures, especially U.S. and Asian pop cultures, enable them to become core consumers of multiple national, regional and global pop cultures. Through their frequent transpacific contacts, they disseminate and mediate cultural information across borders, sometimes far more effectively than the mainstream media does. They also participate in the construction of popular culture through their work in the media or entertainment industries on both sides of the Pacific.

The multiple roles of Asian-American youths in transpacific flows of popular culture indicate changes in the global cultural landscape. The boundary-collapsing power of globalization has subverted our long-held notion of culture, which is generally understood as shared meanings, values and customs of a group of people who live within bounded territories, and "hybridization" and "creolization" have become typical characteristics of contemporary culture (Gupta and Ferguson 1994; Hannerz 1992, 1996). Moreover, advancements in technology, which have widened the scope and accelerated the speed of the circulation of information and products to an unprecedented degree, have induced contradictory tendencies. On the one hand, they strengthen the West's, especially Hollywood's, cultural hegemony as the global media industries are mostly controlled and owned by Western capital and as the content of popular culture is still largely of Western origin. On the other hand, they have expedited the regionalization of cultural flows, such as intra-Asian cultural circulation, which challenges the unidirectional cultural flows from the West to the rest, partly because global media industries divide the world into regional markets and tend to regionally distribute programs, many of which are produced locally (Morley and Robins 1995; Iwabuchi 2002). In addition, some Asian countries, with the development of their economy and media industries, have produced marketable popular cultural products such as film, music and animation, which first circulated at the local and regional levels and then gradually expanded to the global market (Iwabuchi 2002; Park 2006; Yau 2001). Cultural influences from the "periphery" to the "center" are not uncommon nowadays, as illustrated by the noticeable African, Latin or Asian influences on contemporary U.S. pop culture (Hannerz 1992). Asian-American youths' multiple roles signify their critical involvement in this transpacific "cross-fertilization of culture" (Iwabuchi 2002). In addition, the consumption of "homeland" popular culture reconnects them to their "homelands" through images mediated by "electronic capitalism" such as television and cinema (Appadurai 1996), which potentially provide a ground on which to construct a new kind of transnational community based on shared imagination and consumption (Anderson 1983; Park 2004).

Drawing on ethnographic accounts of Korean American youths' consumption of South Korean popular culture (whose popularity is called Hallyu, or the Korean Wave) in Los Angeles and Chicago, this chapter explores the role of (im)migrant youths in the transnational flows of popular culture and its ramifications. It discusses: (1) how young Korean Americans consume, disseminate and construct popular culture across the Pacific; (2) how Korean American youths' consumption of South Korean culture is interrelated with their search for identity and community; (3) how the transpacific cultural flows are affected by the interplay of various structural forces including the market and the state and how they signify the changing global cultural landscape and power relationships.

Globalization and the emergence of the Korean Wave in metropolitan U.S. cities

U.S. hegemony in the popular cultural realm has long been undisputed as symbolized by the dominant power of McDonald's, Coca-Cola and Hollywood overseas (Watson 1997; Marchetti 2000; Morley and Robins 1995). Interestingly, in contrast to the plethora of literature on the (mostly negative) impact of Americanization on other local cultures, scholars have largely ignored the influence of foreign popular cultures on the U.S., implicitly leaving the impression that the U.S., as the center of cultural hegemony, is almost immune to the overwhelming power of cultural globalization (Dorfman and Mattelart 1975). However, the U.S. is not free from foreign cultural influences, although they may not be as strong and visible as American culture represented by Hollywood elsewhere (Desser 2003). Indeed, from the incipient stage of its foundation, this "country of immigrants" has always been subject to foreign cultural influence even though the influence from the northern and western European countries has remained mostly dominant. Yet, since the late twentieth century, the acceptance and visibility of non-European cultural influence in U.S. society have become more apparent as the number and politico-economic power of non-European American populations have increased. Nowadays, it is not unusual to see, for instance, Asian, African or Latin cultural influences on American popular culture such as in fashion, food, films, music and art.

The prevalence of foreign cultural influence is more strongly felt in ethnic spaces and among transnational (im)migrants in metropolitan cities. Historically, (im)migrants' consumption and retention of their heritage culture are nothing new. But contemporary media capitalism, combined with technological development and individuals' movements across borders, has enabled extensive and speedy exchanges of cultural information between the countries of origin and transnational (im)migrants. The speed and volume of these exchanges enable simultaneous and almost unlimited cultural consumption, which connects the countries of origin and (im)migrants more immediately. Moreover, since ethnic spaces in the U.S. are no longer enclosed and isolated islands from the larger society as they once were, cultural practices and information available in ethnic spaces are easily transmittable to the larger society. In this sense, urban ethnic spaces and transnational (im)migrant populations are significant nodal points for the circulation of foreign cultures in the U.S. and important sites for examining cultural globalization of the U.S. (Park 2004).

In major U.S. cities such as Los Angeles, New York and Chicago, ethnic Korean TV channels are established, and depending on the region and the size of the ethnic media market, they air ethnic programs, most of which are imported from South Korea, for hours every day. Additionally, cable TV and radio stations are available. Ethnic newspapers, whose news used to be transmitted from Korea via satellite and either mailed or delivered to subscribers' doorsteps every day, are nowadays available electronically.[3] The proliferation of ethnic video rental shops, bookstores and various types of ethnic cultural spaces (including cafés, clubs, clothing stores, hair salons, etc.) also contributes to Korean Americans' easy and extended access to "homeland" popular culture. Time lag in the transmission of information between South Korea and Korean American communities in metropolitan cities is minimal. For example, through the Internet, news can be shared concomitantly on both sides of the Pacific. The Internet also provides the fastest way to watch the latest episodes of TV dramas and show programs aired in South Korea (within a few hours or even concomitantly). The same programs are available at Korean video rental stores in metropolitan cities within a day or two. Spatiality as well as temporality are compressed, bringing the "homeland" and Korean Americans tightly together (Harvey 1989). As print capitalism facilitated the formation of nationalism by connecting people through imagination, this type of simultaneous sharing of information through the media seems to pave the way for a new kind of imagined transnational community (Anderson 1983).

The growing availability of cultural information from Korea has increased young Korean Americans' exposure to and consumption of Korean popular culture over the years. Yet, there are some variations in terms of genre, intensity and frequency of their consumption depending on factors such as generation, living arrangement, self-identity, socio-cultural grouping and Korean proficiency. For example, consumption of certain types of Korean popular culture requires a degree of Korean proficiency, which limits the participation of non-Korean-speaking people. Also, if one lives with a family, there is a better chance of being familiarized with Korean popular culture because watching Korean videos is one of the most popular pastimes among first-generation Korean Americans.

The Korean American youths in my ethnographic research largely consist of three groups: the U.S.-born generation, the 1.5 generation and *yuhaksaeng* (students who study abroad).[4] The *yuhaksaeng* group in particular is a key player in the consumption, dissemination and, to some extent, creation of transpacific popular culture because of their multi-site living arrangements and frequent travel. Indeed, through the transpacific traveling of the *yuhaksaengs* and their family members (generally mothers), the latest trends on both sides of the Pacific are smoothly transmitted to the other side.

The increasing visibility of South Korean popular culture in the U.S. is also partially interrelated with market and state forces. In the early 1990s, the South Korean government created an official ideology/policy called *segyewha* (globalization). It is largely a new nation-building ideology proposed by the Kim Young Sam government, but it soon exerted tremendous influence on every aspect of South Korean life (Segyewha Committee 1995; G. Park 1996; J. Park 2000a). Although the original *segyehwa* discourse disappeared when South Korea underwent an economic crisis in the late 1990s, globalization has accelerated ever since.

Interestingly, while Korea was still undergoing the economic crisis, the Korean Wave emerged in East/Southeast Asia. Encouraged by this success in the Asian region, the Korean media industry has also made an effort to penetrate the U.S. market, as exemplified by the opening of Korean films at regular movie theaters in major U.S. cities in the early 2000s (for example, the showing of *Shiri* and *Chunhyang*). In more recent years, Korean singers and bands such as *Bi* (Rain) and Wonder Girls have debuted and toured the U.S. The current sensational success of Psy is an indication of the continuing efforts by Korean media industries to enter the U.S. media scene. Simultaneously,

Korean TV dramas and movies also made their way into the homes of some Asian-Americans (mostly those whose countries of origin have experienced Hallyu) as the popularity of Korean popular culture in those people's countries of origin has generated a demand for Korean popular culture in the U.S. as well.

Korean American youths' consumption of Korean popular culture is inter-related with the growing availability and improved quality of Korean cultural products supported by the state ideology, market interest, the development of information technology and globalization of the media. But there is another critical factor that has facilitated Korean American youths' patronage of Korean popular culture: their socio-cultural position in the U.S. and their need for a niche and a sense of belonging.

Limited cultural citizenship and the search for space and identity

Molded in the "model minority" stereotype, younger-generation Asian-Americans are generally viewed as a "problem-free" and "smart" group of people who are valedictorians and computer whizz kids.[5] By virtue of their membership in this over-generalized and imposed category called "Asian American," Korean American youths are also considered "model" students who excel in school and have a rosy prospect for future jobs. Although some live up to these celebrated images of success, a closer look at Korean American youths reveals that, contrary to the public images, many young Korean Americans struggle with social, economic, psychological and academic issues. For example, behind the much-hailed success stories of valedictorians and Ivy League school graduates, there is a considerable number of high school and college drop-outs and college graduates who constantly shift from one tem-porary job to another or who simply do not work at all. It is not unusual to encounter a recognizable number of *paiksu* (the unemployed) who "kill time" at Korean cafés, billiard halls, PC *bang*s (Korean-style Internet cafés) and comic book stores in the Los Angeles and Chicago "Koreatown" areas at any given time. They hang out at those ethnic public spaces either with friends or by themselves, looking for something to do or a place to belong to. Some do that as a temporary pastime during a transitional period between job changes or post-graduation, whereas others do it regularly, full-time.[6]

Kihun is a 25-year-old 1.5-generation *paiksu* whom I met in Chicago.[7] He came to the U.S. in his mid-teens and went to a small private liberal arts col-lege in the Midwest. After graduating from college, he came back to Chicago and has lived with his parents since then. He has been home for more than a year, has worked at odd jobs on and off, but for the most part he has been a *paiksu*. Life as a *paiksu* was not idle, however. According to Kihun, staying at home and listening to others' (mostly parents') comments about his unem-ployment or advice on how to find a job is one of the hardest things for a *paiksu* to bear. So he makes himself busy, staying outside of home as much as possible. Relying on the generosity and resources of others, including friends and *sŏnbae* (senior alumni), he hung out at ethnic public spaces all the time, except for occasional stints at part-time jobs, especially at his *sŏnbaes'* stores in poor urban neighborhoods. He aspires to have a white-collar job someday, but the prospect of realizing that wish seems remote.

I met Chansik, a 1.5-generation part-time college student in his early twenties, at a comic book rental store in Chicago. He was one of the "regulars" at the store, who hung out there during their free time and/or after work. Many of the regulars make themselves "at home" at the store, even eating meals ordered from nearby restaurants.[8] According to Chansik, he hung out at ethnic public spaces such as the comic book store because he did not know what to do with his life and future. He said:

> We [1.5 generation] don't have dreams. That is the sorrow and limit of the 1.5 generation. Although you try, things do not work out as you intended. Also, I don't know where to start. I am afraid ... I don't know what to do. Most of all, I don't have any experience ... Because we live with other ethnic groups, there is no room or flexibility like in Korea. You cannot fit in. Things are cut out, disconnected.

Chansik described himself as an "ordinary" person, who, unlike those "who are goal-oriented and have ability to overcome obstacles," cannot accomplish what is expected of him, such as socio-economic success, even if he tries. Besides his ordinariness, he was a minority. He was indeed very conscious of his "life as a minority." He pointed out that Asian Americans can reach only a certain level in institutions, such as supervisor, but they never become higher-level decision makers. Chansik has witnessed so many cases like that that he has become discouraged and disillusioned. Indeed, based on their personal experiences, both Chansik and Kihun are intimidated and frustrated by the gulf between the ideal and reality, and the larger society and the ethnic community. Without many alternatives, they float like ghosts in the ethnic public spaces as temporary or full-time *paiksu*.

The sense of alienation is not, however, felt by those less successful or jobless young Korean Americans alone. Many younger-generation Korean Americans who are academically successful and socio-economically competent also feel that way. For instance, a 1.5-generation professional, Cathy, who is a graduate of one of the country's most prestigious universities, told me about her experiences during her high school and college days:

> I even was on the pom-pom squad, you know, that type of thing. But I don't think you really felt that you were a part of that school. You always felt that you are running around the periphery. And in college ... you go to a good school, but there is a difference. I think a lot of difference in

terms of the roots. For example, my roommate, white Anglo-Saxon Protestant, her father went to the school and her father was a contributor and her uncle went to the school. And there is history and heritage, whereas for us there was none. So we really didn't feel a part of belonging to the institution or to the place as a social being.

This painful recollection of a bright, ambitious and outgoing 1.5-generation woman illustrates the lack of social space, sense of belonging and socially equal heritage for them in the larger U.S. society. This sense of alienation is also found among the U.S.-born generation. A second-generation artist in his mid-twenties, Brian, expressed his sense of marginality:

Oh, I consider myself an American conditionally, kind of ... Not fully American. I don't feel fully American ... I don't feel fully assimilated into American life and culture. I think I did before; when I was younger, I really felt like I'm just like anybody else, but as I get older, I've started to realize that there's no way that anybody who is a different race really is going to fully assimilate themselves into American culture, society, just because it is so ... everything is so white-dominated and everything from whatever the ideal is, like sexual ideal or even like intellectually, I think the stuff we talked about earlier. So yeah, I consider myself a conditional American ... Like a visitor, a visitor.

Ethnic public spaces are frequented by a complex mix of groups including the above-mentioned sub-groups of youth. Despite differences in generation, academic and social success, gender and class background, many young Korean Americans feel that they have been marginalized; their identity has been simultaneously denied and imposed, and their heritage has not weighed equally. They may be legal citizens of the U.S., but their cultural citizenship was not fully granted as their socio-cultural entitlement and membership are, more often than not, overlooked and negated (Flores and Benmayor 1997; Ong 1996). Cultural citizenship is "the right to be different (in terms of race, ethnicity, or native language) with respect to the norms of the dominant national community, without compromising one's right to belong, in the sense of participating in the nation-state's democratic processes" (Rosaldo and Flores 1997: 57). In other words, "different but equal" is what cultural citizenship advocates. It also emphasizes the importance of having a space where people of different heritages can feel safe and comfortable. Korean ethnic spaces, in this sense, are sites where Korean American youths can feel comfortable, secure and entitled. Thus, backed up by the emotional comfort, Korean American youths often find a sense of belonging and assurance of their identity in such spaces.

Identity is a complex and elusive yet critical boundary marker that defines us and differentiates us from others. For transnational (im)migrant youths, identity is an even more contested issue because they tend to juggle with a "multiplicity of subject positions" (Brah 1996: 123) as they are located between nation-states, races, generations and classes across borders. Moreover, "identity is a question of memory, and memories of 'home' in particular. Film and television play a powerful role in the construction of collective memories and identities" (Morley and Robins 1995: 91). In this light, Korean American youths' consumption of Korean popular culture can be construed as a pursuit of collective memories and, most of all, home. But in contemporary globalized society, home is not necessarily grounded in a territory (Bammer 1994). Instead, it may be a search for a sense of home where individuals can "feel at home" with the emotional comfort and safety usually associated with the notion of home (Morley and Robins 1995: 87). By consuming popular culture from the "homeland" at an ethnic space where one feels secure and entitled, transnational youths can experience, albeit temporarily, a sense of belonging to an imagined community and a home where memories are shared and constructed through the mediation of the media and consumer goods.

Crossing boundaries and building bridges: the emergence of new relations and the complexity of power relations in transnational cultural flows

Consumption tightly connects the local and the global through the globalized production and circulation of commodities and information. It also constructs individual and collective identities based on "socially differentiated (racialized, classed, and gendered) senses of separation" (Crang and Jackson 2001: 338). In other words, identities manifested and mediated by consumption patterns and preferences are indicative of the differentiated social relations and positions in which individuals are situated. Young Korean Americans' consumption of Korean popular culture reveals their "socially differentiated senses of separation" rooted in their transnational position and ethnic/racial minority status; thus, the dynamics of their social relations in which the local, national and global forces intersect are reflected on and generated by it.

While Korean American youths' consumption of Korean popular culture indicates their "socially differentiated senses of separation," it also builds bridges between groups, generating new senses of connection. For example, it brings South Korea and its culture closer to the (im)migrant youths, laying the foundation for a sense of community. Watching Korean TV dramas helps the (im)migrant youths keep up with the latest socio-cultural trends and issues in Korea. Some (especially, *yuhaksaengs*) even consult with their friends and relatives in Korea regarding which dramas to watch; thus, tastes, references and knowledge are almost simultaneously shared through common consumption of cultural products across borders, which, in turn, reinforces a sense of connectedness (Park 2004).

Consumption of Korean popular culture also mediates generational relationships. Watching Korean TV dramas is a typical pastime for first-generation

Korean Americans. By joining their parents or grandparents in this family pastime, some Korean American youths ended up developing better intergenerational understanding and relations. Sandy, a second-generation college student whose family lives in Los Angeles, told me that her relations with her mother grew closer as they watched Korean dramas together. She said that she had realized that there were things in Korean that she could not understand or translate into English, such as the concept of *"han"* (a complex concept that combines compressed sorrow, accumulated anger and, potentially, their transcendence). Discussions of such a concept with her mother and viewing TV dramas together with her (and occasionally crying together over a sad story) connected Sandy and her mother strongly since not only did they share time and emotion but also Sandy developed a better understanding of her mother's way of thinking based on her Korean upbringing.

Korean popular culture connects Korean American youths of different backgrounds (including generation) and elicits a sense of camaraderie among them. As I pointed out earlier, they have a growing chance of intermingling with one another through ethnic public spaces and of sharing cultural references. Some even think that there is a unique "sense of fun" that only Korean American youths, as co-ethnics, can understand and share by hanging out at ethnic public spaces and consuming ethnic popular culture. Through these ethnically specific activities, spaces and references, Korean American youths encounter more chances to socialize with and feel closer to one another, crossing whatever sub-group boundaries they may have.

Friendship-building through the consumption of ethnic popular cultures moves beyond the boundary of the Korean American group, and Korean American youths are often connected to other Asian-American youths through shared consumption of Korean as well as Asian popular cultures. Over the years Korean popular culture has become a source of shared reference and connection among some East/Southeast Asian-American youths due to Hallyu. Also, it is not uncommon for the urban Asian-American youths to be familiar with various popular cultural trends in different parts of Asia. These Asian popular cultures, most prevalently circulated in their respective (im)migrant communities, often spread to other Asian-American communities as the youths frequently exchange information and are curious about something new and different. Oftentimes, better mutual understanding and social relationships are inculcated by such cultural sharing. The shared cultural consumption also expands to the larger society through personal networks and the media. Curiosity or word-of-mouth sometimes leads non-Asian Americans into the realm of Korean pop culture. Some become avid followers who also develop interest in Korea in general, which is likely to create new types of transnational connections.

There are complicated power relations embedded in transnational flows of Korean and Asian popular cultures in the U.S. The Korean comic book rental store is one such example of how these power relations reveal. Unlike

American comic book stores, which are geared toward the selling of comic books, Korean comic book stores focus on renting. Thus, they are equipped with thousands of books rented for either home or in-store viewing. Clients in comic book stores are mainly in their teens up to their thirties (female clients tend to be in their teens and twenties), but younger or older clients are occasionally present (especially men in their forties and fifties). All of the comic books available in rental stores are written in Korean. At one time, a large proportion of them had Korean titles and Korean author names, although the situation has significantly changed over the past several years.[9] For this reason, some parents even rent comic books for their children in order to help them learn Korean in an easy and more entertaining manner. However, the Korean titles and author names of comic books published before the copyrights were strongly observed could be deceptive in some cases because the books' contents are actually of Japanese origin (in other words, pirate copies), and due to hasty, rough translation, certain expressions and grammar follow Japanese convention instead of Korean (Park 2000b). The illegal circulation of pirate copies under the façade of Korean titles and author names during the time when Japanese comics were banned in Korea, as well as the long working relationships between Korean and Japanese comic artists/animators (which affected the drawing styles, story development, etc.), has intensified the "natural" penetration of Japanese styles into Korean comics. Thus, by consuming "Korean" comics, Korean Americans are exposed to the Japanese way of thinking and aesthetics embedded in the disguised form of Korean comics in Korean comic book stores.

There is another layer of cultural influence here. A considerable proportion of the stories and backgrounds of Japanese comics are real or fictive Western countries, indicating Japan's long-held fascination with the West (Schodt 1983; Levi 1996; Park 2010). Character names and features resemble those of "Westerners," and sometimes stories are borrowed from Western classics or historical facts (such as European fairy tales and the Russian revolution). Korean American readers, therefore, learn about the West through the Japanese lens while they also learn about Japan through the Korean lens (in the form of Korean-language comics).

In addition, translated Chinese martial arts novels and comics as well as translated Western novels are usually carried by comic book stores, adding more layers to the transnational cultural encounters. In other words, juxtaposition and hybridization of cultures are clearly manifest in the texts that Korean comic book stores carry. Whether these are considered to be examples of cultural hegemony (of the West and Japan) or (Korea's) "domestication" of foreign cultural products is open to debate (Tobin 1992). In either case, it is clear that there are ironic complexities embedded in cultural products and information in a globalized era in which culture has been hybridized, localized and appropriated through continuous encounters and flows in the midst of lingering cultural hegemony.

Since the directions of cultural flows are multi-faceted and the interplay between hegemonic cultural influence and local response constantly "hybridize" given cultural information and products, traditional cultural "centers" and "peripheries" are situated in a different way than before. Indeed, what intrigued me in my observation of the recent transpacific flows of popular culture between the U.S. and South Korea is the transformation, albeit temporary, of center/periphery relations. To illustrate, cultural information and trends that originated in traditional cultural "centers" such as the U.S. become reformulated and redefined in cultural "peripheries" such as Korea, as they get sifted through local cultural codes, lenses and practices. These Koreanized (localized) cultural trends and information are then imported back to the "center" again and consumed and disseminated not only in ethnic spaces but also in the larger society, becoming part of the "center," which then will be exported to the "periphery" again. Moreover, nowadays it is not uncommon for Hollywood studios to look for content and inspiration for their products in Asia and elsewhere. Hollywood's remake of a few Korean films, including *yŏpgijŏkin keunyŏ* (*My Sassy Girl*) and *Siwolae* (*The Lake House*), indicates such blurred boundaries of and complex relations between the center and the periphery.

Given these changing environments, can Korean American youths be creators of transnational popular culture? In the realm of Korean popular music, Korean Americans and *yuhaksaengs* have left their footprints by introducing new styles of music and becoming an integrated part of the local music scene. Their successful integration went hand-in-hand with the "star system" methods of discovering and making a star, which has become more systematized in South Korea (Russell 2008). Since the late 1990s, almost all of the top idol groups in South Korea have had at least one Korean American member (for example, groups such as H.O.T., G.O.D., Shinhwa and S.E.S. have Korean American members). Moreover, transnational Koreans educated in American institutions or strongly influenced by the American music style have played a crucial role in the construction of South Korean music trends. Seo Taiji and Boys and Psy belong to this category.

The star- and trend-making power of the media industry aside, the changes in South Korean state policy have enabled Korean American youths' active involvement in the Korean entertainment industry. The *segyehwa* (globalization) discourse had fundamentally transformed South Korea's worldview and reality. It opened new doors for overseas Koreans as it regarded them as forerunners and assets of South Korea's expanding politico-economic and cultural spaces, epitomized by the intended construction of a "de-territorialized" global Korean community (Basch *et al.* 1994). In conjunction, changes in the laws regarding the status of overseas Koreans unwittingly benefitted Korean American entertainers, allowing them to become engaged in commercial activities with less restrictions (Park and Chang 2005).

While the Korean state and market provided an incentive for Korean American youths to go to Korea, their limited socio-cultural membership in the U.S. propelled such a decision. In the entertainment business aspiring Asian-American actors and musicians face serious obstacles as there have not been enough space, markets and role models for them yet (Hamamoto and Liu 2000). Asian-Americans are still largely deemed unmarketable (unless they are martial artists) and are more often than not typecast. The situation seems to have improved slightly in recent years, with a little more visibility of Asian/ Asian-American actors/actresses as lead characters in major films and TV dramas. Yet, Asian-American actors are still generally used as token and stereotypical characters, and in the music business they are almost nonexistent. In this situation, aspiring artists head for South Korea. Some of them expressed their wish in public, remarking that they hoped to come back to the U.S. after becoming successful in Korea and then Asia. Given the changing global popular cultural landscape, Hollywood's growing interest in the Asian market, and increasing transnational collaboration in the production of popular culture, their aspiration and hope may actually come true in the near future.[10] Then, it will be another indication of the transforming directions of cultural influence, a reverse move from the "periphery" to the "center."

Although the contribution of Korean American entertainers, particularly musicians, to Korean popular culture could be acknowledged, it is questionable whether they are creative agents of transnational popular culture because, so far, what they have done is not far from disseminating information (for example, hip-hop and rap) from the traditional "center" to the "periphery." They still largely remain studious students or imitators of Western artists in the same genre instead of independent artists with their own voices and colors that are grounded in the locality and individuality. This maturation will take time, but it is undeniable that the role of Korean American youths in the flows of transnational culture on both sides of the Pacific has become significant.

Conclusion

Korean American youths' consumption of South Korean and other Asian popular cultures is intertwined with the general trend of cultural globalization, which has been facilitated by the interplay among global media, the market, the state and technology. At the same time, Korean American youths' marginalized status in the U.S. and their quest for community and identity have intensified their consumption of the now more readily available "homeland's" popular culture. In contemporary society, individuals, particularly displaced people, try to "construct imaginatively their new world." In this context, their "homeland" is often remembered and re-imagined and becomes a "symbolic anchor of community" through the remembrance (Gupta and Ferguson 1994: 11). The media mediates such remembering in a critical way, connecting the "homeland" and the (im)migrants through the compressed time and spatiality.

132   Jung-Sun Park

But since the media is full of hybridized and creolized information and perspectives, which change constantly, its mediation between the transnational (im)migrants and their "homelands" adds more complexity and contradiction rather than provides a simple foundation for a coherent imagined community.

As a core consumer group of global popular culture, transnational (im)migrant youths are key players in the transnational cultural flows, as exemplified by Korean American youths' roles as consumers, disseminators and potential creators of popular culture across the Pacific. The extensive popular cultural flows indicate a condensed and rapid transformation of the transpacific cultural landscape between Asia and North America. In this context, Korean American youths' roles as cultural mediators and creators will become more salient and significant. How they position themselves and participate in the construction of an imagined transpacific cultural community thus will become an important part of their identity politics and search for space and community.

Notes

The author gratefully acknowledges the UCLA Asian American Studies Center for permission to publish this article, with a slight revision, based upon "Korean American Youth and Transnational Flows of Popular Culture across the Pacific," *Amerasia Journal*, 30(1), 2004.

1 I borrowed this expression, (im)migration, from Rouse (1995).
2 Nowadays, the lives of a growing number of transnational (im)migrants span more than two countries (host and native lands) as their continuous movement across borders includes more than one host society. In other words, the traditional notion of immigrants who move from one country to another where they settle for good no longer holds true. Thus, contemporary transnational (im)migrants' involvement with the multiple host and native societies is much more complex than before.
3 Until the mid-1990s, sample copies of newspapers were directly shipped from Korea by air every day and then reprinted locally, causing considerable time lag in the dissemination of news.
4 Due to the dominance of post-1965 immigration among Korean Americans, most U.S.-born Korean American youths are second generation, although third- and even fourth-generation Korean American youths are found among the descendents of the early twentieth-century Korean immigrants. 1.5 generation usually refers to those who immigrated to the U.S. in their pre-teens or early teens with their parents. The *yuhaksaeng* category ranges from early (or pre-) teens (*chogiyuhaksaeng* – young students who study abroad: they are often called the "parachute kids") to postgraduate students, but I focus on those in their teens and early twenties in this chapter. In a strictly legal sense, most *yuhaksaengs* are Korean because they are not immigrants. But, sooner or later, many of them tend to acquire U.S. permanent residency or citizenship. So they are potential Korean Americans at least, and, in actuality, they (especially the *chogiyuhaksaengs*) share many similarities with the 1.5 generation.
5 For a critique of the "model minority" myth, see Hurh and Kim (1989).
6 This does not necessarily mean that most young Korean Americans who hang out at ethnic spaces at odd hours are unemployed. Young professionals, students and even travelers frequent those spaces, too.
7 All names are pseudonyms.

8 The catchphrase of the comic book store printed in its advertisement reads: "Let's blow off the stress of immigrant life!"
9 Within the past decade, there has been a significant increase in the number of Japanese comics officially translated by Korean publishers. These Japanese comics have dominated the South Korean market, so the comic books currently available at Korean comic book stores in the U.S. also reflect these changes.
10 Yunjin Kim and Daniel Henney, both of whom are Korean Americans, first made their fame in Korea. Their success in Korea (and Asia) led them to get a role in Hollywood.

References

Anderson, B. (1983) *Imagined Communities*, London: Verso.
Appadurai, A. (1991) "Ethnoscape: Notes and Queries for a Transnational Anthropology," in R. Fox (ed.) *Recapturing Anthropology*, Santa Fe: School of American Research.
——(1996) *Modernity at Large*, Minneapolis: University of Minnesota Press.
Bammer, A. (1994) "Introduction," in A. Bammer (ed.) *Displacements: Cultural Identities in Question*, Bloomington: Indiana University Press.
Basch, L., Glick Schiller, N. and Szanton-Blanc, C. (1994) *Nations Unbound: Transnational Projects, Postcolonial Predicaments, and Nation-states*, Langhorne: Gordon and Breach.
Brah, A. (1996) *Cartographies of Diaspora*, New York: Routledge.
Crang, P. and Jackson, P. (2001) "Geographies of Consumption," in D. Morley and K. Robins (eds) *British Cultural Studies*, Oxford: Oxford University Press.
Desser, D. (2003) "Consuming Asia: Chinese and Japanese Popular Culture and the American Imaginary," in J. Lau (ed.) *Multiple Modernities: Cinemas and Popular Media in Transcultural East Asia*, Philadelphia: Temple University Press.
Dorfman, A. and Mattelart, A. (1975) *How to Read Donald Duck: Imperialist Ideology in the Disney Comic*, New York: International General.
Flores, W. and Benmayor, R. (1997) *Latino Cultural Citizenship*, Boston: Beacon Press.
Glick-Schiller, N. and Fouron, G. (1990) "Everywhere We Go We are in Danger: Ti Manno and the Emergence of a Haitian Transnational Identity," *American Ethnologist*, 17 (2): 329–47.
Gupta, A. and Ferguson, J. (1994) "Beyond 'Culture': Space, Identity and the Politics of Difference," *Cultural Anthropology*, 7(1): 6–23.
Hamamoto, D. and Liu, S. (2000) *Countervisions*, Philadelphia: Temple University Press.
Hannerz, U. (1992) *Cultural Complexity: Studies in the Social Organization of Meaning*, New York: Columbia University Press.
——(1996) *Transnational Connections*, London: Routledge.
Harvey, D. (1989) *The Condition of Postmodernity*, Oxford: Basil Blackwell.
Hu-Dehart, E. (1999) *Across the Pacific: Asian Americans and Globalization*, Philadelphia: Temple University Press.
Hurh, W. and Kim, K. (1989) "The 'Success' Image of Asian Americans: Its Validity, and Its Practical and Theoretical Implications," *Ethnic and Racial Studies*, 12(4): 512–38.
Iwabuchi, K. (2002) *Recentering Globalization: Popular Culture and Japanese Transnationalism*, Durham: Duke University Press.
Kearney, M. (1995) "The Local and the Global: The Anthropology of Globalization and Transnationalization," *Annual Review of Anthropology*, 24: 547–65.
Levi, A. (1996) *Samurai From Outer Space: Understanding Japanese Animation*, Chicago: Open Court.

Marchetti, G. (2000) "Buying American, Consuming Hong Kong: Cultural Commerce, Fantasies of Identity and the Cinema," in P. Fu and D. Desser (eds) *The Cinema of Hong Kong: History, Arts, Identity*, Cambridge: Cambridge University Press.

Morley, D. and Robins, K. (1995) *Spaces of Identity: Global Media, Electronic Landscapes and Cultural Boundaries*, New York: Routledge.

Ong, A. (1996) "Cultural Citizenship as Subject Making: New Immigrants Negotiate Racial and Ethnic Boundaries," *Current Anthropology*, 37(5): 737–62.

——(1999) *Flexible Citizenship: The Cultural Logic of Transnationality*, Durham: Duke University Press.

Park, G. (1996) *Globalization: Capital and Culture in Change*, Seoul: Nanam.

Park, J. (2000a) "Change in South Korean Citizenship and Its Implications," paper presented at the 52nd Annual Meeting of Association for Asian Studies, San Diego, California.

——(2000b) "Transnational Flows of Popular Culture Across the Pacific: Japanese Comics and Animation in South Korea and the U.S.," proceedings of the Asia Youth Forum 2000, Seoul, Korea.

——(2004) "Korean American Youth's Consumption of Korean and Japanese TV Dramas and Its Implications," in K. Iwabuchi (ed.) *Feeling Asian Modernities: Transnational Consumption of Japanese TV Dramas*, Hong Kong: Hong Kong University Press.

——(2006) "The Korean Wave: Transnational Cultural Flows in East Asia," in C. Armstrong, G. Rozman, S. Kim and S. Kotkin (eds) *Korea at the Center: Dynamics of Regionalism in Northeast Asia*, Armonk: M.E. Sharp.

——(2010) "The Success and Limitations of Japanese Comics and Animation in the U.S.: Can Korean Manhwa and Animation Follow Suit?," in D. Black, S. Epstein and A. Tokita (eds) *Complicated Currents: Media Flows, Soft Power and East Asia*, Melbourne: Monash e-Press.

Park, J. and Chang, P. (2005) "Contention in the Formation of National and Ethnic Identities in Global Context: The Case of the Overseas Korean Act," *Journal of Korean Studies*, 10(1).

Rosaldo, R. and Flores, W. (1997) "Identity, Conflict, and Evolving Latino Communities: Cultural Citizenship in San Jose, California," in W. Flores and R. Benmayor (eds) *Latino Cultural Citizenship*, Boston: Beacon Press.

Rouse, R. (1995) "Thinking through Transnationalism: Notes on the Cultural Politics of Class Relations in the Contemporary United States," *Public Culture*, 7(2): 353–402.

Russell, M. (2008) *Pop Goes Korea*, Berkeley: Stone Bridge Press.

Schodt, F. (1983) *Manga! Manga!: The World of Japanese Comics*, New York: Kodansha International.

Segyehwa Committee (1995) *Segyehwaui Bijŏngwa Chŏnryak* (Visions and Strategies of Segyehwa), Seoul: Seoul Press.

Tobin, J. (1992) "Introduction," in J. Tobin (ed.) *Re-Made in Japan*, New Haven: Yale University Press.

Watson, J. (1997) *Golden Arches East: McDonald's in East Asia*, Stanford: Stanford University Press.

Xavier, J. and Rosaldo, R. (2002) *The Anthropology of Globalization*, Malden: Blackwell.

Yau, E. (2001) *At Full Speed: Hong Kong Cinema in a Borderless World*, Minneapolis: University of Minnesota Press.

Chapter 8

Digitization and online cultures of the Korean Wave

"East Asian" virtual community in Europe

Sang-Yeon Sung

In an era of digitization, new, independent yet unpredictable patterns of identification are produced and circulated through online cultures across national borders. The Korean Wave (Hallyu) is a new kind of cultural phenomenon, fostered through highly developed digitization and online cultures, such as YouTube, Facebook and Twitter, among East Asians within and outside the region. Digital technologies enable East Asians to share and engage with cultural content that evokes so-called "Asian values" (Sung 2008). East Asians who are mostly immigrants or students in Europe construct a strong pan-Asian community by consuming Korean popular culture, which offers them a collective regional identity as a substitute for the dominant culture (Sung 2012). By exploring how East Asian immigrants in Europe construct a collective regional identity through the Korean Wave popular culture, this chapter considers the nexus of transnationalism, nationalism and regionalism in the uneven power structure of the West.

The Korean Wave started with the importation of television dramas through cable channels, but now its circulation has been accelerated by the use of the social media and online culture. The growing number of K-pop fandom in the United States and Europe and the worldwide popularity of Psy's *Gangnam Style* are the examples of this flow. Through the visibility of *Gangnam Style*, K-pop has not only gained international attention but also evoked strong confidence in the South Korean music industry to plan a new strategy for penetrating the global market. The Korean Wave is complex and unpredictable. However, one feature remains predominant – the role of East Asian consumers within and beyond the region. Although the Korean Wave has reached international audiences around the world, its main consumers are East Asians, who create a transnational consumer group and play a significant role in circulating the Korean Wave in various local settings. Considering that increasing numbers of East Asians live in Europe and the Korean Wave helps shape their distinctive community (Sung 2012), this chapter explores their consumption behavior and consequences in Europe, based on an ethnographic case study in Austria. The numbers of East Asians currently living in Austria are 2,500 (Koreans), 3,000 (Taiwanese), 2,500 (Japanese) and 15,673

(Chinese). The size of the Chinese community can be estimated as up to 30,000 when the official data consider illegal migrants and refugees. There are three groups of East Asian migrants living in Austria – students, migrant workers and corporate expatriates – and many of these migrants tend to become immigrants after their study or contract is over.

The Korean Wave provides Asian societies with reassurance that, even within an increasingly globalized world, Asian identity remains strong (Sung 2008 and 2012). The Korean Wave phenomenon is intertwined with important contemporary issues such as national, regional and transnational identities. It offers opportunities to analyze multi-dimensional and complex intercultural relationships formed under the force of globalization. This chapter therefore explores socio-political factors underlying its consumption by East Asians and the ways by which it has influenced the construction of their transnational identities as being East Asians at the same time as being marginalized Austrians. They nourish Asian sentiments by consuming Korean popular culture, and this brings them comfort and closeness to their hometowns, strengthening their bonds of sharing the same cultural context, their mutual understanding with each other and their consciousness of being Asian. Consumption is a particularly felicitous point of departure for examining the symbolic aspects of collective identity (Lamont and Molnar 2001). Although consuming popular culture can be considered as leisure and entertainment, not a significant part of daily activities (Chua 2006), the weight of pop culture in East Asians' daily lives and growing exchanges of East Asian pop culture affect identity construction for East Asians, who no longer struggle to integrate or understand the pop culture of the dominant society, but choose what they think is more suitable for them. Therefore, exploring their consumption behavior and consequences can be an important source for understanding their sense of community and identity. This chapter considers how East Asian immigrants in Europe, particularly in Austria, construct a collective regional identity through their engagement with the Korean Wave popular culture.

This chapter is based on my ethnographic research on the Korean Wave consumption among East Asians in Austria. Not much ethnographic study of the Korean Wave in Europe has occurred; however, because of K-pop's growing popularity in Europe, some have attempted to explore this popularity in local contexts. For example, research on the reception of K-pop in Paris was explored (Cha and Kim 2011) as the visibility of Korea's largest entertainment company's "SM Town World Tour" in June 2011 turned out to be quite successful in attracting local attention. However, the ethnographic study of K-pop reception in Europe needs to be carried out according to local specifics because local environments, patterns of social integration and histories make K-pop consumption unique in each location. This ethnographic study focuses on how and why East Asians consume Korean popular culture and how it constructs and connects them as East Asians, by drawing on data from personal in-depth interviews, emailed questionnaires and website interviews (at www.sysung.at). The subjects of interviews were first- and second-generation Chinese, Japanese and Taiwanese whose ages were between 20 and 65 and who were currently living in the Austrian capital. Additionally, interviews and observations of the East Asian community done by student groups at the University of Vienna are incorporated into this study. The research excluded Koreans because the intention of this project was to understand how Korean pop culture functions in reflecting East Asian culture, and whether other East Asians feel comfortable and close to Korean pop culture as if it were their own.

The main research questions of this study are: Does the media consumption of K-pop play a central role in the articulation of transnational East Asian identity? Why are East Asians engaged with it and not much with the culture of the host society? Do they feel "Asian" while consuming it? Do social media and online culture play a significant role in transnational East Asian identity? The data show how these immigrants articulate their transnational identities as East Asians while struggling to integrate into a host society of Europe. East Asian immigrants in Austria are maintaining part of the East Asian community by consuming Korean pop culture, which they consider Asian, and therefore Korean popular culture plays a significant role in the articulation of transnational East Asian identity.

Media consumption, migration and identity in a digital age

Due to the growing usage of online culture, migrants today make sense of transnational lives through their online consumption, and the relationship of the media and migration has become the key to understanding transnational identity. For East Asian migrants in Europe, who have moved voluntarily, media consumption plays an integral role in daily life as a major means of connecting them socially. Recent studies recognize the significance of mediated migration, the media's role as a significant variable in migratory processes and practices (King and Wood 2001). Media consumption can be understood as a key cultural mechanism creating the emergence of individualized identities, both imagined and enacted (Kim 2011).

Rapid economic growth in globalizing East Asia has diversified and shifted the patterns of international migration towards movement of the highly skilled and knowledge intensive into Western countries (Lucas 2005). If the classical study of immigrants has been focused on the struggle of assimilation and integration in the host society and culture, studies of immigrants today closely recognize how immigrants construct their identity and feeling at home across national borders. If immigrants had maintained their collective group identity and an isolated attitude towards, and at best, a polite relationship with, their host societies (Hübinette 2009), digitization and online culture not only enable immigrants today to connect strongly with their homelands, but also to stay connected with other East Asians, while staying (dis)connected with the dominant culture they are living in. Their engagement and selection of Korean popular culture gives them a chance to choose which cultural product they intend to consume, and this reflects how they identify themselves and negotiate with the dominant society and power structure.

Anthropologists and ethnomusicologists have focused their research on the role that popular culture and music play in the construction of cultural identity (Cohen 1993 and 1997; Mathews 2000; Tandt 2002). Research has tended to concentrate, however, on how Western culture, specifically that of the United States, has influenced local societies and local identity construction, but not the other way around. The study of the Korean Wave in East Asia or among East Asians outside the region opens a new window on the study of globalization and identity, because it focuses not only on West-to-East influences but also on how East Asian nations are influencing each other, and even on how Eastern culture may influence Western culture through new consumption practices. Consumerism and identity are key terms for cultural analysis today, all the more so in the context of globalization (Tandt 2002). Identity is conditioned through its ongoing interactions with others; thus, identity is how the self conceives of itself and labels itself (Giddens 1991). Cultural identity is a matter of how people conceive of who they are through the choices they make in the cultural supermarket (Mathews 2000), and an understanding of culture crucially involves consumption (Paasi 2003), especially in a digital age now.

The explosion of user-created media content on the web has created a new media universe. As more and more people are using social media such as Facebook and Twitter, their favorite pop music and the television drama that they watched the previous night can spread instantly in online spaces. This powerful use of social media has created a new kind of cultural flow and connected East Asian immigrants in Europe with popular cultural products that are similar to their own cultural background. Their movements, fashion styles, living habits and public postures can show a certain cultural content, and such situations may be sustained in "cultural proximity" (Straubhaar 1997).

My research on the Korean Wave in Austria shows that Korean popular culture represents East Asian popular culture for several reasons. First, unlike Japan, which for many East Asians has created negative historical memories, Korea remains a fairly neutral or positive country because it has not had political conflicts with them. Therefore, they do not feel uncomfortable consuming Korean popular culture. Second, Korean popular culture contains "Asian values" more than other Asian products, and this makes consumers feel nostalgic towards "Asia." Third, after living in Europe for a while, they are somehow used to being identified as "East Asians" because Austrians do not recognize sharp differences among Asian cultures, so they feel more connected with each other, compared to how they felt before moving to Europe.

Through social media, they tend to have more communications with friends in East Asia, which updates them with cultural trends there and enables them to keep up with popular music and television dramas. Most of the cultural products they desire are provided free on YouTube or other Internet websites. As multiple channels of consuming Korean cultural products increase, East Asians tend to consume more Korean popular culture, compared to Western culture or the mainstream culture from their host society. For example, some students at the University of Vienna are fans of Korean popular music and film, and this interest in Korean popular culture has been spread mostly through Facebook. Students consume popular culture in many ways. Internet online culture provides the easiest and most convenient way to obtain products and news; without it, East Asians in Austria would be unable to consume all the cultural products they want with the same speed as in their homelands. However, patterns of acquisition differ by age; older generations still prefer to copy CDs or VCDs and share the copies with their friends. Respondents in this study mentioned that they use the Korean Wave to stay in touch with their families in Asia and to keep up with cultural trends. Ms. Chen said during her interview:

> Most the Korean dramas that are popular in Taiwan, I watched it. My friends would tell me which one was famous in Taiwan, and I usually make a copy or buy it from Taiwan and bring it here. I can watch it over and over. It is really touching my sentiments.
> (Interview with the author, December 15, 2009)

Consuming Korean television dramas connects her with her friends back home in Taiwan. She added that her love of Korean dramas made her more interested in other Korean cultural forms, such as Korean cuisine, and electronic goods, such as Samsung Galaxy and Notebook. Through the Internet and social media, East Asian immigrants receive news, download music videos or dramas, participate in the dissemination of pop culture by posting their opinions, and maintain connections with their homelands by consuming a culture that they consider fresh and familiar (Iwabuchi *et al.* 2004). Asian immigrants struggling to integrate or understand the culture of their host society may be an old story now. In recent decades, sharing East Asian pop culture has created a specific sense of community according to consumption patterns. Facebook plays a strong role in disseminating K-pop in Austria among East Asians, as many interviewees said that they have strong connections with each other via Facebook and fan club sites. Though fan club sites are for those who are very active, joining Facebook fan sites represents a more casual exploration of personal preference. Most K-pop fans said that they get information of the latest album releases and updates on popular music videos from fan club sites.

East Asia or East Asian culture is not a central interest to many Austrians, who lack sufficient knowledge and information to appreciate it. Most of the news disseminated by the mass media relates to European countries. Because the local interest in Vienna lies mostly in Austria and neighboring countries, little news about the rest of the world is disseminated. The Asian region is seldom mentioned, and most inhabitants of Vienna consequently know little about East Asian tradition or popular culture. So the sudden popularity of Psy's *Gangnam Style,* which hit the top spot on Austrian music charts, was a surprising phenomenon. This one artist's popularity through social media brought significant attention to K-pop, Korea and even East Asia.

The Korean Wave among East Asians in Austria

Many interviewees agreed that Korean pop culture contains strong Asian sentiments, which all East Asians can assimilate, and their main reason for purchasing Korean pop culture is because of these values. Many interviewees complained of how difficult it was to integrate into Austrian society because of different cultural values and the lack of knowledge of Asian culture. They claimed that the Internet makes it easier for them to feel close to East Asia. Hann-Wei Chen, a second-generation Taiwanese living in Austria, commented:

> Korean TV series still convey traditional Confucian values that might be one reason for success in East Asian countries, foremost in China and Taiwan, where modern TV series mostly lack of these values ... Many Asian traditions, such as Confucianism, come from China, but they were better preserved by Korean culture. There might be a longing for the good old times.
>
> (Website interview with the author, February 11, 2010)

According to this male interviewee, even the trendy Korean soap operas focus on the importance of family values or respecting elders, and this makes Asians feel connected because it points out a marked difference between Western and Eastern values. By consuming Korean pop culture, he says, Asians feel more connected to their homeland, "Asia," and feel close to Korea. The older generation's love of Korean television drama was well expressed by many interviewees, especially Ms. Zhang, a 60-year-old Taiwanese:

> I love Korean dramas. I watched almost everything that was popular in Taiwan. Every time I go back home, my friends will burn the Korean drama to me. *Jewel in the Palace* is my favorite one. I am just amazed how they can make the drama so realistically. They are just so touching. I cry all the time when I watch.
>
> (Interview with the author, December 3, 2009)

Ms. Chang, a 45-year-old Taiwanese, said:

> I watch Korean drama many times. I also like Korean films. They are really well made, and it portrays more Asian life than Japanese ones.

Japanese ones are just trendy and well made, but sometimes it is not realistic in Taiwanese life. Korean dramas are more "Asian" to me. Maybe that is why I watch Korean drama so often: because I miss home.

(Interview with the author, September 5, 2009)

Ms. Chung, a 63-year-old Taiwanese, said:

My friends all love Korean drama. Even my mother in Taiwan watches Korean drama every day. Because it is so popular in Taiwan, I watched it several times, too. I think it is very sophisticated and well made. I am not a fan of dramas, but *Dae Jang Geum* (*Jewel in the Palace*) was so well made that I watched it all through. Koreans are very talented people.

(Interview with the author, December 12, 2009)

Interviews show that the Korean cultural content carries Asian values and sentiments, and this motivates East Asians in Vienna to watch Korean television dramas. According to the interviewees, Korean pop culture's merit is to express values and sentiments that no other East Asian pop culture expresses. Especially for those living abroad, this cultural sentiment is an important factor in the decision to purchase Korean television dramas. As pointed out by Mr. Chen, the Confucian values are originally from China, but because they are so well expressed through the Korean television dramas, they help East Asians feel a sense of home. According to the interviewees, after watching Korean dramas, they fell in love with Korean style or Korean food. For example, they have started to eat spicier food and tend to patronize Korean restaurants more often because they have seen Korean food in the dramas, and that made them want to taste it. According to Ms. Chung:

I moved to Vienna thirty years ago. At that time, I felt very lonely and it was very hard to adapt to Austrian life. But nowadays, it is very nice. Even though I am sitting at home, I can watch or listen to any Asian products, and I feel so good and comfortable to live abroad. I don't feel so distanced from my home town.

(Interview with the author, December 12, 2009)

Ms. Zhang commented:

The life of overseas Asians became very different than before. People tried very hard to adapt to the lifestyle here, but now you feel so close to your home country. You can follow their trend by Internet and you can almost download everything from Internet. We live here but share more Asian trends.

(Interview with the author, December 3, 2009)

As mentioned by Ms. Zhang and a few others, Korean popular culture is a substitute culture for many East Asians in Vienna because they feel isolated or lonely. Interviewees did not directly express or point out their difficulties, but claimed that Korean popular culture gives them comfort while having an uneasy time trying to integrate in a host society of Europe.

Unlike Taiwanese and Chinese immigrants, Japanese immigrants hesitated to admit that Korean popular culture provides them with a feeling of home, but they agreed that Korean television dramas made them nostalgic and reminded them of old-time Japan. They also agreed that Korean pop culture contains strong Asian values which are lacking in modern Japanese pop culture but which are important features their parents' generation longs for. Many Japanese mentioned that they love Korean pop culture because it inspires nostalgic feelings of Asian-ness. Akemi Oki, a 40-year-old Japanese woman in Austria, said:

> I like Korean soap opera because all the story and contents are more sentimental than Japanese ones. In Japan, it is hard to find these stories like Korean soap opera anymore. In my mother's generation, we used to have these Asian-feeling dramas, but [they are] no longer popular in Japan. The Asian sentimental stories are no longer produced. That is the main reason that our mothers' generation feels very close to Korean television dramas, because it reminds them of their childhood while watching Korean soap opera. No other foreign products can attract Japanese as much as Korean dramas.
>
> (Interview with the author, March 22, 2009)

She pointed out that Korean popular culture has an Asian core, and that is the main reason for Japanese to consume it. Yet, she refused to identify herself as "East Asian," forcefully calling herself "Japanese." To my question whether she felt there was some bonding between East Asians through the Korean Wave, she again emphasized: "I am Japanese, and not Asian" (interview with the author, March 22, 2009). However, by viewing Korean soap operas, she became attracted to Korean food: "I am eating *kimchi* almost every day now. Combination with sushi and *kimchi* is really the best. My mother in Japan loves Korean food, too. She even went to Korea several times" (interview with the author, March 22, 2009). Akiko, 45 years old, married to an Austrian, and a resident of Vienna for 15 years, showed great affection for Korean pop culture:

> I love Korean men. Bae Yong Joon [hero in *Winter Sonata*] is the most attractive man I ever saw. We cannot find this kind of actor in Japan. So tall and has this intelligent look! Japanese women love Korean actors ... I sometimes watch Korean drama all night. It is so romantic. I sometimes

Online cultures of the Korean Wave 143

think how can Korean men be so romantic when they are Asian. I sometimes miss Asia when I am watching Korean dramas.

(Interview with the author, March 22, 2009)

Korean movies and dramas typically feature love and family issues, but unlike their Western counterparts, they emphasize filial piety. Chinese and Japanese people rediscover an Asian identity by watching Korean television dramas, while identifying with Confucianism and humanism. These dramas illustrate a balance between tradition and modernization, and emphasize "care and respect mediated by tight social ties in family and nation" (Yoon 2008). These themes in Korean films and dramas can be very familiar to East Asians. According to interviewee Yi Chung:

> In our church, we have a lot of people who watch Korean drama regularly. I know [a] few friends who watch it very often. I am not in [*sic*] fan of dramas, but I can understand why they like Korean drama so much. It deals with a lot of ethics we forget in the modern days, like respecting our parents or value of traditional culture. Like in the story of *Jewel in the Palace*, Koreans really well delivered their traditional culture. Everybody loves Korean food after watching that drama!
>
> (Interview with the author, December 3, 2009)

Their attraction to Korean popular culture is not only based on Asian sentiment, but also another important reason is that Korean popular culture indicates cultural hybridity. Culture is neither produced nor consumed in a single country today. K-pop fits perfectly into the demands of a globalized world. A product designed for global markets does not necessarily contribute to the formation of genuine cultural links between East Asians, other than common consumption habits, said one interviewee. The less identifiable a particular cultural item is with a single country, the more cultural acquisition is possible for everybody around the world. This means, hybridity sells. What all the responses have in common is the view that Korean popular culture combines high quality, which can rival that of Western cultural products, with an Asian voice and face, which makes it easier to identify with the content of the products. According to an interviewee identified as C, who refused to give his name:

> I first started to like Korean pop music because of their look and performance. After getting to know more, it is really [a] Western blend of Asian pop music. I think that is the most attractive part of Korean pop music. You kinda get every mixture of culture.
>
> (Interview with the author, March 1, 2010)

Jenny (a nickname) emphasized that Korean pop music is very trendy:

Korean pop is really up to date. I love their fast beat and their well-made videos. I like Mandarin pop as well, but only because I can understand the lyrics. I still love to listen to K-pop, although I don't understand the lyrics. It is never boring.

(Interview with the author, February 9, 2010)

Another interviewee, Tomas (a nickname), said:

Although I am only half-Japanese, I love Japanese and Korean pop culture. I feel very comfortable viewing or listening. Korean or Japanese pop are no longer really boring. My Austrian friends also like them a lot. I think because they are not something like transnational – visually more Western, but still have this Asian thing.

(Interview with the author, January 29, 2010)

Generally, the older generations (forties to sixties) favor Korean television drama, while the younger generations (25–40) prefer Korean popular music because of the hybridity and trendiness. Gerhard, 26 years old and half-Japanese, said: "Korean pop music has nice beat, and the singers are nice looking" (website interview, January 29, 2010). A Chinese student who refused to be identified by name said: "There are a lot of attractive Korean singers and they are good dancers" (website interview, January 29, 2010). Students who participated in website interviews said that they were great fans of Korean pop music, and they liked it because it is very trendy. All the singers or groups they liked – namely 2NE1, Super Junior, Wonder Girls and Big Bang – are the Korean Wave stars in China, Taiwan and Japan. Because students are often on the Internet, they seem fully aware of pop music trends in East Asia and they follow these trends in Austria, too. Although K-pop does not contain strong Asian values in the way that television dramas and films do, and although most of the students who like K-pop also enjoy J-pop or Taiwan-pop, it can arguably be said to bring East Asians together. Unlike other national pop styles, K-pop is often used at East Asian parties and Asian bars that advertise K-pop nights in Austria.

Koreans feel a need to portray Korea in a positive light to non-Koreans. This could be a reason why the Korean Wave does not display elements unique to Korean culture or elements of traditional culture that producers feel may not be modern enough. As one of the interviewees claimed, a deep-seated desire among Koreans is not to appear backward, and this attitude can be seen in the cultural products that Koreans export. Many interviewees revealed that, through their consumption of Korean pop culture, their image of South Korea had changed greatly. Most interviewees commented that they had had neither negative nor positive feelings towards South Korea, but that experiencing Korean pop culture had interested them in Korean culture and Koreans. Some were unsure whether the image of South Korea was positive or ambiguous, but most said it had changed during the previous ten years. Many reasons were mentioned for this change, among which was the Korean Wave popular culture.

The Korean Wave as a national, regional and global phenomenon

Arguments concerning hybridization of global–local interactions often focus on how the non-West responds to the West, and usually neglect how the non-Western countries have reworked distinctive and multiple modernities (Ong 1996). The globalization of media and popular/consumer culture is often based upon an assumption of the Western/American domination, and the arguments are focused on how the "Rest" resists, imitates or appropriates the products of the West. An alternative way to view globalization can connect the concepts of national and regional in the complex processes of globalization. Globalization even encourages local people to rediscover the local that they have neglected or forgotten in their drive towards Western-imposed modernization (Featherstone 1993; Robertson 1995). Globalization can be considered as intertwined and mutually constituting processes that also enhance the idea of valuing national or regional culture, as well as containing tensions and contradictions.

As indicated in the case study above, transnational mobility is now regarded as a defining characteristic of East Asians abroad; global culture is viewed as a key component of East Asians living in Europe; and the idea of globalization is employed to build the nation and the region of East Asia. The hybrid products that have been called the Korean Wave may look similar to American products, but they are said to possess the distinction of evoking a sense of familiarity among East Asians at home and abroad. Non-Western people who have so far confirmed their existence only through the West are finding new opportunities to construct an alternate consciousness through the sharing of popular cultural flows (Cho 2005). The Korean Wave represents a new type of cultural flow, mainly spreading through the Internet and social media and bringing cultural proximity to East Asians in Europe. Instead of merely assimilating or resisting Western cultures, East Asians at home and abroad are now active participants in their regional cultural flow and consumption as intersected with identity formation. As marginalized and excluded, East Asians in Europe may imagine and construct a transnational consumer group whose engagement with the Korean Wave demonstrates a longing to be part of a regional "East Asian" community.

This case study indicates an emerging cultural taste in Europe among East Asian immigrants for media cultural products that may routinely reinforce links with their home countries and with the region of East Asia. Korean popular culture has clearly become a cultural icon of contemporary East Asia, and this popularity has led overseas East Asians to consume the Korean Wave phenomenon through the Internet and share their emerging cultural taste through social media, even in a foreign land of Europe. By sharing similar contents that contain their values and sentiments, they struggle to create their own sense of community, distinct from the dominant culture or group of their host society. Many interviews with, and much observation of, East Asians reveal that consuming Korean popular culture provides comfort to those living in a foreign society where they feel isolated and find it hard to integrate. Many pointed out that Austrian culture is hard to assimilate, and Austrians' lack of knowledge of East Asian cultures makes them feel distant from their host society. The feelings of marginalization and distance initially motivated them to search for their identity as being "East Asians" by consuming the Korean Wave culture that is popular in their hometowns.

For these East Asians in Europe, engagement with the Korean Wave popular culture in everyday life may be a significant marker of self-identity. The participants in this study have different tastes and preferences by genre and nation, but all of them agree that they prefer to watch or listen to East Asian pop culture including the Korean Wave, which keeps them in closer touch with their hometowns. Instead of admiring Western popular culture or a host society of Europe, they are finding new opportunities to construct an alternate consciousness and structure of feeling by sharing a popular culture similar to their own. In this sense, the Korean Wave plays a significant role in rediscovering and rebuilding an East Asian identity in Europe.

References

Cha, H. and Kim, S. (2011) "A Case Study on Korea Wave: Focused on K-pop Concert by Korean Idol Group in Paris, June, 2011," *Multimedia, Computer, Graphic and Broadcasting Communications in Computer and International Science*, 263: 153–62.

Cho, H. (2005) "Reading the Korean Wave as a Sign of Global Shift," *Korea Journal*, 45: 147–82.

Chua, B. (2006) "East Asian Pop Culture: Consumer Communities and Politics of the National," *Cultural Space and Public Sphere in Asia*, 27–43, Seoul: Conference Publication.

Cohen, S. (1993) "Ethnography and Popular Music Studies," *Popular Music*, 12(2): 123–38.

——(1997) "Identity, Place and the 'Liverpool Sound'," in M. Stokes (ed.) *Ethnicity, Identity and Music: The Musical Construction of Place*, Oxford: Berg.

Featherstone, M. (1993) "Global and Local Cultures," in J. Bird, B. Curtis, T. Putnam and G. Robertson (eds) *Mapping the Futures: Local Cultures, Global Change*, London: Routledge.

Giddens, A. (1991) *Modernity and Self-identity*, Cambridge: Polity.

Hübinette, T. (2009) "To be Non-white in a Colour-Blind Society: Conversations with Adoptees and Adoptive Parents in Sweden on Everyday Racism," *Journal of Intercultural Studies*, 30(4).

Iwabuchi, K. (2002) *Recentering Globalization: Popular Culture and Japanese Transnationalism*, Durham: Duke University Press.

Iwabuchi, K., Muecke, S. and Thomas, M. (2004) "Introduction," in K. Iwabuchi, S. Muecke and M. Thomas (eds) *Rogue Flows: Trans-Asian Cultural Traffic*, Hong Kong: Hong Kong University Press.

Kim, Y. (2011) *Transnational Migration, Media and Identity of Asian Women: Diasporic Daughters*, London: Routledge.

King, R. and Wood, N. (2001) *Media and Migration: Constructions of Mobility and Difference*, London: Routledge.

Lamont, M. and Molnar, V. (2001) "How Blacks Use Consumption to Shape Their Collective Identity: Evidence from Marketing Specialists," *Journal of Consumer Culture*, 1: 1–31.

Lucas, R. (2005) *International Migration and Economic Development: Lessons from Low-Income Countries*, Cheltenham: Edward Elgar Publications.

Mathews, G. (2000) *Global Culture / Individual Identity: Searching for Home in the Cultural Supermarket*, London: Routledge.

Ong, A. (1996) "Anthropology, China, and Modernities: The Geopolitics of Cultural Knowledge," in H. Moore (ed.) *The Future of Anthropological Knowledge*, London: Routledge.

Paasi, A. (2003) "Region and Place: Regional Identity in Question," *Progress in Human Geography*, 27(4): 475–85.

Robertson, R. (1995) "Globalization: Time-Space and Homogeneity-Heterogeneity," in M. Featherstone, S. Lash and R. Robertson (eds) *Global Modernities*, London: Sage.

Straubhaar, J. (1997) "Distinguishing the Global, Regional and National Levels of World Television," in A. Streberny, D. Winseck, J. McKenna and O. Boyd-Barrett (eds) *Media in Global Context: A Reader*, New York: Arnold.

Sung, S. (2008) "Introduction: Why are Asians Attracted to Korean Pop Culture?," *Korean Wave*, Seoul: Jimoondang.

——(2012) "The European Reception of Gugak: Performing Korean Court Music in Vienna, Austria," in H. Um and H. Lee (eds) *Rediscovering Traditional Korean Performing Arts*, Seoul: Korean Arts Management Service, 25–31.

Tandt, C. (2002) "Globalization and Identity: The Discourse of Popular Music in the Caribbean," in R. Young (ed.) *Critical Studies: Music Popular Culture Identities*, Amsterdam: Rodopi.

Yoon, S. (2008) "The Cultural Identity of Asian Communities: Korean Hallyu Television Dramas and Their Receptions among Asian Media Audiences," paper presented at The International Association for Media and Communication Research in 2008.

Chapter 9

Hybridization of Korean popular culture
Films and online gaming

Dal Yong Jin

Korean popular culture has been considered a very distinctive non-Western culture in the global market as well as the regional market. Two cultural genres – Korean cinema and online gaming – have been unique due in large part to the degree of their appearance in the global markets. The global penetration of these cultural products – one in the audiovisual sector and the other in the new media sector – is noteworthy, given that these two cultural products have rapidly grown, based on their canny appropriation of cultural globalization, known as hybridity. As local-based cultural industries, they have utilized hybridization as one of the most important production strategies in order to penetrate the global and the regional markets. From storytelling to special effects, and from hiring local staffs to adopting local cultural taste, these two cultural genres have vehemently developed hybridization strategies.

Interestingly enough, these two cultural products have shown very different results in the global cultural markets in the early twenty-first century. Korean films alongside television programs had been among the most significant cultural genres driving the Korean Wave in the first several years of the 2000s; however, they have experienced a deep recession in very recent years. Contrary to this, domestic online gaming has been a latecomer on the bandwagon of the Korean Wave; however, the online game industry has rapidly increased its export to the global markets and has enjoyed massive popularity. Although hybridization has not been the sole factor for the growth and/or the fall of local popular culture in the global markets, it is significant to understand the nature of hybridization appropriated in the production of local popular culture and its implications to the local cultural industries, because hybridization has become the most significant approach that many local cultural producers are increasingly relying on in the globalized society.

This chapter documents the hybridization process of local popular culture with cases of Korean cinema and online gaming. It investigates the hybridization process of these two cultural genres in order to understand whether local popular culture has been influenced by Western norms or whether the process has created local cultural products that are representing and promoting local culture. This chapter maps out whether hybridity has created the third

Hybridization of Korean popular culture 149

culture, which is resisting Western dominance in the realm of local culture, by analyzing hybridized Korean films and online games. It finally articulates whether hybridity embedded in local popular culture can reduce an asymmetrical power relationship in the realm of culture between Western (mainly the U.S.) and non-Western (primarily developing) countries.

Hybridity in Korean popular culture

Contemporary cultural theories contain polarized ideas on whether culture is becoming increasingly homogeneous or heterogeneous under the scenario of globalization. The swift rise and fall of certain Korean popular culture, including Korean cinema and online gaming, have also been identified with several theoretical frameworks, including cultural imperialism and hybridization. In particular, cultural globalization and/or hybridity, which emphasizes either power to challenge and break the dominant culture of Western countries or power to sustain and develop local identities, has become a crucial theory (Wang 2006).

In postcolonial discourse, the concept of hybridity occupies a central place (Meredith 1998). Hybridization or hybridity refers to the construction of new culture that emerges from the interweaving of elements between the colonizer and the colonized, challenging the validity of any fixed cultural identity (Bhabha 1994). Since the early 1990s, hybridization has greatly influenced local popular culture because the heterogeneous creative mixings of the global and the local lie at the center of much of the globalization discourses (Ritzer and Ryan 2004: 42–7). As an alternative theoretical framework to cultural imperialism and/or Americanization, emphasizing homogenization of popular culture in the local due to the dominant role of Western popular culture, hybridization primarily claims that the new global order has to be understood as a complex and overlapping order, while defying existing center–periphery models (Kraidy 2002; Nederveen Pieterse 2004; Ryoo 2009). In other words, hybridization has been defined as the ways in which forms became separated from existing practices and recombine with new forms and practices (Rowe and Schelling 1991: 231, cited in Nederveen Pieterse 1995). Closely related to the concept of hybridity, Robertson (1995) proposed the concept of glocalization to understand cultural globalization. This concept emphasizes the interaction between the global and local, explicating that the local strategically incorporates the global by particularizing the universal (Cho and Lee 2009).

Whether on the subject of hybridization or glocalization, what we have to understand is the nature of hybridization because different perspectives interpret it in much different ways. With the case of films, for example, Turow (2009: 52) describes "hybridity as mixed cultures or the process of mixing genres within a culture and across culture." Several previous works considered hybridity to describe mixed genres and identities in popular culture (Tufte 1995; Kolar-Panov 1996). For these scholars, hybridity mainly implies physical fusion of two different styles and forms, or identities. However, what they did not focus on is whether the fusion of two cultures truly avoids a homogeneous culture heavily influenced by Western countries (Jin 2010a). It is inevitable that cultures often generate new forms and make new connections with one another in the course of hybridization. Several scholars, therefore, argue that hybridization cannot be considered as merely the mixing, blending and synthesizing of different elements that ultimately form a culturally faceless whole (Wang and Yeh 2005; Ryoo 2009).

Bhabha (1994) and Nederveen Pieterse (2004), in particular, claim that hybrid culture is not necessarily pure, but should create the new culture. For Bhabha (1994), hybridity is the process by which the colonial governing authority undertakes to translate the identity of the colonized (the Other) within a singular universal framework, but then fails, producing something familiar but new (Papastergiadis 1997, cited in Meredith 1998). This new mutation is the indeterminate spaces in between subject-positions that are lauded as the locale of the disruption and displacement of hegemonic colonial narratives of cultural structures and practices (Bhabha 1994). Bhabha indeed points out that hybridity should open up a third space within which elements encounter and transform each other as signifying the in-between, incommensurable (that is, inaccessible by majoritarian discourses) location where minority discourses intervene to preserve their strengths and particularity. As Bhabha (1994: 53) argues, "hybridity is an interpretive and reflective mode in which assumptions of identity are interrogated." However, the third space is also a mode of articulation, a way of describing a productive, and not merely reflective, space that engenders new possibility (Meredith 1998). The third space has to enable other positions, neither dominant, nor controlled, to emerge. It is also crucial to understand that hybridity symbolizes power which has the potential of empowering, dangerous or transformative force to the local culture (Werbner 1997).

As a few scholars (Kim 2011; Mori 2009; Ryoo 2009) point out, hybridization has also occurred in the Korean cultural industries as local cultural producers, such as online game developers and film directors, as well as music producers engage with Western popular culture. By analyzing the major characteristics of Korean films and online games through the lens of hybridity, this chapter sheds light on the current debates on hybridization, which has been a major norm in Korean popular cultural practices.

Global penetration of Korean films and online games

The Korean film and online game industries have shown very different trajectories in the twenty-first century. As one of the major cultural genres leading the Korean Wave, the film industry had played a key role between the late 1990s and the first several years of the 2000s in the Hallyu phenomenon until it experienced a deep slump in recent years. The Korean film industry had rapidly increased its export of films, from $31 million in 2003 to $76 million in 2005, which was a 145% increase during this period. However, starting in 2006, the export of domestic films had plunged from $24.5 million in 2006 to $13.5 million in 2010, although it slightly increased to $15.8 million in 2011 (Korean Film Council: KOFIC 2012a). The market share of domestic films has indicated the same trend. This was as low as 15.9% in 1993 (KOFIC 2009). Due to favorable government policies and the rapid involvement of domestic big corporations, such as Samsung and Daewoo, the market share of domestic films had increased to 63.8% in 2006, and Korean cinema was considered as one of the most successful film industries in the world. The situation has changed since 2006 immediately following the FTA (Free Trade Agreement) with the U.S.; the market share dropped to 42.1% in 2008. Due to the recent successes of a few domestic films, though, it increased to 52% in 2011 (KOFIC 2012b).

On the contrary, the online game industry has rapidly reigned supreme among the Korean cultural industries in terms of export to foreign countries, including Western countries. While Western countries, including the U.S. and European countries, as well as Japan have emphasized console games, which are the largest in terms of the global market share in the video game sector, Korea has fundamentally developed online games (Jin 2011). In particular, the Korean online game industry has expanded its exportation of domestic online games in the global video game markets, and the export of online games has far exceeded that of other cultural sectors, including films. Unlike domestic television programs and films, the local online game industry has exported several games to Western countries, including the U.S. and France as well as Asian countries.

Korea's online game industry has substantially increased its foreign export, from $182 million in 2003 to as much as $2.1 billion worth of games in 2011 (Korea Creative Content Agency: KCCA 2012: 17–19). The online game industry as the largest sector in the game industries consisted of 97.6% of exports in 2010 (KCCA 2012). In the video game sector, the online game industry accounted for as much as 88.7% of the market share, followed by mobile (7.1%), console, arcade and PC games. Several Korean online games have especially penetrated the global game markets, and massively multiplayer online role-playing games (MMORPGs) and casual games are two successful genres. Numerous domestic games, including "Maple Story," "Lineage I," "Lineage II" and "Aion," began knocking on the door of overseas markets, including the Western markets (Jin 2011). The "Lineage" games developed by NCSOFT have especially shown a unique presence in the global markets. Aion, developed by NCSOFT, also rapidly penetrated North America and Europe. Due to Aion, earnings from the U.S. and Europe were $46 million in the fourth quarter of 2009, which accounted for 24% of its revenue (NCSOFT 2010). In recent years, overseas sales accounted for 35–45% of the company's sales. NCSOFT has set up foreign subsidiaries for the operational service of games, and it has also tried to acquire local firms for the development of online games (Strom 2012: 326).

There are several elements to the rise and fall of Korean cinema and the swift growth of online gaming. In particular, government policies have directly impacted these two major cultural industries. Since the mid-1990s, the Korean government has developed its neoliberal cultural policies, emphasizing small government; however, the government has also supported the film and game industries with its legal and financial arms, which have been fundamental resources for the growth of Hallyu. Supportive and protective government policies until the early 2000s were certainly major factors for the growth of the Korean film industry. As Jihun Lee, Head of Publishing at veteran online game publisher Webzen explains, "the pool of talent and government support made for an excellent investment environment" (Wallis 2012). However, the film and online game industries have also developed their own unique strategies to advance the quality of their cultural products, and they have eventually extended their exportation of these cultural products.

In particular, several factors are clustered for the growth of the online game industry in the Korean context, including favorable government policies, a competitive market structure, a swift development of information and communication technologies (ICTs), the transnationalization and globalization of the game industry, and people's mentalities about accepting new technology and online gaming (Jin 2010b). Korea's online game corporations have been supported by extensive government intervention, and the online game market is being driven by the swift development of ICTs, in particular broadband subscribers.

Globalization and transnationalization are also fundamental factors for the growth of the online game sector. Over the last decade, many foreign-based game giants, such as Blizzard Entertainment, Electronic Arts (EA), Microsoft, Nintendo and Sony, have swiftly invested in the Korean game market in the midst of neoliberal globalization. Both competition and collaboration with these global developers have certainly advanced the quality of domestic games, which has resulted in the global popularity of several online games. In addition, hybridization has become one of the most significant elements because both the online game industry and the film industry have certainly engaged with hybridization strategies in both structure and content.

Understanding hybrid Korean films

While Korean cinema has witnessed the rise and fall of its film industry, it has also experienced a dramatic change in film content. It becomes crucial to determine the overall trend of Korean cinema in content in order to understand the major features of contemporary Korean films. In particular, it is significant to analyze domestic films according to hybridity because it gives a crucial frame to map out the changing nature of Korean cinema. As a few

Hybridization of Korean popular culture 153

critical culturalists (Lee 2008; Otmazgin 2009) point out, Korean popular culture is not really Korean in the sense that it has not evolved from Korean traditional values but is rather a mixture of influences; therefore, Korean popular culture, including films and online gaming, should be analyzed through the lens of hybridity.

Most of all, two major elements for the hybridization of domestic films are genres and stories, which are closely related. As Turow (2009) claims, again, the term hybridity can be used to describe mixed cultures or the process of mixing genres within a culture. Therefore, the changing patterns in genres are critical to understanding the hybridization of domestic films. Korean films have shown their unique hybridization processes in both genres and themes. The characteristics of the top 10 highest-grossing films have significantly changed over the last two decades. While the majority of independent films are not hybrid, nor commercially successful, the domestic films that made the top 10 list of each year show that they are mostly commercial and hybrid films. In 2006, when Korea changed its screen quota system, for example, among the top 10 grossing films only two genres – drama and comedy – represented Korean cinema. During the year, *The Host*, enticing more than 13 million moviegoers, and *Tazza, Hanbando, Maundy Thursday* and *Barefoot Gibong* were all dramas, and *200 Pound Beauty, My Boss, My Teacher, Marrying the Mafia 3, Forbidden Quest* and *My Scary Girl* were comedy movies (Table 9.1).

Compared to this, in 2012, several genres made the top 10 list, including comedy (*The Grand Heist, All About My Wife* and *Dancing Queen*), crime/ action (*The Thieves* and *Nameless Gangster*), drama (*Masquerade* and *Unbowed*), melodrama (*Architecture 101* and *The Concubine*) and horror (*Deranged*) (Table 9.2). Unlike 2006, the top 10 grossing films in 2012 show a variety of genres, and this kind of change has continued over the last 15 years, meaning that Korean cinema has dramatically shifted its major genres, in particular from dramas to commercially successful Hollywood genre movies.

Table 9.1 Top 10 grossing movies in 2006

	Korean films	*Nationwide admission*	*Genre*
1	The Host	13,019,740	drama
2	Tazza: The High Rollers	6,847,777	drama
3	200 Pound Beauty	6,619,498	comedy
4	My Boss, My Teacher	6,105,431	comedy
5	Hanbando	3,880,808	drama
6	Marrying the Mafia 3	3,464,516	comedy
7	Maundy Thursday	3,132,320	drama
8	Forbidden Quest	2,576,022	comedy (sexy)
9	Barefoot Gibong	2,347,311	human drama
10	My Scary Girl	2,286,745	romantic comedy

Source: Korean Film Council (2007) *Korean Film Industry White Paper 2006*, Seoul: KOFIC

154   Dal Yong Jin

Table 9.2 Top 10 grossing films in 2012

Ranking	Korean films	Nationwide admission	Genre
1	The Thieves	12,982,573	crime/action
2	Masquerade	11,523,893	history/drama
3	The Grand Heist	4,909,937	comedy/history
4	Nameless Gangster	4,694,595	crime/drama
5	All About My Wife	4,598,583	comedy/melodrama
6	Deranged	4,515,833	horror
7	Architecture 101	4,107,078	melo/romance
8	Dancing Queen	4,039,462	comedy/drama
9	Unbowed	3,443,533	drama
10	The Concubine	2,636,320	historical melodrama

Source: Korean Film Council (2013) *Korean Film Industry White Paper 2012*, Seoul: KOFIC

Indeed, there has been a significant change in genres in Korean cinema over the past several decades. Over the period 1995–2012, among 180 top-listed domestic films, drama was the most popular genre. The number of dramas during the period was 74 (41%), followed by comedy 51 (28.3%) and action 28 (15.5%). Interestingly, horror/thriller became the fourth most popular genre with 19 films (10.5%). These four major film genres accounted for 95.5% of the annual top 10 grossing films during this period in Korean cinema. The others were science fiction (SF) 3 (*Yonggary*, 1999; *2009 Lost Memories*, 2002; *D-War*, 2007) melody/romance 2 (*Close to Heaven*, 2009; *Architecture*, 2012), documentary 1 (*Old Partner*, 2009), adult (*Rehearsal*, 1995) and western 1 (*The Good, The Bad, the Weird*, 2008). This implies that only a few film genres are successful in Korean theaters because film producers make similar movies that the audiences prefer, instead of developing experimental and non-entertaining genres.

Until the mid-1990s, drama, including melodramas, comprised the largest portion of domestic movies each year. Dramas were receiving warm attention from moviegoers. The early Korean dramas not only hybridized Korean and Hollywood signifiers (costumes, languages and soundtracks) but also mixed Hollywood melodramatic tropes and realist Korean aesthetics and issues. Therefore, this specific genre is well developed, rich with unique national values, such as the division of the country, democracy and social values (e.g. class issues, income divide and Confucian mentalities), which are distinctive to Korean culture, at least until the early 1990s. However, Korean cinema has been commercialized, emphasizing economic imperatives as in the case of Hollywood movies, rather than serious social issues and/or national values, in the midst of globalization (Jin 2010a).

The nature of drama itself has changed over the past decade or so, because unlike during the 1970s and 1960s, dramas between 1995 and 2012 were not melodramas, which had been the most important genre in Korean cinema. From the mid-1990s until 2012, dramas were mostly connected to crimes, street gangs and rotten cops, instead of family and social issues. While some of the recent dramas also reflect socio-cultural values embedded in Korean society, such as the Korean War (*The Front Line*, 2011, *71: Into the Fire*, 2008, *Welcome to Dongmakgol*, 2005, *Taegukgi*, 2004, *Silmido*, 2003), and socio-cultural issues (*Silenced*, 2011, *Barefoot Gibong*, 2006, *Maratoon*, 2005) many dramas are also crime action movies (*Nameless Gangster*, 2012, *The Unjust*, 2010, *Running Turtle*, 2009, *Another Public Enemy*, 2005, *Friend*, 2001) (Jin 2010a). It is therefore very rare to see melodramas or melo-romance movies. Only a few such movies have made the top of the box office each year, including *Architecture 101* (2012), *Close to Heaven* (2009), *My Wife got Married* (2008), *You are My Sunshine* (2005) and *All for Love* (2005). Interestingly, unlike in previous decades, SF/fantasy (*D-War*, 2007) and horror/thriller (*Deranged*, 2012, *The Client*, 2011, *Moss*, 2010, *Thirst*, 2009, *Typhoon*, 2005, *The Big Swindle*, 2004, *Memories of Murder*, 2003, *2009 Lost Memories*, 2002) are some of the major Hollywood genres which have made it to the top of the movies in domestic box office. Of course, that does not mean that melodramas and/or romance movies have disappeared in Korean cinema, because several movies are hybrid in genre between comedy and romance, and between comedy and drama.

Whereas it is not surprising to see the change in genres through the hybridization process, what we have to consider is whether these commercialized films touch on several significant themes, such as ideological conflicts (the Korean War and the South/North Korea division), political issues (democracy) and traditional culture (national beauty and arts). As Heather Tyrrell (1999) points out, national cinema concerns itself with the lives and struggle of people in the nation, while entertainment predominates in Hollywood's commercial themes, including action, horror, western and comedy; newly hybrid Korean films are not concerned about ordinary people's lives and their struggles. The film industry could be considered an achievement for domestic cinema in the sense that it had attained a comparable status of special effects proficiency with Hollywood (Jin 2005). The problem was that Korean filmmakers mainly could not create new forms of culture. Hollywood films as global standards reign supreme, while a local cinema primarily tries to copy or follow what Hollywood has done. The primary trajectory of globalization, not only in capital and structure but also in content, is still from the West to the local (Jin 2010a).

Other than genres and themes, Korean films have strategically hybridized in several ways. Several film production corporations have especially utilized Hollywood style action and special effects in order to create blockbuster-style domestic movies. As it is in several national film industries, hybridization has become one of the major strategies in Korean cinema since the late 1990s. Although hybridization is not new, the Korean film industries have rapidly appropriated hybridization since *Shiri* (directed by Jae-ku Kang) – the first Hollywood-style big-budget blockbuster movie – was made a national success. While there are many hybrid movies, several movies, including *The Thieves*

(2012), *Masquerade* (2012) and *D-War* (2007), have been very successful in the domestic box office. Regardless of their success in the domestic market, they have not been able to penetrate the Western markets, although they have made flimsy appearances in North America and Western Europe.

The nature of the hybridization of the three movies is not much different. They were arguably not successful in creating the third space because they were not resisting Hollywood. Instead, they tried to make another form of Hollywood films, which are homogenized, not authentic. As Kraidy (2002: 317) argues, "politically, a critical hybridity theory considers hybridity as a space where intercultural and international communication practices are continuously negotiated in interactions of differential power." This means that "hybridity" is not merely the synthesizing of different elements to form a culturally blended whole, nor should it be construed as an in-between zone where global and local power relations are neutralized in the obscurity of the mélange. Rather it is "the dialogical re-inscription of various codes and discourses in a spatio-temporal zone of signification" (Kraidy 1999: 472). The key point to remember is whether Korean cinema has advanced its power while resisting global power, and in this regard it is premature to say that the Korean film industry has created an equal power relationship with the global force, which is the weakest link of the contemporary Korean films.

Hybridization of local online gaming

There are several socio-cultural contexts that contribute to the rapid growth of Korean online gaming, and the hybridization of the text has been one of the most significant factors. In particular, Korean online game corporations have developed their hybrid game genres, including MMORPGs. Although several other genres, including casual games and first-person shooter (FPS) games, were temporarily popular in Korea in 2007 and 2008, domestic online game producers have continued to develop MMORPGs, which naturally encompass hybridization strategies (KCCA 2010: 64). Due to the fact that MMORPGs require a very large number of players who interact with one another from many different countries, the storylines, themes and genres are hybrid in most MMORPGs.

As a basic storyline, several MMORPGs created in both Western and non-Western countries, including "World of Warcraft" and "Lineage," hybridize their games. The majority of MMORPGs are based on traditional fantasy themes, as in the case of "Dungeons & Dragons"; however, many MMORPGs utilize hybrid themes and genres that merge fantasy components with those of sword and sorcery and science fiction. As will be detailed later, domestic MMORPGs, including "Lineage I," "Lineage II" and "Aion," have appropriated hybridity in their games, which has resulted in success in the global game markets. Due to their late arrival in the global cultural markets, several MMORPGs also draw thematic material from comic books, which is another form of hybridity. Indeed, online gaming has been hybridized, and MMORPGs are mostly hybrid.

More specifically, "Aion," as the most recent MMORPG which has been globally successful, shows the nature of hybridity in local online gaming. There are several elements that Aion has made a global success. NCSOFT developed "Aion" based on its hybridization strategy, meaning the developers integrated Western game storylines with Korean cultural settings. Aion combines player versus player (PvP) and player versus environment, including computer (PvE), which is a concept the developers call PvPvE in a fantasy game environment. NCSOFT realized that Korean online gamers like PvP games, characterized by graceful movements and community interactions, and they encourage role players to take roles within a social hierarchy and engage in coordinated strategies or other collective activity, while U.S. players like PvE (Martinsons 2005). NCSOFT combines PvP and PvE in order to attract two major customers. The PvPvE gameplay of Aion revolves around battles within the Abyss and Balaurea (Pino 2012).

Prior to Aion, "Lineage" games are also very successful in the global markets based on their hybrid natures. "Lineage" mixes Western stories with Korean mentalities. They take place against a backdrop of medieval fantasy. Since it is set in the Kingdom of Aden in medieval Europe, the basic storyline is naturally Western. However, NCSOFT integrates Western game storylines with Korean cultural settings, which emphasize solidarity, affiliation and family matters which are based on Confucian values (Kim 2005). "Lineage's" popularity has been based on innovative hybridization – a mix of a global role-playing game storyline with local mentality (Jin 2011).

Likewise, the glocalization process for domestic online games is one of the most significant hybridization strategies in terms of structure. In order to penetrate American and European game markets, several game developers and publishers have development studios in Europe and the U.S. For example, Aion added several traditional local clothes in a few countries, including China and Taiwan, and recruited and hired local vocalists in order to provide familiarity to local users in these countries. In the case of the North American market, NCSOFT hired 16 fantasy novelists and asked them to revise stories, words and storylines in the game in order to avoid any awkwardness for American users. In Russia, NCSOFT added Russian adages during the translation of the original stories. As such, NCSOFT has substantially appropriated both hybridization and glocalization strategies in developing and promoting Aion in the global markets. Consequently, Aion became one of the most popular online games in North America (Choe 2012). NCSOFT sold about 700,000 packages in September 2012, and it was the first time that any domestic game came top on the list. According to data from market research firm NPD Group, Aion was the top-selling PC game in the U.S. in September 2009, followed by "The Sims 3" (Electronic Arts), "Champions Online" (Atari) and "World of Warcraft" (Blizzard Entertainment) (Molina 2009; NPD Reports

158 Dal Yong Jin

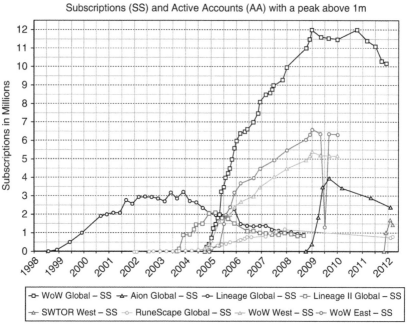

Figure 9.1 Subscription to MMORPGs.
Source: MMODate.net (2012). MMODate Charts. http://users.telenet.be/mmodata/Charts/Subs-1.png

2009) (see Figure 9.1). Nexon, the largest Korean online games developer, including such games as "KartRider" and "Maple Story," headquartered in Tokyo, Japan in order to penetrate the global markets easily while appropriating glocalization strategies (Song 2011). Korea's online game corporations have deliberately utilized the glocalization process to attract global game users.

As one online game magazine (mmosite.com 2011) aptly put it, the success of Korean online games achieved in North America is simple; localization strategy. For example, NCSOFT has never sent any Korean technical staff to the U.S. since its U.S. branch was established. The games of its U.S. branch were developed independently all by local employees. Such strategy accounts for the perfect performance that NCSOFT has been achieving in North America. Foreign game users, therefore, do not see any serious cultural antagonism and/or resistance in Korean online games because they easily identify them as part of their own culture and games. The glocalization strategy as part of hybridization certainly becomes a crucial factor for the growth of local online games in other countries. Korean game developers have strategically developed identity-less local games in the global markets in order to appeal to global

Hybridization of Korean popular culture   159

game users, which has resulted in the popularity of local online games in many different global markets.

Hybridity primarily describes mixed genres and identities (Turow 2009), and the game industry itself is a hybrid sector. With the case of Japanese console games, Mia Consalvo (2006: 120) especially points out:

> The game industry is a hybrid encompassing a mixture of two different businesses and (more importantly) cultures to a degree unseen in other media industries. Just as different national identities have been mixed in the hybrid, so too the realms of business and culture are converging in novel ways. The particularities of the video game industry and culture can be recognized in the transnational corporations that contribute to its formation and development; in the global audience for its products; and in the complex mixing of format, style and content within games.

The point is whether hybridity opens up "a third space" within which elements encounter and transform each other as signifying the in-between, incommensurable location where minority discourses intervene to preserve their strengths and particularity, as Bhabha (1994) points out.

In this regard, it is certainly indicative of the hybridization of the online game industry. Several Korean game firms have utilized the fundamental characteristics of online games coupled with the Korean mentality in the process of updating and developing games. The popularity of local games is dependent on their sophistication, using cultural authenticity rooted in Korean society (Jin 2010b). The Korean online game industry has arguably developed the third space by mixing the two different cultures between the local and the global (Western), although it is not perfect in the creation of the third space. Several online games have relied on Western storylines; however, publishers and developers have melded them with Korean mentalities in producing games. While admitting that local game developers are not powerful enough yet to become the subject in the complicated and dynamic processes of hybridization, these game developers have conducted relatively solid performances to create unique game contents (Jin 2010b and 2011).

However, it is also crucial to understand that the nature of online gaming is not yet a fully confirmed example of bottom-up hybridization. As Kraidy (2002) points out, one of the major issues during the hybridization process is whether local developers have initiated the process, which means whether domestic online games have been sites of resistance against imperialist powers. The Korean online game industry has certainly adapted itself to fit patterns of Western cultural consumption, but it has arguably done so largely according to an American-inspired localization model. O'Byrne and Hensby (2011: 126) claim that "hybridization rejects the simplicity of cultural imperialism and homogenization in favor of a concern with the reception and indigenization of cultural forms – an active interplay between core and periphery." However, the most conspicuous shortcoming in the discourse of hybridity is that it does not address questions of power and inequality:

> Relations of power and hegemony are reproduced *within* hybridity, for wherever we look closely enough we find the traces of asymmetry in culture, place, and descent. Hence, hybridity raises, rather than erases, the question of the terms and conditions of mixing. Meanwhile, it is also important to note the ways in which relations of power are not merely reproduced, but refigured in the process of hybridization. Thus, according to the context and the relative power and status of elements in the mixture, hybridity can be asymmetric or symmetric.
>
> (Nederveen Pieterse 2007: 219)

Power relations are an important variable in the production of a hybrid culture (Zanariah and Ishak 2011). While local game firms do ostensibly globalize their games through hybridization, decisions about where it will expand have been made by Western users because many local firms develop games in Western countries according to their taste (Lin 2011; Jin 2010a). Local game corporations have also strategically adopted borderless storytelling and backgrounds to attract Western gamers as well as game users in their country. However, it is also true that local game firms have been influenced by Western game publishers as well as users, and this hybridization process partially hurts local identities, although it proves both commercial successes and contraflow.

Conclusion

This chapter has discussed cultural globalization with the cases of local films and online games. The Korean cultural industries have appropriated hybridization strategies in order to create cultural products that foreign audiences as well as domestic audiences enjoy. In a way of mixing two different cultures in themes and stories, cultural industries corporations have jumped onto a hybrid bandwagon, and Korean popular culture, both films and online games, has seemingly hybridized in mingling with two different cultures. Hybridization of popular culture has been imperative because the cultural industries have to create hybrid culture which is a global norm in some sense.

What we need to consider is whether hybrid culture in the cases of Korean cinema and online gaming is a simple mixture of two different cultures, can or cannot resist global forces, or whether they are symbolizing the third space, because hybridity should be the site of resistance against imperialist powers (Kraidy 2002). Korean cultural industries firms have experienced difficulties in creating new forms of movies and online games. As the genres and themes of Korean movies and online games demonstrate, many film producers and game developers have developed money-making genres, such as comedy and horror in films, and MMORPGs in online games. Hybrid movies and games have

Hybridization of Korean popular culture 161

made commercially oriented entertainment cultural products through both structural hybridization and convergence of culture.

However, it is doubtful whether Korean popular culture could resist Western influence in content, because many Korean cultural industries corporations cannot produce a politically and culturally unique third space. Domestic films and online games have made popular products targeting global audiences from the beginning; therefore, they utilize Western stories, including scenery, clothes and armor, while adapting Korean mentalities, such as Confucian values emphasizing collectivism as evidenced in several MMORPGs and films. With a few exceptions, they have not been able to create the third space, preserving locality while resisting global forces. Of course, hybridization does not always lead to equal cultural exchange (Crothers 2013: 31), meaning the global flow of cultural products remains uneven and markedly one-sided in favor of Western popular culture and cultural producers.

The primary concern of hybridity is not the physical mixing of two different cultures, but the creation of new forms of culture, not homogenized, but a mixed third space resisting global domination. Local cultures should create unique combinations as they incorporate foreign and globalizing influences, such as those coming from the U.S., in order to actualize cultural globalization (Penney 2011: 86). Hybridity also should function as part of a power relationship between center and margin, hegemony and minority, and indicate a blurring, destabilization or subversion of that hierarchical relationship (Nederveen Pieterse 1995: 56). That means local producers and developers must play a key role in creating the third culture, which is built on the base of local culture and local initiative. As seen in the cases of local cinema and online gaming, local producers and developers cannot guarantee pluralism and diversity yet. While Korea has rapidly increased its global visibility with a few cultural products, including films and online games, the country is still not powerful enough to become the subject in the complicated and dynamic processes of hybridization (Wang 2006), which local producers and developers have to overcome in order to create new local-driven global culture.

Note

Some of the analysis above was previously conducted for the article titled "Critical Interpretation of Hybridization in Korean Cinema: Does the Local Film Industry Create the Third Space," *Javnost – The Public*, 17(1) (2010): 55–72. Here, I extended the analysis to map out the overall trend of hybridization in genres during this whole period.

References

Bhabha, H. (1994) *The Localization of Culture*, New York: Routledge.

Cho, J. and Lee, H. (2009) "The War over D-War: An Investigation of the Global Production, Distribution, and Reception of a Strategically Hybridized Cultural Text," paper presented at the International Communication Association, Chicago, May 21–27.

Choe, S. (2012) "Reasons for the Success of Aion in the Global Market," *Economy Chosun*, December, http://economyplus.chosun.com/special/special_view_past.php?boardName=C00&t_num=4205&img_ho=62 (accessed January 4, 2013).

Consalvo, M. (2006) "Console Video Games and Global Corporations: Creating a Hybrid Culture," *New Media and Society*, 8(10): 117–37.

Crothers, L. (2013) *Globalization and American Popular Culture*, Lanham: Rowman & Littlefield.

Jin, D. (2005) "Blockbuster-ization vs. Copywood: The Nation-State and Cultural Identity in Korean Cinema," *Journal of Media Economics and Culture*, 3(3): 46–72.

——(2010a) "Critical Interpretation of Hybridization in Korean Cinema: Does the Local Film Industry Create the Third Space," *Javnost – The Public*, 17(1): 55–72.

——(2010b) *Korea's Online Gaming Empire*, Boston: MIT Press.

——(2011) "The Digital Korean Wave: Local Online Gaming goes Global," *Media International Australia*, 141: 128–36.

Kim, J. (2005) "Lineage: The Prince of Online Gaming," *Kyunghyang Shinmun*, December 12.

Kim, M. (2011) "Riding the Korean Wave of Multiculturalism: Review and Future Prospects," in D. Kim and M. Kim (eds) *Hallyu: Influence of Korean Popular Culture in Asia and Beyond*, Seoul: Seoul National University Press.

Kolar-Panov, D. (1996) "Video and the Diasporic Imagination of Selfhood: A Case Study of the Croatians in Australia," *Cultural Studies*, 10(2): 288–314.

Korea Creative Content Agency (2010) *2010 Korean Game Whitepaper*, Seoul: KCCA.

——(2012) *2012 Contents Perspective*, Seoul: KCCA.

Korean Film Council (2009) *Korean Film Industry White Paper 2008*, Seoul: KOFIC.

——(2012a) *Summary of 2011 Korean Film Industry*, Seoul: KOFIC.

——(2012b) *Korean Cinema 14*, Seoul: KOFIC.

Kraidy, M. (1999) "The Global, the Local, and the Hybrid: A Native Ethnography of Glocalization," *Critical Studies in Mass Communication*, 16: 456–76.

——(2002) "Hybridity in Cultural Globalization," *Communication Theory*, 12(3): 316–39.

Lee, K. (2008) "Mapping out the Cultural Politics of the Korean Wave in Contemporary South Korea," in B. Chua and K. Iwabuchi (eds) *East Asian Pop Culture: Analyzing the Korean Wave*, Hong Kong: Hong Kong University Press.

Lin, Y. (2011) "Playing as Producing: Convergence Culture and Localization of EA Digital Games in Taiwan," in D. Jin (ed.) *Global Media Convergence and Cultural Transformation: Emerging Social Patterns and Characteristics*, Hershey: IGI Global.

Martinsons, M. (2005) "Online Games Transform Leisure Time for Young Chinese," *Communications of the ACM*, 48(4): 51.

Meredith, P. (1998) "Hybridity in the Third Space: Rethinking Bi-cultural Politics in Aotearoa/New Zealand," paper presented to Te Oru Rangahau Maori Research and Development Conference, July 7–9, 1998.

Ministry of Culture, Sports and Tourism (2011) *2010 Contents Industry Whitepaper*, Seoul: MCST.

Ministry of Culture and Tourism (2006) *Establishment of Film Development Fund*, December 22.

Mmosite.com (2011) "Korean MMOs Occupying North America," August 30. http://news.mmosite.com/content/2011-08-0/korean_mmos_occupying_north_america.shtml (accessed November 4, 2012).

Molina, B. (2009) "NPD: 'Aion' Tops PC Sales in September," *USA Today*, October 23. http://content.usatoday.com/communities/gamehunters/post/2009/10/npd-aion-tops-pc-sales-in-september/1#.UMasIoNWyuI (accessed December 5, 2012).

Mori, Y. (2009) "Reconsidering Cultural Hybridities: Transnational Exchanges of Popular Music in Between Korea and Japan," in C. Berry, C. Liscutin and J. Mackintosh (eds) *Cultural Studies and Cultural Industries in Northeast Asia,* Hong Kong: Hong Kong University Press.

NCSOFT (2010) *Investor Relations, 4Q 2009,* Seoul: NCSOFT.

Nederveen Pieterse, J. (1995) "Globalization as Hybridization," in M. Featherstone, S. Lash and R. Robertson (eds) *Global Modernities,* London: Sage.

——(2004) *Globalization and Culture,* Boulder: Rowman & Littlefield.

——(2007) "Hybridity," in G. Ritzer (ed.) *Blackwell Encyclopedia of Sociology,* Vol. 5, Hoboken: Blackwell.

NPD Reports (2009) "Aion #1 in September," http://aion.ign.com/articles/news/4494/NPD-Reports-Aion-1-for-September.

O'Byrne, D. and Hensby, A. (2011) *Theorizing Global Studies,* New York: Palgrave Macmillan.

Otmazgin, N. (2009) "A Tail that Wags the DOG? Cultural Industry and Cultural Policy in Japan and South Korea," *Journal of Contemporary Policy Analysis,* 13(3): 307–25.

Penney, J. (2011) "KEVIN07: Cool Politics, Consumer Citizenship, and the Specter of Americanization in Australia," *Communication, Culture and Critique,* 4(1): 80–98.

Pino, L. (2012) "Aion Overview Morningstar Gamers," July 31. http://mstarga mers.com/mmorpg/aion (accessed December 5, 2012).

Ritzer, G. and Ryan, M. (2004) "Americanisation, McDonaldisation, and Globalisation," in N. Campbell, J. Davies and G. McKay (eds) *Issues in Americanisation and Culture,* Edinburgh: Edinburgh University Press.

Robertson, R. (1995) "Glocalisation: Time-Space and Homogeneity-Heterogeneity," in M. Featherstone, S. Lash and R. Robertson (eds) *Global Modernities,* London: Sage.

Ryoo, W. (2009) "Globalization or the Logic of Cultural Hybridization: The Case of the Korean Wave," *Asian Journal of Communication,* 19(2): 137–51.

Song, J. (2011) "Games Developer Nexon Lines up IPO in Japan," *Financial Times,* November 7. http://www.ft.com/cms/s/0/52d0e952-0923-11e1-8e86-00144feabdc0 .html#axzz2FdcxhyuP (accessed December 5, 2012).

Strom, P. (2012) "Internationalisation of the Korean Online Game Industry: Exemplified Through the Case of NCSOFT," *International Journal of Technology and Globalization,* 6(4): 312–34.

Tufte, T. (1995) "How to Telenovelas Serve to Articulate Hybrid Cultures in Contemporary Brazil," *The Nordicom Review,* 16(2): 29–35.

Turow, J. (2009) *Media Today: An Introduction to Mass Communication,* London: Routledge.

Tyrrell, H. (1999) "Bollywood versus Hollywood: Battle of the Dream Factories," in T. Skelton and T. Allen (eds) *Culture and Global Change,* London: Routledge.

Wallis, V. (2012) "The Original Hallyu: The Korean Video Game Industry," Septeber 23. <http://10mag.com/korean-video-game-201209/> (accessed December 5, 2012).

Wang, G. and Yeh, E. (2005) "Globalization and Hybridization in Cultural Products: The Cases of Mulan and Crouching Tiger, Hidden Dragon," *International Journal of Cultural Studies,* 8(2): 175–93.

Wang, W. (2006) "A Critical Interrogation of Cultural Globalization and Hybridity: Considering Chinese Martial Arts Films as an Example," paper presented at the annual conference of the International Communication Association, Dresden, Germany, June 16.

Werbner, P. (1997) "Introduction: The Dialectics of Cultural Hybridity," in P. Werbner and T. Modood (eds) *Debating Cultural Hybridity: Multi-cultural Identities and the Politics of Anti-racism,* London: Zed Books.

Zanariah, S. and Ishak, A. (2011) "Cultural Hybridity: Adapting and Filtering Popular Culture in Malaysian Television Programmes," *Malaysian Journal of Media Studies,* 13(1): 1–15.

Chapter 10

K-pop dance trackers and cover dancers

Global cosmopolitanization and local spatialization

Liew Kai Khiun

Introduction: K-pop and the visibly conscious image generation

> But now the mirror image has become detachable from the person mirrored, and it is transportable. And where is it transported? To a site in front of the masses. Naturally, the screen actor never for a moment ceases to be aware of this. When he stands before the apparatus, he knows that in the end he is confronting the masses. It is they who will control him. Those who are not visible, not present while he executes his performance, are precisely those who will control it.
>
> (Benjamin 2008: 33)

For two days over the weekend of June 23 and 24, 2012, the ground floor of Plaza Singapura, one of Singapore's more popular malls, turned into a performance venue for a Korean pop music dance competition. Korean pop music or K-pop is performed by pop artistes trained in South Korea. Amidst the mix of supporters and casual weekend shoppers in the audience, 20 groups of mostly local teenagers took their turns to perform the dances of K-pop groups. With the logos of corporate sponsors emblazoned on the board behind the stage and a concurrent sales promotion of the latest Samsung smartphones nearby, it was difficult to ignore the commercial purpose of the event. As prosumers and "immaterial laborers" of the globalizing K-pop industry, whatever rewards these juvenile hopefuls would receive would be minute compared with the sales receipts generated by such events. Seemingly innocent of such hegemonic undercurrents, the contestants were more absorbed in rehearsing their steps at the corner of the mall, cheering for fellow groups, watching recorded playbacks from their parents' camcorders and posting updates on Facebook. Standards of performances varied among the contestants from the awkward and poorly prepared to more polished groups executing highly synchronized moves. With the mingling of plump and toned bodies, masculine and androgynous forms, males and females from different ethnic groups, the teenage amateur dancers of the era of the social media have turned an otherwise commercial venue into a more autonomous and cosmopolitan site of public participation.

Nonetheless, the familiarity of these contestants with K-pop texts and choreographies is indicative of a more independent method of mastery of dances and lyrics, as well as the formation of groups through the social media in the cyberspace. Even though the prospect of being a Seoul-based K-pop star may just be a distant possibility, the commonly dismissed manufactured and plasticized genre of manicured pop idols has in some ways served to energize the local space by bringing out a more vernacular and organic parti-cipation. In contrast to the earlier forms of transnational cultural flows from the region that were more essentialized along ethnic contours, I will argue that Hallyu has freed up more cosmopolitan imaginations and participation when its first wave arrived in the city-state through television dramas (Liew and Fu 2006). The second wave has been very much defined by K-pop and its accompanying fan cover dances. Through social media, Hallyu continues to act as an unintentional platform for social convergence and multicultural cosmopolitanism. While K-pop industry girl and boy groups tend to consist of fair/creamy-skinned "East Asian"-looking singers, its fan cultures have in contrast a significantly more visible inclusive and cosmopolitan profile. In striving to perfect the dance choreographies of their K-pop idols, the fan cover dances should not be seen as mimics, but a showcasing of their moves through YouTube from the fans' bedrooms to the public arenas. In uploading their fan cover dances to YouTube, they are scripting these dances according to their varied experiences and locations. Idealized and reified, official and corporate discourses on cosmopolitanism have often been framed along the contrived and tokenized assemblages that often mask the systematic and structural inequalities and hierarchies. In contrast, vernacular and more organic forms of cosmopolitanism are more spontaneous undertakings with open opportunities for more pluralistic engagements and inclusive participation that would bring otherwise under-represented and invisible groups meaningfully out in the public sphere. This chapter demonstrates that the popularity of K-pop dances has been crucial in injecting new meanings, agencies and bodies into the tightly managed and functionalistic spaces of Singapore.

Writing in 1936, Benjamin's *The Work of Art in the Age of its Technological Reproducibility* pointed out the synchronicity in the development of the mechanical analogue media of film, photography and radio on the evolution of modern mass culture. The rapid ease of replication and transportability of images by the mechanical apparatus altered the social relations between the artiste and the increasingly faceless mass audience in the intensified process of estrangement felt before one's appearance (*Erscheinung*) (Benjamin 2008: 33). Following Baudrillard's concept of the simulacrum as a mirror to the real, Holt (2001) positions the imagination of children's novels as a "looking glass world" opposite the world of "living pictures." Unlike the replicated and consumed images of Benjamin's world, however alike in appearance, the image seen in the mirror to the real tends to possess dissimilar subjectivities.

In the context of the discussions on the media image as replicated and copied by Benjamin, and in the postmodern hyperreal simulacrum by Holt, this chapter demonstrates that the proliferation of K-pop-inspired cover dances and flash mobs in cyber and physical spaces presents a networked image more visibly conscious of its own presence and subjectivity. With the emphasis on exploring the politics of the appropriation of K-pop dance choreographies through the specific case study of Singapore, this chapter seeks to triangulate the relationships between the virtual, domestic and public spaces in the new cosmopolitan places engendered.

Hallyu and K-pop 2.0

A confluence of market strategies as well as the rise of the social media has probably aided K-pop's role in bringing Hallyu to new heights in both Asia and the rest of the world. Although the export of K-pop began alongside the export of Korean dramas in the late 1990s, the dynamics shifted in 2008 with the confluence of aesthetical and technological determinants in what Cha and Kim (2011: 155–6) observe as the move from the "formation" years to the more advanced stage of diversification. On the industry level, Korean record labels like JYP, YG Entertainment, SM Town and Leon, several of which are helmed by former singers, have been training a new breed of highly manicured and youthful Korean boy and girl groups executing visibly simple synchronized dance choreographies easily imitated by lay viewers (Lawlietta 2009).

To widen the supply of aspiring artistes as well as to give fans the prospect of not only getting to know their stars, but also becoming one in the future, the K-pop industry has been hosting auditions and singing contests within and outside Korea. At the same time, the introduction of video-streaming digital technology on YouTube in 2005 marked the beginning of a new trend in the circulation of popular music flows and texts. Through the video clips on YouTube, viewers are no longer reliant on the mainstream print and broadcast media in determining their viewing preferences. This is especially true for the generation of youths born into the Internet age in the 1990s. While Korean television dramas defined the first generation of Hallyu fans in the living room, YouTube has introduced new fans to the world of K-pop through the convenience of increasingly mobile smartphones. Studies in K-pop fan cultures have also moved from the conventional fan clubs to that of participation in the social media (Jung 2011a and Jung and Hirata 2012). From this generation too emerges that of the cover-dance performer eager to not only relive the televisual experience but to re-perform the Music Video dances to a larger audience via YouTube. Psy's *Gangnam Style*, which has garnered more than 1.5 billion views as of April 2013, is perhaps the strongest indicator of YouTube's significance in projecting K-pop's global reach. It is a reach that has been further multiplied by live performances, cover dances and parodies of the clip.

168 Liew Kai Khiun

The global phenomenon of K-pop cover dances has created a need to revisit the discussions of the performative negotiation of the subjective body with the hegemonic disciplinary mechanisms of neoliberal global capital (Merriman 2010; Antebi 2009). From the countless performances of its cover dances, what role has K-pop served either as a disciplinary cookie cutter, or as a skill for the constant struggle of the subjective body defining its presence within the city? In terms of the appropriation of K-pop dance choreographies, this postmodern element is invoked through the conscious and constant mutation by fan cover dances of the original performances of these groups. As would be reflected in the movement from "Sound" to "Dance" Trackers, as well as from "Official" to "Cover" Dancers in the next section, K-pop is clothed with a more culturally colorful cosmopolitan profile by fans who are otherwise in the wrong body shape, uniform, ethnicity and gender to be Hallyu stars.

Sound and dance trackers, official and cover dancers

In order to see the new patterns of appropriating Hallyu, the post-2008 fans would be categorized as dance tracker in contrast to their predecessors who are henceforth dubbed sound tracker as seen in Table 10.1. While serving as broad temporal markers, such categories are neither rigidly established nor do they suggest the replacement of one generation by the other. The sound trackers' engagement with the material comes from the definite seating position from the television screen as their cognitive and optical senses coordinate with the audiovisual images on the television box. With genres touching on history, crime, politics and family, most Korean television dramas cater to an adult market accustomed to serialized narratives where soundtracks served to anchor their memories and dramatize the text. Given this televisual experience

Table 10.1 The sound tracker and dance tracker

Sound tracker	Dance tracker
Adult	Adolescent
Text	Body
Television	YouTube
Cognitive	Physical
Narrative	Choreography
Television serial	Music video
Soundtrack	Dance track
Resolution	Synchronization
Moment	Movement
Tears	Sweat
Experience	Performance
Star chaser	Star dancing
Fan tribute	Fan dance

from the living room, the sound tracker would mainly be an adult who had watched the dramas broadcast in the first Hallyu wave. This is because the dramas would be aimed at a broader demographic base across the family rather than the smaller juvenile crowd won over in Hallyu 2.0.

Audiences would wait for the dramatic moments of cliffhangers and resolution where romantic courtships are ascertained, family disputes resolved and kingdoms saved. These are the moments where tears are expected to be shed by the audiences overwhelmed by profession of romantic love and devotion. Finally, other than tourist visits and language lessons to be more deeply involved in extending the screen experience and pleasures, the opportunity for the sound tracker to participate in a larger collectivity would be through the fan club and playing the role of a "star chaser," a Chinese term used to describe the more fanatical fan following. In cyberspace, the soundtrack is a signifier for fan tributes and memories of the televisual moments. Fan videos on websites and video-streaming portals are used as tools to immortalize the presence of prominent drama serials like *Autumn in My Heart*, *Winter Sonata* and *Dae Jang Guem*, which were synonymous with the first wave of Hallyu. Compared to the MVs of post-2008 K-pop groups that average nearly 30 million views within a year of their release, these soundtracks do not go beyond one million views on YouTube. Uploaded as early as April 1, 2006 (less than a year after the portal was established), "My Memory," the theme song of *Winter Sonata*, only managed to garner about 870,000 views some six years later on YouTube. This reflects the relatively lesser reliance on the social media by the sound tracker of the first wave of Hallyu.

An emerging generation of what I call "dance trackers" is more engaged with the world of K-pop. This is because K-pop caters to the teenage market in the same way Korean dramas cater to the adults. In contrast to the traditional viewer, dance trackers are fans who seek more physical engagement from the world of Korean entertainment. They closely scrutinize the dance choreographies of the music videos. In focusing on the dance track instead of the soundtrack for more reasons than familiarizing themselves with the faces of individual members of the groups, fans of K-pop aim to observe and practice the distinctive choreographies of the music videos. Unlike the sound trackers' emphasis on experiencing the dramaturgical resolutions and moments of Korean drama, which are often teary events, K-pop cover-dance fans strive to replicate and perfect the dance styles of their favorite groups. With a larger group of fellow enthusiasts, synchronization is the goal that has to be achieved with much more coordinated practice.

K-pop music videos on YouTube act as instructional tutorials and demonstrations, which is also key to the promotion of a K-pop dance culture with innumerable uploads of relevant amateur performances. Apart from the stylized music videos, K-pop groups would also release basic unedited video recordings of dances on YouTube, featuring members in more casual outfits in dance studios as choreographical references. These dance practices are in some ways the first main source in which aspiring dancers are able to see a full frontal version of the dance patterns without the filmic interruptions of cut-aways and zooms of actual MVs. Consolidated online into channels devoted to K-pop "mirror dances," with subscriptions reaching to about 35,000 people, and 11 million views, channels like "DanceVersionHD" and "MirrorHD" have morphed into semi-pedagogical repositories of K-pop dance choreographies. Internet websites like learnkpopdance.com have also been instrumental in providing viewers with more organized searches of the relevant male and female K-pop MVs featuring fuller dance versions in different settings. They provide centralized platforms for uploads of individual K-pop cover dances performed and put up by cover dancers around the world hoping to seek greater recognition. Featuring some 160 selected cover dances in its playlist, the site continually receives more hyperlinks of cover dances and discussions in the comments section. Hence, while the dance tracker may play the role of a star chaser, it is apparent from their video postings that they aspire to dance like the stars. Such aspirations of fan cover dancers in turn have been acknowledged by both the artistes and industry that would occasionally showcase samples of some of these performances. The girl group T-ara, for instance, has publicly acknowledged their cover-dancing fans with a montage of a selection of cover-dance clips from 37 countries in their music video "Sexy Love" less than a month after the release of the track (Carolicity 2012). Serving as archival footages, video technologies have been acknowledged to be critical visual cues for the retention and transmission of non-literary dance choreographies (Caroll 2008), giving both practitioners and audiences more convenient working memories to recall movement configurations (Pullen 2011; Stevens, Ginsborg and Lester 2011). Aside from lengthening temporalscapes, video-streaming technologies have given the dancing body new mobilities into new frontiers, physical and virtual (Grainge 2011; Brookes 2010).

As well as the difference between television drama and music video fans, it is important to distinguish the cover dances of the dance trackers with the official versions of the dances by the artistes as seen in Table 10.2.

Table 10.2 Official and cover dances

Official dance	*Cover dance*
Auditioned	Joined
Artiste	Hobbyist
Korean-ness	Trans-ethnic
Gendered	Trans-gendering
Studio	Place
New release	Cover dance
Choreographed	Learned
Cinematic POV	Camcorder Frontal View
Concert	Flash mob
Globalize	Localize

Selected from thousands of candidates in public auditions, isolated from their networks of friends during years of intensive training in dance, singing and even learning foreign languages before making their debuts, professional K-pop artistes are carefully manicured and tightly monitored by their managers. With their thematized fashions, toned bodies and porcelain skins, the K-pop artiste is supposed to exude the image of a stylized Seoul-based form of Korean urban modernity. Even as some groups are made up of artistes from China and Southeast Asia, so keen is the emphasis on a racialized idea of Korean-ness or "East Asian-ness" that no K-pop group has yet to include a member who does not fit into the predominantly ethnocentric "Oriental" look.

In terms of the gendering process, even with some members made deliberately to look androgynous, the separation of sexes into both singularly male and female groups has been a rigid convention as suggested by Jung (2011b) as part of the sculpturing of gender identities in the presentation of the concept of the metrosexual, urbane and androgynous "soft masculinistic," "*chogukjeok* Pan-East Asian" K-pop boy groups. Typically, the male groups will be immaculately suited and elaborately costumed with shapely toned arms revealed at times from sleeveless tuxedos, or clothes that will eventually be ripped to show their bare chests like the signature movement of the members of Beast. At the other end are female groups distinguishing the trademark of K-pop with the cabaret display of long slender legs from their short pants. While groups like T-ara and 2NE1 have been defined more by their funky disco beats and tribal dancehall rap respectively, it is likely that they would be showing off their legs in their dances, a style that has been defined by Girls' Generation. Nonetheless, the emphasis on projecting the lower body serves to underline a more sanitized sexuality than that of the upper body that would have been construed as too explicit for mainstream consumption.

Produced mainly in studio environments with well-decorated stages, props and costumes, most music videos of K-pop groups do not feature any recognizable locations and localities. With highly secretive training preparations and marketing, the industry would bank on teasers, new releases of singles followed by live performances before the fuller album emerges. By that time, the group will be perfectly trained to perform choreographed set pieces that would be devoid of any mistakes. Indeed, the fans would not expect any mistakes from their favorite groups' performances. Mediated by the cinematic angles from a rapid succession of fast cuts to broad shots and close-ups, the visual, stylized, larger than life images of the stars represent the last stage of the perfected manufactured artiste ready to enter live concerts around the world.

At the other side of the spectrum are fans who desire to be cover dancers of these K-pop groups. These fans take to their feet as a tribute to their stars. They also express the desire to appropriate the spatiality created by their favorite artistes' choreographies. Unlike the K-pop artistes, the cover dancers come from various backgrounds including self-taught hobbyists, amateur performers and professional instructors capitalizing on the newfound popularity of K-pop to advertise their classes. In this respect, the Internet has proved to be a useful site for aspiring cover dancers to learn K-pop dance steps by themselves. They do so through "mirror dancing," which involves the viewer learning from dance tutorials where the images are "horizontally flipped" to create a mirror effect that can be more intuitively followed.

Even as its portrayals have been systematically racialized and sexualized, the socio-cultural profiling of dance choreographies has also been creatively delimited by both dancers and the wider public in the popular realm (Ghandnoosh 2010; Hanna 2010; Ovalle 2009). Similar trends have also been seen in the expansion of K-pop into the wider world. Unlike the evident show of Korean-ness, there is more fluid multicultural display online as well as offline of aspiring talents.

While the cover dances on YouTube and other public displays seem to be visibly fronted by people from East and Southeast Asia, there is also some representation from Caucasians, Indians and African Americans. In addition, a more playful and deliberate subversion of the prescribed gender roles of K-pop groups is also increasingly witnessed where men would do cover dances of female groups and vice versa. In what is called the "mash up" dances, fan performers would even mix parts of the choreographies of the male and female groups together in their attempts to create more hybridized versions. Cover dancers have also taken advantage of the increasing ease of video editing tools to generate their own montages on YouTube whereby multiple perspectives are created in the condensing of different dance moves recorded separately into one image.

One particularly popular cover dance on YouTube comes from the re-performance of the song "Twinkle" by three members from the girl group Girls' Generation (SNSD). In this cover dance, styling her hair and clothes differently in each segment, the performer by the username of "ckcpip" simulates the moves of the three artistes before pulling them together giving the illusion to the viewer of three separate performers. As she mentioned in her YouTube clip, it took this Eurasian female performer in her early twenties from presumably the United Kingdom an entire day to stage the reproduction and another to edit and render to her approximately 10,000 subscribers (May 5, 2012).

In Taiwan, T-ara's otherwise cutesy sounding "bo peep bo peep" has been segued into quasi-religious pop songs with Sino-Tibetan Buddhist themes and was performed in festivals by dancers dressed in the costumes of popular folk deity Nalakuvara, who is also popularly known as Santaizi (Liou 2012). In Thailand and the Philippines, the feminine dance choreography of Wonder Girls' *Nobody* was performed by Thai gay men to demonstrate their effeminacy as "Wonder Gays" (Käng 2012) and by male prisoners in the Philippines as part of their physical exercise and rehabilitation program (Schwartzman

2009). From the intimate space of the bedrooms and living rooms to the dance studios and public arenas, the most striking deviation of the mirror dances from the artistes that they are following lies in the fan-performers' deeper sense of place and body.

Recorded usually with a simple recording of broad frontal camera angle, viewers are able to see an undecorated actual space instead of the staged elaborate settings of mainstream music videos. Lastly, just as in the anticipated concerts for K-pop artistes, the collective public event in the flash mob or dance competition becomes the high point of the cover dancer who participates in localizing the context of the music in their immediate surroundings. These multi-layered spatial and digital appropriations of space can perhaps be placed broadly as part of Jensen's (2011) conceptualization of a new form of "imagined mobilities." Fueling such mobilities is the development of Information and Communicative Technologies (ICTs) that Jauhianen (2007) adds to Lefebvre's (2004: 89) notion of the diversity and multiplicity of everyday life within the urban context creating the sensation of place through the "movement of a street or the tempo of a waltz." Superseding the more corporeal automative mobility of transport and travel, imagined mobilities encompass the aural and the sensual in the molding of "ambient power." As reflected in the case study of Singapore's experience with K-pop, these K-pop cover dances at home and on the streets have been instrumental in molding the aforementioned ambient power.

Choreographing controlled spaces: K-pop in Singapore

As the Singapore government tries to position itself as a "world class," "international" city-state, the local becomes parochialized and peripheralized. While it is easy to spot the association of "Western" with desired "international," the place of the transnational circulation of regional popular culture flows to the republic problematizes such identifications as K-pop that is foreign yet not sufficiently "global" to planners. Being part of the historical migratory network between Southern China and India as well as Southeast Asia, vernacular culture in Singapore has been largely transnational in nature as migrants in the colonial port city drew influences and linkages from their historic motherlands. In the post-war decades, through the intermediaries of Hong Kong and Taiwan, the mainly ethnic Chinese society drew its contemporary popular culture resources and affiliations from Japan for the past decade. The prominence of regional popular entertainment products in the mediascape of the republic reflects not just the dearth of quality local competition, but also the acceptance of a cultural flow that is transnational and locally popular (Ng 2003; Kong 2002). This chapter uses several case studies in the Singapore context to highlight the cosmopolitan characteristics of the dance tracker and the cover dancer operating within the K-pop industry.

174 Liew Kai Khiun

Homes and schools: closet and high school dancers

Inspired by K-pop dance choreographies, there are voluminous uploads of cover dances performed by individuals in Singapore in the comfort of their domestic environments, a trend reflecting on the ease of utilizing digital video cameras and new media platforms. As these amateur dancers exhibit their mastery of new K-pop dance moves on YouTube, they also flash out their living rooms and bedrooms of their apartments openly online. In the case of a regular performer by the username of "Weiying Won," her performances reveal the whitish tropical glare and layout of the furniture in the living room space with the conventional family portraiture taken usually upon the children's graduation, enabling viewers familiar with Singapore to identify this as a typical public housing apartment in the republic. Evidently familiarized with the dance choreography, she would usually perform in front of the camcorder in the gap between the sofa and the television set. In one of her cover dances on T-ara's *Roly Poly* (Won 2012), apart from concealing part of the furniture with what looks to be a piece of old cloth, little to no attempt was made to wallpaper the background to create a stage effect. Completely at ease with her own domestic surroundings without the screen presence of the rest of the family, she commences a seemingly uninterrupted dance in front of the camera. To demonstrate her ability to follow the steps, she inserts two smaller clips of related official MVs of *Roly Poly* that serve as referential points for prospective viewers.

Besides other performances recorded from the confines of bedrooms and living rooms in public housing apartments, innumerable clips from YouTube also feature cover dances carried out in the more public areas of the republic's public housing estates where close to 90% of the populace reside. In these areas which Chua (1997) describes as highly planned, hierarchized and functionalistic modernist environments, these cover dancers and their YouTube recordings have created new spatial openings, imaginations and publics in cyberspace.

A more collective effort can be seen in the informal dance groups of assembled teenagers at high school level such as the cover dance performances of WondershiDae and STARREseconds on YouTube. Reflecting the very transient nature of these informal dance bodies, WondershiDae disbanded in 2011 while STARREseconds still appears to be participating in competitions. Even if the various groups have been faithful to their favorite K-pop groups' official choreographies, the compositions of these bodies departs from the strictly East Asian or "Chinese" looking girl and boy K-pop groups with their mixed ethnic and gender backgrounds (two men and one ethnic Indian woman).

As seen in Figure 10.1, the maintenance of femininity in Girls' Generation's song notwithstanding, the mixed group has basically de-racialized and de-gendered the original presentation of the text. Filmed within the premises of a

K-pop dance trackers and cover dancers 175

Figure 10.1 Cover dance of SNSD *Hoot* by WondershiDae and STARREseconds. http://www.youtube.com/user/WonderShiDaeSG?feature=watch (accessed December 24, 2012)

school, this clip, commanding an unusually high 27,000 views for an informal group from Singapore, serves as their performance to the cyber-community which, to them, is seemingly as important as the actual competitions they have participated in at malls.

Coordinated and corporatized flash mobs

Figures 10.2 and 10.3 are examples of two fundamentally different K-pop-inspired flash mobs in Singapore with the former being a Samsung-commissioned Girls' Generation (SNSD) cover dance and the latter an assortment of moves from different SMTown K-pop groups by enthusiasts. Engaging professional dancers dressed in costumes similar to those used by SNSD as well as paid bystanders with the corporation's placards, the flash mob organized by Samsung at Orchard Road, Singapore's shopping district, served more as an advertising showcase. In contrast, the flash mob in Figure 10.3 was coordinated more informally at the iconic tourist area of the Marina Bay by fans performing to petition SMTown to stage its K-pop concert in Singapore. Unlike the well-toned bodies of Samsung's commissioned dancers, the cover dancers at Marina Bay were more spontaneously attired. As the slightly plump turbaned Sikh man dancing in the flash mob reveals, the "petitioners" have pulled together a more cosmopolitan and diverse group of K-pop performers. After attracting nearly 65,000 views, their efforts appeared to have paid off when the first SMTown mega-concert was staged at Marina Bay in November 2012.

Figure 10.2 Girls' Generation (SNSD) cover dance flash mob organized by Samsung. http://www.youtube.com/watch?v=XJltX8tlyOY (accessed December 25, 2012)

Figure 10.3 Flash mob for petition to bring SMTown concert to Singapore on June 25, 2011. http://www.youtube.com/watch?v=xOwvIdF7tsg (accessed December 25, 2012)

In as much as these K-pop-inspired flash mobs have promoted business interests, the collective emphasis of synchronized K-pop dances has also helped younger generations of Singaporeans to negotiate their presence in the public space more confidently without permission. While imitating slick and sexy dance moves of pretty boy and girl groups may add to the glamour of the

K-pop dance trackers and cover dancers   177

place, the arrival of Psy's *Gangnam Style* to Singapore presents more irreverent and naughty possibilities of subverting the public space. The next section demonstrates how this unintended export of K-pop has equipped Singaporeans with the performative skills of *Gangnam Style*'s signature "horse riding" move.

Singaporean-izing Gangnam Style

Appearing within a month of its posting, the proliferation of local parodies of the *Gangnam Style* in Singapore on YouTube reflected the global virality of Psy's MV. Including flash mobs performing on the streets, as well as kindergarten and college performances in addition to the live performance of Psy in the republic on December 1, inputting the keywords "Gangnam Style Singapore" on YouTube yielded 2,660 related results as of the end of 2012. While formulaic cover dances of mainstream K-pop groups seemed to be performed by teenagers and young adults, the apparent boisterousness of *Gangnam Style* choreography has resulted in widespread popularity on YouTube and inspired fan cover performers to conjure more creative parodies. Among them are two outstanding versions by Singaporean Vloggers The Asianparent and Dee Kosh (Figure 10.4).

Unlike most parodies where characters lip-synched the original lyrics, these two versions have changed the lyrics completely into Singapore's lingua franca, the English language, as well as its more endearing creolized vernacular version, "Singlish." Similar to other parodies, both deploy the sense of playful mockery with scenes of well-suited lead dancers in nondescript children's

Figure 10.4 Singaporean Style by Dee Kosh.
http://www.youtube.com/watch?v=VFqLy27OSd4 (accessed December 25, 2012)

playgrounds, haughty bare-bodied unshapely men in sunglasses in swimming pools, and characters moving in awkward "horse-riding" dances next to public landmarks. However, both the "Singaporean Style" and "Kancheong Style" are more intent on verbalizing their performative acts to broader social critique. The aesthetics of the choreography here become peripheral compared to the lyrics in these two productions, for the lyrics in these parodies hit out at the pressures of urban living in Singapore. Compared to the reminders of parents to give their children a decent childhood over stressing them with educational demands by The AsianParent who featured a politically correct ethnic mix of children doing the *Gangnam Style*, Dee Kosh's version is thematically more randomized. Articulating dissatisfactions with the ruling party and complaining about stringent laws and social profiling in the republic, at 2.8 million views this cruder version has garnered a million more eyeballs than "Kancheong Style," which was officially endorsed and mentioned by the Prime Minister on Children's Day (Insing 2012). In contrast, Dee Kosh's parody, posted on August 11, 2012, two days after the country's annual National Day parade which is often characterized by highly uplifting patriotic songs and mass displays, playfully mocks the authorities with sexual innuendoes in Singapore Style.

Differing from the attempts at perfecting the original in conventional K-pop cover-dance performances, the idea of reproducibility in *Gangnam Style* parodies in Singapore, and probably elsewhere, lies not in the desire for mirroring the official ideal. With female teenagers between the ages of 13 and 17 (mainly K-pop fans) and male adults from 35 to 54 years of age with little knowledge of the genre comprising the majority of viewers of this clip (Dee Kosh 2012), *Gangnam Style* in Singapore has become a more universal phenomenon that may or may not necessarily be identified with the rest of K-pop in Singapore.

Conclusion: K-pop apparatus and the building of networked public passions

In the local segment of TVN's debut regional K-pop star-hunt contest in 2011, two women, Jasmine Tan, aged 16, and Maressa Zahirah, aged 23, were chosen from hundreds of contestants to represent the republic for the final knockout round in Seoul. Tan was spotted for her relatively outstanding cover dances, Zahirah for her vocals of slower K-pop songs. Although both lost out to their Filipino counterparts in the final round, they had a taste of the intensive training regime undertaken by aspiring K-pop artistes (Sim 2011). These song and dance competitions are unusual not so much because of the crowds involved, but because of the participation of those undeterred by the seeming bias of the K-pop machinery towards youthful teenage recruits with porcelain fair skin and facial features. At 23, not only is Zahirah over-age, but from an ethnic Malay background with a seemingly darker skin complexion.

She seemed to be disadvantaged in these contests, as it was rumored that "non-ethnic Chinese looking participants would not qualify." Nonetheless, wanting to "prove people wrong," Zahirah persevered and made it to the top 20 together with three other ethnic Malay females (Tan 2011). Not content with being performers, the contestants sought to be transportable images asserting their humanity from Seoul. Thus, both Zahirah and Tan, and many other contestants in the region were keen to seize the opportunities to take control of the screen. Even as the K-pop corporate machinery sought to extract maximum consumer involvement, it ironically equipped its consumers with new cultural literacies. The contestants of these K-pop contests were able to explore these new cultural literacies through the pre-verbal language of dance and the new media tools of the digital age to project their bodies more autonomously into the physical and cyberspaces.

Highly networked to the digital social media with personally managed multi-referenced Facebook, YouTube and Twitter accounts, Zahirah and Tan are the generation of cover performers that Hallyu 2.0 has engendered. De-centering and transcending the geo-social and cultural boundaries of the highly manufactured and rigidly regimented industry, these K-pop fan performers have used the text as a kinesthetic tool to re-articulate and reaffirm their own presence in what Martin (2006) calls the "passionate public."

With Psy's *Gangnam Style*, K-pop has been given a brief power surge into the otherwise Western-dominated circuits of global popular entertainment. The countless parodies generated by this music video bring the popularity of dance choreographies that the K-pop industry has generated to the forefront of public attention. In some ways, the multitude of cover dances and flash mobs by fans around the world underpins the significant cosmopolitanization of the otherwise manicured and mannequin-ish K-pop boy and girl groups. The seeming simplicity of these synchronized dance choreographies has provided choreographic possibilities and cultural elasticity for its appropriation and re-performances by cover dancers. More than imitative acts, these performers use K-pop dances to reinterpret, reinscribe and recalibrate the socio-cultural contours to which they have been subjected within their individual local contexts. In bringing out and asserting individual differences, the cover dancers have collectively insisted that K-pop acknowledges the diverse cosmopolitan landscapes and dance-scapes of the places it reaches.

References

Antebi, S. (2009) "The Talk Show Uploaded: YouTube and the Technicity of the Body," *Social Identities: Journal for the Study of Race, Nation and Culture*, 15(3): 297–311.

Benjamin, W. (2008) *The Work of Art in the Age of its Technological Reproducibility and Other Writings on Media*, London: The Belknap Press of Harvard University Press.

Brookes, P. (2010) "Creating New Spaces: Dancing in a Telematic World," *International Journal of Performance Arts and Digital Media*, 6(1): 49–60.

Carolicity (2012) "T-ara Releases Cover Dance MV for Sexy Love," *AllKpop*, September 14. http://www.allkpop.com/2012/09/t-ara-releases-cover-dance-mv-for-sexy-love (accessed December 28, 2012).

Caroll, S. (2008) "The Practical Politics of Step Stealing and Textual Poaching: YouTube, Audio-visual Media and Contemporary Swing Dancers Online," *Convergence: The International Journal of Research into New Media Technologies*, 14(2): 183–204.

Cha, H. and Kim, S. (2011) "A Case Study on Korean Wave: Focused on K-pop Concert by Korean Idol Group in Paris, June 2011," *Communications in Computer and Information Science*, 263: 153–62.

Chua, B. (1997) "Modernism and the Vernacular: Transformation of Public Spaces and Social Life in Singapore," in J. Ong, C. Tong and E. Tan (eds) *Understanding Singapore Society*, Singapore: Times Academic Press.

ckcpip. (2012) "[KCC Cover] Twinkle", May 5, online available HTTP: <http://www.youtube.com/watch?v=qQJl5d9lNwM> (accessed December 31, 2012).

Dee Kosh (2012) "Singaporean Style (Gangnam Style Parody)," August 11, http://www.youtube.com/watch?v=VFqLy27OSd4 (accessed December 26, 2012).

Ghandnoosh, N. (2010) "Cross Cultural Practices: Interpreting Non-African American Participation in Hip Hop Dance," *Ethnic and Racial Studies*, 33(9): 1580–99.

Grainge, P. (2011) "A Song and Dance: Branded Entertainment and Mobile Promotion," *International Journal of Cultural Studies*, 15(2): 165–80.

Hanna, J. (2010) "Dance and Sexuality: Many Moves," *Journal of Sex Research*, 47(2–3): 212–41.

Holt, J. (2001) "Deconstructing the Mirror Image: The Crisis of Logic in the Looking Glass World," *Lore*, 1(3), http://rhetoric.sdsu.edu/lore/1_3/holt_mirror_final.htm (accessed April 22, 2013).

Insing.com. (2012) "PM Post Gangnam Style Parody Video on Facebook," October 4, http://news.insing.com/tabloid/pm-lees-gangnam-style-post/id-d3603f00 (accessed December 26, 2012).

Jauhianen, J. (2007) "Seasonality, Rhythms and Post Post-modern Everyday Urban Landscapes," in H. Palang, H. Sovvali and A. Printsmann (eds) *Seasonal Landscapes,* London: Springer.

Jensen, A. (2011) "Mobility, Space and Power: On the Multiplicity of Seeing Mobility," *Mobilities*, 6(2): 255–71.

Jung, S. (2011a) "K-pop, Indonesian Fandom, and Social Media," in R. Reid and S. Gatson (eds) "Race and Ethnicity in Fandom" Special Issue, *Transformative Works and Cultures*, 8, http://journal.transformativeworks.org/index.php/twc/article/view/289/219 (accessed December 29, 2012).

——(2011b) *Korean Masculinity and Transnational Consumption: Yonsama, Rain, Old Boy, K-pop Idols*, Hong Kong: Hong Kong University Press.

Jung, S. and Hirata, Y. (2012) "Conflicting Desires: K-pop Idol Flows in Japan in the Era of Web 2.0," *Electronic Journal of Contemporary Japanese Studies*, 12(2), http://japanesestudies.org.uk/ejcjs/vol12/iss2/jung.html (accessed December 28, 2012).

Käng, D. (2012) "Kathoey 'In Trend': Emergent Genderscapes, National Anxieties and the Re-Signification of Male-Bodied Effeminacy in Thailand," *Asian Studies Review*, 36(4): 475–94.

Kong, L. (2002) "Popular Music in a Transnational World: Constructing Identities in Singapore," 38(1): 19–38.

Lawlietta (2009) "The Secret Behind Kpop Choreography," *Allkpop*, September 9, http://www.allkpop.com/2009/09/the_secret_behind_kpop_choreography (accessed December 26, 2012).

Lefebvre, H. (2004) *Rhythm Analysis: Space, Time and Everyday Life*, London: Continuum.

Liew, K. and Fu, K. (2006) "Hallyu in Singapore: Korean Cosmopolitanism or the Consumption of Chineseness?," *Korea Journal*, 45(4): 206–32.

Liou, Y. (2012) "The Fusion of Secular and Sacred Elements in the Music of the Record Industry in Taiwan," 3rd Inter-Asia Popular Culture Studies Conference, Taipei, July 3–5.

Martin, R. (2006) "Productive Pleasures: Episode of a Critical Public in Cuban Dance," *Space and Culture*, 9(3): 254–60.

Merriman, P. (2010) "Architecture/Dance: Choreographing the Inhabiting Spaces with Anna and Lawrence Halpin," *Cultural Geographies*, 17(4): 427–49.

Ng, B. (2003) "Japanese Popular Music in Singapore and the Hybridization of Asian Music," *Asian Music*, 34(1): 1–18.

Ovalle, P. (2009) "Urban Sensualidad: Jennifer Lopez, Flashdance and MTV Hip Hop Regeneration," *Women and Performance: A Journal of Feminist Theory*, 18(3): 253–68.

Pullen, K. (2011) "If Ya Like It, That You Shoulda Made a Video Beyonce Knowles: YouTube and the Public Sphere of Images," *Performance Research*, 16(2): 145–53.

Schwartzman, N. (2009) "Filipino Prisoners Dance to Wonder Girls' Song," *Asian Correspondence.com*, April 8, http://asiancorrespondent.com/23379/filipino-prisoners-dance-to-wondergirls-song/ (accessed January 31, 2012).

Sim, F. (2011) "Two Singaporeans Earn a Shot at Kpop Stardom," *Yahoo Singapore Entertainment*, October 24, http://sg.entertainment.yahoo.com/blogs/singapore-showbiz/two-poreans-fly-seoul-k-pop-dreams-104828744.html (accessed December 31, 2012).

Stevens, C., Ginsborg, J. and Lester, G. (2011) "Backwards and Forwards in Space and Time: Recalling Dance Movement from Long Term Memory," *Memory Studies*, 4(2): 234–50.

Tan, K. (2011) "I Want to Prove People Wrong," *The New Paper*, October 26, http://www.asiaone.com/News/AsiaOne%2BNews/Singapore/Story/A1Story20111025–306999.html (accessed December 31, 2012).

——(2012) "The Ideology of Pragmatism: Neoliberal Globalization and Political Authoritarianism in Singapore," *Journal of Contemporary Asia*, 42(1): 67–92.

The Asianparent (2012) "Singapore Gangnam Style with children – Super Kancheong Style (Kan Cheong)". Online. September 28. Available HTTP: <https://www.youtube.com/watch?v=y5xEZCLWrs> (accessed May 30, 2013)

Won, Weiying (2012) "티아라 T-ara Roly Poly Dance Cover by Weiying" July 7. https://www.youtube.com/watch?v=dwlIP3sFSeE (accessed May 30, 2013).

Part III

Perspectives inside/outside

Chapter 11

Cultural policy and the Korean Wave

From national culture to transnational consumerism

Hye-Kyung Lee

It has been over a decade since the Asian media first reported on the Korean Wave, which referred to a transnational demand for, and passionate consumption of, South Korean popular culture. By now the Korean Wave has become part of the common lexicon not just for media commentators and cultural businesses but also ordinary Korean people and overseas fans of Korean popular culture. Its soaring recognition is manifested by the growth in the volume of academic writings on this topic. The search term "Korean Wave" finds 1,940 articles on Google Scholar as of February 23, 2013 while "Hallyu," the Korean equivalent to the Korean Wave, leads to 400-plus writings on DBpia, a Korean web search site specializing in scholarly writings, as of March 10, 2013. Researchers who contemplate the Korean Wave from external angles tend to make sense of it in relation to globalizing forces and Korean popular culture's consumption beyond the country, focusing on the deregulation and transnationalization of the media industries especially in Asia; Korean popular culture's hybridity and its appeal in overseas markets, its contextualized reception by overseas fans, the formation of common cultural sentiment among Asian media consumers, and their cross-border sharing of Korean pop culture via online and digital means of reproduction and distribution (Chua and Iwabuchi 2008; Iwabuchi 2010; Jung 2011; H. Kim 2002; Ryoo 2009; Shim 2006). Those who look at the inside of the phenomenon pay more attention to the increased production and export capacity of Korean cultural industries, government cultural policy and the understanding of the Korean Wave within Korean society (Cho 2005; Choi 2013; Kang 2007; Shim 2006 and 2008; Sohn 2011). While policy- and industry-oriented research seeks practical measures to boost the phenomenon, critical media and cultural studies writers have raised concerns with its neoliberal and consumerist features as well as its evocation of nationalistic responses both in and outside the country (Choi 2013; Iwabuchi 2010; Kang 2007; D. Lee 2010; K. Lee 2008). They also point out the limitations of the Korean Wave in facilitating meaningful transcultural practice and dialogue where diversity and reflexivity are promoted.

This chapter is intended to further the critical interrogation into the Korean Wave by investigating the state cultural policy's responses to it from a historical perspective. The cultural policy's full embrace of the phenomenon to the degree where the Korean Wave itself becomes a policy paradigm will be reflected in the historical transformation of the relationship between the state and popular culture. The current policy for the Korean Wave shows both continuation and discontinuation from cultural policy before its rise, where popular culture was an object of state control (military regimes from the 1960s till 1993) and became redefined as a domestic industry needing state support and protection (from 1993 till 2003). The move from the first to the second phases corresponded to the transformation of Korean society, which is summed up as political democratization and economic neoliberalization. Meanwhile the coming of the current phase (from 2004 on) implies that the cultural industries policy is taking an unprecedentedly transnational and consumerist turn. Cultural policy's politically and ideologically charged understanding of popular culture, which weakened throughout the 1990s, has given way to the view that sees popular culture – or the wider "K-culture" – as an effective instrument for cultural export and nation branding. Such neoliberal and consumerist orientation in cultural policy, however, did not outdate its long-standing developmental approach: governmental planning and investment have intensified in order to address the policy goal of helping Korean cultural industries fit in the increasingly globalized economy and expanding their overseas markets. The Korean Wave assists the country's popular culture to consolidate its legitimacy as an export industry and creates a new public–private interface in which an array of projects are planned and carried out across the country and beyond, feeding multi-faceted governmental and commercial aspirations. The policy goes beyond domestic cultural policy in the sense that it treats overseas fandom of Korean popular culture as a new parameter that defines the success of the country's cultural industries. The policy is keen to enlarge the "display" elements of the Korean Wave, these being either economic or soft power impacts. Meanwhile, the questions necessary to bring the Korean Wave phenomenon to cultural policy "proper" in Williams' sense (1984) – for instance, questions of quality, diversity and public interest – are losing their footing in the current policy discussion.

Popular culture as an object of state control

Since the 1960s until today, Korea has been characterized as a developmental state, where the state assumes the leading role in the economic advancement of the country by exercising various capacities and strongly regulating market forces (Weiss 1998). Although the developmental nature of the Korean economy has diminished with the rise of neoliberal public policy since the financial crisis in 1997, the state-driven approach still dominates many areas including cultural policy, where the state is the biggest resource provider, planner and coordinator. Such attributes of cultural policy are clearly observed in its dealings with the Korean Wave. The Korean developmental state began with the establishment of the military and authoritarian Park Chung Hee government (1961–79), which pursued the "modernization of the homeland" through "economic development" and "anti-communism" as the two fundamental principles of the country. Whilst being successful in fostering export industries and leading rapid economic progress, it was a severely oppressive regime that did not allow political opposition or civil and labor activism. Its cultural policy took extremely statist and interventionist approaches. In particular, it had a very tight ideological and moral hold on popular culture such as TV, film and pop music. During this period, Korean cultural policy's primary goal was to revitalize "national culture," which was thought to be under serious threat from the rapid process of the Westernization and industrialization of the country. Although national culture was often understood as Korean traditional culture and arts, the ambiguity around its nature made it a policy rhetoric that was politically and ideologically interpreted and applied. Furthermore, it was the government itself which tried to reinvent national culture through various state cultural projects including supporting Korean "spiritual culture" (which was broadly renamed as Korean studies in later years) and traditional arts, "purifying" and restoring cultural properties, organizing national arts and folklore events, sanctifying the country's heroes, emphasizing the country's history of resistance against foreign invasions, reinventing Taekwondo and so on (W. Kim 2012; Oh 1998). Mass-produced popular culture was deemed as external and potentially damaging to national culture. It was generally understood in terms of "pathology," "decadence" and "non-discriminatory acceptance of Western culture" and was projected as an object of state regulation (Ministry of Culture and Public Information 1979). This explains why the *Public Performance Law* (1961), *Motion Picture Law* (1966) and *Recorded Music Law* (1967) were more interested in state control, not support for the industries: tight regulations were put on popular cultural content as well as the industries' production and distribution businesses, particularly import and export. Empowered by the above laws, out of 22,758 domestic songs submitted between May 1975 and September 1979, the Arts and Culture Ethics Committee (1966–75) and its successor the Public Performance Ethics Committee (1976–96) rejected the lyrics of 210 songs and requested the lyrics to 4,654 songs to be revised for various reasons such as "decadence," "ill-health," "nihilism" and "sad tone" (Ministry of Culture and Public Information 1979: 268–9). Similarly many songs by John Lennon and Bob Dylan were banned simply for their social messages such as anti-war. Youth culture, associated with popular cultural consumption and showing some proximity with the youth revolt in the Western world, was severely suppressed and criminalized throughout the 1970s (W. Kim 2012).

Never allowing popular culture to express social and political awareness and reflexivity, the authoritarian government was keen on its instrumental uses in justifying the regime and disseminating its ideologies. By providing guidelines, financial incentives and prizes, state cultural policy systematically encouraged "healthy" activities such as collective singing at village/workplace choirs, exhibitions of photographs positively depicting industrialized Korea and the production of "excellent" films, which referred to films that successfully represented and promoted state ideologies and policies, such as the spirit of the October Yushin (which made Park's presidency virtually permanent and gave him the right to appoint one-third of parliamentary members), patriotism, virtues of diligence and frugality, the modernization and industrialization of Korean society and national cohesion (W. Kim 2012). In such a policy environment, TV, films and animations portraying the bright sides of Korean society and sending anti-communist messages were produced and some of them – for example, anti-communist animations for cinema – also enjoyed commercial success (J. Kim and J. Kim 2007). In the 1980s the government's moral control became somewhat loosened resulting in the rise of 3S (Screen, Sports and Sex) in popular culture. However, the suppression of politically sensitive content intensified as the government was alarmed by the surging democratic and labor movements. The lack of civil actors meant that the state predominated in the discourse of popular culture. Although political and labor activism at the end of the 1980s was eager to propose alternative cultural politics (Shin 1989), its perspective on popular culture was rather pessimistic. Both the government and progressive cultural activists were more concerned with "national culture," while being wary of either the rebellious or the conformist effects of popular culture on the mind of the public (W. Kim 2012; Oh 1998). News media's overt co-option by the government deepened the latter's suspicion over the functions of the cultural industries. Although activists saw film and popular music's potential as a means of public empowerment, they by and large shared the Frankfurt School's idea of the culture industry. They were more interested in developing "national" and "people's" culture that would combine realism and folk cultural traditions of the country (Chu 2005). Failing to obtain positive recognition and backing from either progressive movements or the wider society and still waiting to see the emergence of a consumer society, Korean cultural industries remained subject to state guidance and control until the early 1990s despite the new cultural policy rhetoric of cultural welfare and public accessibility.

Popular culture as cultural and content industry

The dynamic process of political democratization and economic neoliberalization of the country throughout the 1990s brought substantial changes to cultural policy, laying an important internal condition of the forthcoming Korean Wave. First, the country's cultural sector saw the deregulation of content and the consequently increased freedom of expression with the lifting of the restriction on the publisher registration system (1987), the ban on public access to publications from communist countries and North Korea (1988) and the abolition of censorship on theatre (1988), music (1996) and film (1997). This was a result of continuous negotiation between state authority and the democratic movement. Cultural practitioners in various fields became better organized and strengthened their voices against state control, and the new generation of consumers who were imbued with a freer political and social atmosphere began to emerge as powerful patrons of popular culture. Perhaps the best example is the abolition of music censorship in 1996, which was triggered by Taechun Chung who campaigned against the censorship that banned many of his songs for political reasons and took the case to the constitutional court. Chung's case was buttressed by the loud protest of fans of the popular boy band Seo Taiji and Boys, who were forced to publish an album containing the censored lyrics of a socially themed song. The democratic mood and the rise of the consumer society encouraged cultural producers to explore new motifs and styles, further pushing political, social and moral boundaries. This might explain the renaissance of Korean film and music industries in the 1990s, where films that told politically sensitive stories gained popular responses and new styles of pop music were actively explored (Kang 2007; Shim 2006). The politically and ideologically conceived notion of "national culture" was replaced by the idea of "Korean culture" in which popular culture plays an important role by contemplating the country's contemporary issues and expressing the Korean people's (especially the younger generation's) cultural identities and aesthetic sentiments.

Second, state cultural policy began to perceive popular culture as an industry. Kim Young Sam's civilian government (1993–98), which embraced the theory of post-industrial society, was deeply impressed by the potential market values of popular culture, as seen from the global success of U.S. cultural industries (e.g. *Jurassic Park*'s global income was worth Hyundai's earnings from exporting 1.5 million cars) (Shim 2006). Inventing and spreading a powerful economic justification for cultural "industries," it set up the Cultural Industries Directorate in 1994 within the cultural ministry whose policy priorities included, among others, "the industrialization of culture" as well as "the internationalization of Korean culture." This radical departure from the ministry's traditional attitude should be understood in the context of the broader neoliberal shift in Korean public policy under the name of "new economy" and "internationalization," the core of which was deregulation of the financial sector and integrating the country into the global market economy. The market-driven policy was continued by the President Kim Dae Jung (1998–2003), who in his presidential inauguration speech advocated the cultural industries occupying a section of the country's pillar industries. Trying to "rebuild" Korea in the aftermath of the financial crisis by embracing neoliberal policies, his government gave a huge boost to IT and cultural industries. In 1999, the *Basic Law for Cultural Industries' Promotion* was enacted to provide a policy framework by defining cultural industries and stipulating the promotion of these industries as a "state responsibility," setting a legal grounding for state planning and investment in this area. The same year saw the enactment of the *Recorded Music, Video and Games Law* that defined the promotion of these industries as the state's responsibility and called for governmental actions. The following governments of Roh Moo Hyun (2003–8) and Lee Myung Bak (2008–13) shared the post-industrialist view of Korean society and advocated culture as the country's new engine. This period witnessed the enactment of new laws that aimed to facilitate the growth of individual cultural industries (the *Film and Video Promotion Law* 2006, *Games Industry Promotion Law* 2006 and *Music Industry Promotion Law* 2006) and the *Contents Industries Promotion Law* (2010), which gave further grounding for the government policies for cultural industries.

It is often believed that the 1990s saw a renaissance of Korean popular culture as there was a notable growth of cultural industries in both quantitative and qualitative terms, setting an internal context for the Korean Wave. It was in line with the democratization of the country and the emergence of consumer society equipped with increased disposable income and diversified cultural tastes. The renaissance was also attributed to the active roles played by the government as a cultural planner and resource mobilizer. Yet, the expansion of cultural industries entailed innate tension within cultural policy as it was expected to address both the cultural and economic features of popular culture. The latter gained more currency over time, especially in the 2000s when the industries showed further growth in terms of size, a tendency towards concentration and rapid restructuring due to changes in technological environments (D. Lee 2010). The liberal Roh Moo Hyun government (2003–8), which was backed by the middle and lower classes and civil groups, was ambitious to bring broad social and civil perspectives to cultural policy, proposing three objectives of cultural policy: "creativity," "diversity" and "vitality" and paying attention to cultural education, the culture of equality, cultural diversity and the development of local culture (Ministry of Culture and Tourism 2004). However, this did not greatly affect cultural industries policy as the government was also caught up with neoliberal agendas such as opening up the country's film market to the U.S. and nurturing "content" industries by monetizing culture (Ministry of Culture and Tourism 2005). It was difficult for social and cultural concerns to find a firm place in the policy. They might be an issue for the arts or civil society but not really for popular culture. In this vein, a survey conducted by Korea Culture and Tourism Policy Institute is revealing. Cultural practitioners, media commentators and members of civil groups, despite opinion gaps over other issues, were in broad consensus that the government's cultural industries policy was successful in economic terms, whereas its social and civil benefits were rather doubtful (Y. Lee 2005). While maintaining the developmental approach, the government has continued to pursue the neoliberal goal of commercializing and industrializing culture.

Korean Wave as a cultural policy paradigm

From implicit to explicit policy

The Korean Wave came as an unexpected surprise for the Korean government. Although the "internationalization of Korean culture" was a policy priority under the Kim Young Sam (1993–98) government, it was close to a rewording of "promoting Korean culture abroad," a policy objective the government had pursued for a long time. Throughout the 1990s, policy-makers' main concern was cultural industries' domestic growth and sustainability. When the popularity of Korean TV drama was first detected in Vietnam in the mid-1990s, the government was puzzled but saw it as a one-off fashion: without its assistance, terrestrial broadcasters and entertainment companies had to make efforts to explore overseas markets by themselves (Sohn 2011: 50). Despite increasing news reports on the Korean Wave, the cultural policy response was rather slow and sporadic until 2004 when *Winter Sonata* became a mega hit in Japan. This exceptional phenomenon of overseas demand for Korean popular culture made itself a legitimate object of state policy, and policy-makers began deliberating on its potential cultural, economic and diplomatic benefits. Indicating its overall socio-cultural concerns for cultural policy, the Roh Moo Hyun government (2003–8) expected the Wave to serve as a potential catalyst for transnational cultural dialogue, the development of Northeast Asian culture and increased cultural collaboration within the Asian region (Ministry of Culture and Tourism 2004). Yet, the policy was soon preoccupied with strongly quantity-oriented, pragmatic agendas such as expanding cultural export and enhancing the country's brand power (Ministry of Culture and Tourism 2005). The conservative Lee Myung Bak government (2008–13) actively showed its desire to maximize market and brand values of the Korean Wave. By proposing "Korea, a high-class cultural nation" as its cultural policy goal, it called for the branding of Korean traditional culture and support for the export of Korean cultural contents (Ministry of Culture, Sports and Tourism 2008). Presidential initiatives such as the National Brand Committee and pan-cultural-ministry initiatives such as the Korean Wave Promotion Taskforce indicate how high the Korean Wave sits on the government agenda. Success stories of K-pop and TV drama beyond Asia motivated the government to upgrade the Korean Wave from an Asian to a global project, ultimately aiming at every corner of the world. Since the mid-2000s, the Korean Wave policy has developed into a complex web of activities including planning, funding, investment, market research, marketing, branding, training, consulting, showcasing, events and networking engaging a vast array of governmental actors in and outside the country. The Korean Wave has become a key stream of the state cultural policy and some existing policy initiatives have become part of the Korean Wave project.

Korean culture re-branded as "K-culture"

The emergence of the Korean Wave as a government project happened with the extreme extension of its boundary. It was under the Roh Moo Hyun government that the cultural ministry began to stretch it to traditional culture by branding the latter as "Han (Korean) style," but without making a noticeable impact. The following government was bold enough to put almost all areas with which the cultural ministry is concerned – except religion – under the umbrella of the Korean Wave and gave them the fashionable prefix "K": K-fine art, K-traditional arts, K-literature and so on. Believing that many areas of "K-culture" can ride the Korean Wave, the ministry has recently announced a comprehensive "Korean Wave Plan," under which selected traditional and contemporary cultural sectors will receive various financial, managerial and marketing support from the central government and its agencies. The idea of K-culture evokes an essentialist and nationalist view that sees Korean culture as both an imprint and carrier of Korean people's distinct spirit, identity and character. Trying to discover the specifically Korean nature of the country's pop music, the ministry's *Korean Wave White Paper* argues for a close aesthetic connection between K-pop idol groups' dynamic dance style and that of the country's dance in ancient times (Ministry of Culture, Sports and Tourism 2013a: 27). Another extensive report on the Korean Wave detects distinct Korean spirits *"heung"* (passion) and *"han"* (bitter feeling and regret) as a unique characteristic of K-pop and TV drama (Korean Culture and Information Service 2012: 30–45, 113). While ignoring the effect of cultural globalization, localization and hybridization forces on contemporary Korean culture (K. Lee 2008; Ryoo 2009; Shim 2006), the above view contains highly pragmatic and pliable sides. That is, whatever its origins, the forms and genres of culture are Korean once they are value-added by Korean cultural industries or artists. The logic is similar to the way we decide the country of origin of manufactured goods. Here, fine art and classical music rooted in Western cultural traditions become "K-fine art" and "K-classics" without reservation. Stretching the Korean Wave and bringing the instrumental and externally bounded reasoning to many different areas of culture, the aforementioned "Korean Wave Plan" envisions a future where "K-culture" becomes a universal or world culture that is distributed and consumed widely across national borders. Within this understanding of Korean culture, cultural diversity – diversity within popular culture or in the ethnically non-homogeneous Korean society – hardly seems an issue. Neither the issue of quality nor of excellence is a key part of the discussion.

Korean Wave projects as a kaleidoscope of desires

In the country's mainstream media, the Korean Wave has already replaced "made in Korea." Nowadays numerous things and activities claim a place within the Korean Wave phenomenon: from cosmetic surgery and medical care to green industries, nuclear power stations, national security and elections. Broadly referring to exporting to overseas and attracting overseas users, the Korean Wave works as a powerful signifier that encapsulates the desires and interests of commercial and governmental actors who seek overseas markets, domestic legitimacy and public attention. Perhaps one of the focal points where these desires and interests are manifest is Korean Wave projects at local levels: e.g. the ongoing Hallyu World (Goyang City), the planned Korean Wave Focal Point (North Cholla Province), the canceled Korean Wave Audiovisual Theme Park (Jeju Island), the planned Han Style World (Gosung, Gangwon Province), the planned Korean Wave Drama Zone (Chucheon), the planned Korean Wave Star Street (Gangnam, Seoul) and the canceled Korean Wave Star Street (Chungmuro, Seoul). However, these projects often lack a robust plan and rely on a speculative assumption that the motif of the Korean Wave would be powerful enough to attract private investors and tourists. The Korean Wave Audiovisual Theme Park had simply to be canceled when the contracted company failed to deliver the project despite various favors given by the local government (*Chosun Ilbo* 2012). Hallyu World (formerly Hallyuwood), a mega project consisting of building a Korean Wave themed park, a K-pop arena, a large aquarium, broadcasting facilities, hotels, shopping malls and residential and commercial facilities in Goyang City by 2013, has shown very slow progress due to the economic recession and project companies' financial problems (*Joongang Ilbo Joinsland* 2013). Meanwhile the cultural ministry suddenly canceled its plan to create a Korean Wave Star Street in Chungmuro, Seoul, due to a lack in its budget, frustrating companies and individuals who had already invested in this area in order to gain a Korean Wave premium (*Hankook Ilbo* 2011). Given that these projects involve speculative investment dependent upon trends in the real estate market and deal with multiple commercial actors who pursue their own routes to maximize profit, it seems difficult to know how many economic benefits can be generated for local residents (Choi 2013). This is not to mention the ambiguity around how K-culture, as a supposedly universal culture, can be integrated with local cultural tradition and identity.

The business sector is deeply involved in the Korean Wave policy at the central level, too. Sharing the belief that the Korean Wave opens up new opportunities to raise the profile of Korean companies and products and reinforcing the instrumental and commercial aspirations of this policy, representatives of big corporations (e.g. Hyundai Car, SK, Lotte Hotel, Shinsegae Department Store, Korean Air, Seoul Broadcasting System, etc.) have sat on the Visit Korea Year Committee and the National Brand Committee (Choi 2013). In 2012, the Korean Wave Support Committee was set up to further advance the agenda of linking the Korean Wave to business, involving a number of the most powerful business associations in the country (notably the Federation of Korean Industries), entertainment companies as well as the cultural ministry (Ministry of Culture, Sports and Tourism 2012). Close collaboration between the government and industries has been a typical feature of the Korean developmental state; however, the evolving partnership between governmental actors and cultural businesses is fairly unprecedented. Their motivations do not always coincide but the Korean Wave gives them symbolic and financial incentives to work together. For example, the Visit Korea Year Committee, the Korean Cultural Center Paris and the Paris branch of Korea Tourism Organization sponsored SM Entertainment's (one of the largest talent agencies) *SM Town Live World Tour in Paris* (2011), which attracted a large audience and generated a huge media sensation in Korea. The event was followed by a flash mob requesting YG (another big talent agency) singers be brought to London and this later turned out to have been orchestrated by the Korean Cultural Center in London (*Ohmynews* 2011). While governmental actors are eager to raise the profile of the Korean Wave itself, talent agencies are keen to make their artists' overseas popularity visible and get positive news coverage, which is crucial to accumulating their company value. Thanks to the K-pop sensation, SM's share price rocketed by ten times between 2008 and 2011 (its sharp increases matched by its artists' overseas promotion and tours that were positively reported via the domestic media) and YG successfully floated on the stock market after the aforementioned London flash mob (D. Lee 2012). These companies also attracted capital investment via the Public Fund of Funds' cultural account and proved to be very lucrative. As of January 2013, SM has received investment of more than 12 billion won (approx. $10.7 million) and YG more than 7.4 billion won (approx. $6.6 million) via the Fund, and the return rates are 437.3% and 823% respectively (Ministry of Culture, Sports and Tourism 2013b). Such high return rates encouraged talent agencies themselves to invest in cultural accounts under the Fund. Another interesting example is Gangnam District's Korean Wave Star Street project, the local government's response to the global popularity of Psy's *Gangnam Style*. The street, where SM, JYP and Cube, the three talent agencies, are located, has been chosen (ironically, YG which manages Psy is not located in this district) and will be beautified along with the installation of public artworks, information facilities, hand printing and so on (*Seoul Shinmun* 2012). With no interest in discussing the meanings of "Gangnam" in Korean society and its pop culture scene, it looks like a straightforward tourism project, which is also likely to provide the talent agencies with symbolic values that might assist them to accrue more financial values.

Overseas fans as a source of legitimacy

At the center of the Korean Wave policy there exists overseas fandom as a new but powerful source of the legitimacy of Korean popular culture as a promising export industry and an eligible subject of state cultural policy. Ironically, overseas fans' linguistic and socio-cultural distance from Korean society means that they are insulated from the country's discourse of the Korean Wave phenomenon and its attention to them. Discovering and reporting overseas fans and their enthusiastic engagement with K-pop and TV drama have become a routine of the government agencies involved. This seemingly serves as evidence of the effectiveness of the existing Korean Wave policy and the need for more policy effort in this area. The gravity of overseas fandom in the Korean Wave discourse in media and cultural policy could be well illustrated by the following two examples. In early 2011, MBC began broadcasting *I am a Singer*, an audition program, featuring earlier-generation singers and young singers whose style differed from the mainstream pop music dominated by boy or girl groups. Becoming a big hit, the series triggered negative public opinion about idol groups and the talent agencies that were continuously churning out similar groups. Although the debate on the idol-group-dominated K-pop scene continued (*Hangyoreh* 2011), the criticism soon gave way to a celebration of "K-pop warriors who shook Europe" and their artistic achievement once the popularity of K-pop in Europe began to be reported (*Kyunghyang Shinmun* 2011). Another example is the fiasco around *Right Now*, a song released by Psy in 2010. After *Gangnam Style* proved to be a global media sensation in September 2012, some online users predicted that *Right Now* would be the next mega hit after seeing the rapidly increasing number of views of its YouTube video and overseas fans' positive comments. However, the video's accessibility was limited to those who were 19 or over as it was graded as "R19" by the Ministry of Gender Equality and Family, which had the power to regulate cultural content that could harm young people, due to its strong ("bad") language. Then online users began criticizing the ministry's too strict position and blaming it for overseas fans' restricted access to the *Right Now* video (*Yonhap News* 2012). There was a feeling that the policy would damage Psy's emerging career as a global pop singer. Seriously pressured, the ministry made an incredibly quick move by lifting the restriction from the song and other songs R19-graded for reasons such as inappropriate language for young people. Although there had previously been voices problematizing the ministry's conservative criteria, they did not catch the public's attention until Psy, out of the blue, rose as a K-pop star. Music censorship had long been discussed in terms of freedom of expression and was a key agenda for the country's cultural activism in the 1980s and 1990s. However, it is now reconstructed as an issue of the Korean Wave and market access. This is a new version of cultural consumerism where overseas demands are equated with public interest and market orientation overcomes public policy concerns. This transnational consumerism can be seen as Korean cultural policy and the media's response to neoliberal globalization where the country is emerging as a new center of the production of transnationally popular cultural text and stars. It vividly contrasts with the nationalistic and protectionist approaches taken by the country's cultural industries policy in the past.

Conclusion

The relationship between the state and popular culture in Korea has undergone a dynamic transformation since the 1960s. Through the historical process, popular culture gained substantial autonomy from the state and social legitimacy as both a socio-cultural and an economic force. Reflecting the inherent tension within the country's broader socio-political shift itself, its cultural policy was given the complex task of fostering both cultural and economic dimensions of popular culture. Similarly, reflecting the overall triumph of neoliberal ideologies in public policy, the government has shown more interest in cultural industries' market values and their quantitative growth. The gap between the two pillars of the renaissance of Korean popular culture in the 1990s – democratization and marketization – has been further widening, leading popular culture to be depoliticized and progressive and alternative voices to lose currency. Views and opinions concerning quality, diversity and public interest and the critique of commercialism are seldom heard in the current policy discourse of cultural industries. Popular culture has become "content," a brand-new engine of wealth generation and then an export material. In this process, "Korean culture" replaced the old idea of "national culture." Without engaging in wider discussion about what it meant and would include and how it came into being, it has recently been re-branded as "K-culture," where the essential idea of Korean culture is fused with simplistic universalism and globalism. The surge of the Korean Wave appears to present a new opportunity for Korean popular culture to seal off the internal schism between its cultural and economic components by endowing the latter with symbolic endorsement and repackaging it as a source of national pride, new aesthetics and an advanced image of the country. The Korean Wave has also given cultural industries policy an impetus to expand its remit and continue its developmental roles, driving various projects at both central and local levels and opening up an interface where the policy unprecedentedly collaborates with commercial businesses of cultural production and distribution. Under the current policy for the Korean Wave, even the rhetoric of transculturalism and international exchange are more or less powerless as stress is put on a single-directional and outbound global flow of Korean cultural products. The reasoning of cultural policy as public policy is increasingly subordinated to that of transnational consumerism with overseas markets and consumer demands rising as key criteria for valuing Korean popular culture. Moreover, the transnational consumerist idea of Korean culture feeds the country's understanding of its cultural identity, local cultures and popular cultural aesthetics. In a similar vein, overseas fans of Korean popular culture, unknowingly, act as cultural arbiters whose responses and comments heavily affect the government and mainstream media's view of popular culture. The rapidly expanding field of Korean Wave policy seems to be in need of interventions from critical scholars, civil society and local communities who wish to bring cultural perspectives and public policy concerns to it. Unfortunately, however, the idea of the Korean Wave as Korean culture conquering Asia and then the world and serving consumers beyond national borders is still dominating policy and media discourse of the phenomenon.

Acknowledgment

This research was funded by the Korea Foundation's Field Research Fellowship program (2012–13).

References

Cho, H. (2005) "Reading the Korean Wave as a Sign of Global Shift," *Korean Journal*, 45 (4): 147–82.

Choi, Y. (2013) "The Korean Wave Policy as a Corporate-state Project of Lee Government: The Analysis of Structures and Strategies Based on the Strategic-relational Approach," *Economy and Society*, 97: 252–85.

Chosun Ilbo (2012) "The Abolishment of the *Taeawangsashingi* Set that Dreamt the Korean Wave from Jeju," May 9.

Chu, K. (2005) "Anti-Yushin and Cultural Movement in the 1970s: Focusing on the Location of Folk Entertainment in the Cultural Movement," *Historical Folklore Studies*, 21: 7–72.

Chua, B. and Iwabuchi, K. (2008) *East Asian Pop Culture: Analysing the Korean Wave*, Hong Kong: Hong Kong University Press.

Hangyoreh (2011) "Is the Current System of (Pop) Idol Training Alright?" June 17.

Hankook Ilbo (2011) "Korean Wave Star Street will Move from Chungmuro to a Third Location," December 18.

Iwabuchi, K. (2010) "Globalization, East Asian Media Cultures and Their Publics," *Asian Journal of Communication*, 20(2): 197–212.

Joongang Ilbo Joinsland (2013) "Hallyu World without Substance … Kept Being Emptied for 8 Years," March 12.

Jung, S. (2011) "Race and Ethnicity in Fandom: Praxis," *Transformative Works and Cultures*, 8. http://journal.transformativeworks.com/index.php/twc/article/view/289/219 (accessed March 20, 2013).

Kang, N. (2007) "Neoliberalism and the Korean Wave," *Chinese Contemporary Literature*, 9: 273–302.

Kim, H. (2002) "The Desire and Reality in the Korean Wave Discourse," *Contemporary Criticism*, 19: 216–33.

Kim, J. and Kim, J. (2007) "Effect and Acculturation of Korean Animation by Policy of Korean Culture," *Korean Contents Journal*, 7(12): 55–65.

Kim, W. (2012) "Competition in the Appropriation of 'Things Korean,'" *Society and History*, 93: 185–235.

Korean Culture and Information Service (2012) *Korean Wave: From K-pop to K-culture*, Seoul: Korean Culture and Information Service.

Kyunghyang Shinmun (2011) "The Warriors of K-pop Who Shook Europe," June 11.

Lee, D. (2010) *The Age of Cultural Capital*, Seoul: Culture Science.

——(2012) "The Truth of the SM Entertainment Show in LA," *Pressian* (January 25, 2012). http://www.pressian.com/article/article.asp?article_num=30120123190932 (accessed March 22, 2013).

Lee, K. (2008) "Mapping out the Cultural Politics of 'the Korean Wave' in Contemporary South Korea," in B. Chua and K. Iwabuchi (eds) *East Asian Pop Culture: Analysing the Korean Wave*, Hong Kong: Hong Kong University Press.

Lee, Y. (2005) *Cultural Industries Policy, Evaluation and Prospect*, Seoul: Korea Culture and Tourism Institute.

Ministry of Culture and Public Information (1979) *The Thirty Years of Culture and Public Information*, Seoul: Ministry of Culture and Public Information.

Ministry of Culture, Sports and Tourism (2008) *Cultural Vision*, Seoul: Ministry of Culture Sports and Tourism.

——(2012) "Press Release: The Launch of Collaborative Platform between Korean Wave and the Business Sector."

——(2013a) *Korean Wave White Paper*, Seoul: Ministry of Culture, Sports and Tourism.

——(2013b) "Korean Wave News," http://www.mcst.go.kr/usr/kwave/news/mcst/newsView.jsp?pSeq=2259 (accessed March 20, 2013).

Ministry of Culture and Tourism (2004) *Creative Korea*, Seoul: Ministry of Culture and Tourism.

——(2005) *C-Korea 2010: Cultural Power*, Seoul: Ministry of Culture and Tourism.

Oh, M. (1998) "Cultural Policy and National Culture Discourse in the 1960s and 1970s," *Comparative Cultural Studies*, 4: 121–52.

Ohmynews (2011) "Is the London K-pop Event a Work of the Korean Cultural Center?," July 10, http://star.ohmynews.com/NWS_Web/OhmyStar/at_pg.aspx?CNTN_CD=A0001594309 (accessed March 20, 2013).

Ryoo, W. (2009) "Globalization, or the Logic of Cultural Hybridization: The Case of the Korean Wave," *Asian Journal of Communication*, 19(2): 137–51.

Seoul Shinmun (2012) "1080m Gangnam Korean Wave Street to be Launched by the End of the Year," November 2.

Shim, D. (2006) "Hybridity and the Rise of Korean Popular Culture in Asia," *Media, Culture & Society*, 28(1): 25–44.

——(2008) "The Growth of Korean Cultural Industries and the Korean Wave," in B. Chua and K. Iwabuchi (eds) *East Asian Pop Culture: Analysing the Korean Wave*, Hong Kong: Hong Kong University Press.

Shin, K. (1989) "The Meaning of the Birth of Minyechong," *Arts and Criticism*, 15: 173–83.

Sohn, S. (2011) "Understanding and Evaluation of Public Policy on Hallyu," *The Journal of Cultural Policy*, 25(1): 39–62.

Weiss, L. (1998) *The Myth of the Powerless State: Governing the Economy in a Global Era*, Cambridge: Polity.

Williams, R. (1984) "State Culture and Beyond," in L. Apignanesi (ed.) *Culture and the State*, London: Institute of Contemporary Arts.

Yonhap News (2012) "Lift 19R from Psy's *Right Now*, an Online Appeal Going On," September 20.

Chapter 12

Re-worlding culture?

YouTube as a K-pop interlocutor

Kent A. Ono and Jungmin Kwon

In 2011, *Billboard* and *Billboard Korea* jointly launched the Korea K-pop (Korea Pop) Hot 100. On the *Billboard* homepage, K-pop is listed in the main menu under "International," below Canada, France, Germany and Japan. In the same year, hundreds of European fans held a flash mob in Paris to persuade SM Entertainment, a major Korean pop company, to add another concert after the first concert sold out. JYJ, a Korean pop group, also performed at sold-out shows in South America, setting a new record for the fastest ticket selling time. The following year, Girls' Generation, another Korean singing group, made a huge debut in the U.S. mainstream market by performing on the *Late Show with David Letterman*. Other K-pop singers gained public attention not only in East and South Asia, Europe and the Americas, but also in the Middle East and Africa. K-pop's circulation and popularity had gone global.

The most monumental event in K-pop history happened in December of 2012, when the *Gangnam Style* music video by Psy, a K-pop singer, reached, for the first time in YouTube history, 1 billion views on the video-sharing website – as of April, 2013, it recorded 1.5 billion views, making it the most watched video on YouTube ever. Thanks to the video having gone viral, the song climbed to second place on the *Billboard* Top 100, behind Maroon 5's "One More Night." At the end of 2012, the American Broadcasting Company (ABC) included Psy with Taylor Swift and Carly Rae Jepsen on its 2012 New Year's Eve show, reinforcing and arguably sedimenting K-pop as a global cultural force.

The rapid rise of K-pop seems almost ironic given Korea's colonized position during much of the twentieth century. Korea was colonized by its neighboring country, Japan, for more than 30 years beginning in the second decade of that century. After gaining separation from Japan in 1945, Korea, from the Maginot Line to Communism's southward movement into East Asia, largely remained under economic, political, cultural and social control of the United States (Choi 2006: 85).

In her 1985 essay, "Three Women's Texts and A Critique of Imperialism," Gayatri Spivak described "worlding" as an imperial process of implicitly reinscribing imperial culture into "the Third World" contexts in order to legitimize imperial dominance. Korea, as part of "the Third World," was assuredly worlded by imperial powers. The importation of imperial culture from "First World" nations meant colonial dependence was established through the directional flow of global cultural products (Choi 2006: 77) and unequal trade and consumption practices. Given this history, how might the current diffusion of Korean pop (K-pop) be understood? Might it be that the historical colonial worlding process of First World culture infusing its culture into the Third World is being reversed, with empires functionally participating in their own un-worlding? As a no longer overtly colonized society, to what degree is Korean culture, in its deportation to Western civilization, un-worlding Western colonial societies? Because Korea fell under imperial control historically, is the current popularity of K-pop culture an example of a hybrid colonial form that both worlds and "unworlds" culture? Or, is K-pop itself part of the very worlding Spivak described nearly 30 years ago?

Interestingly, central to this discussion about K-pop's contemporary role as a worlding and/or un-worlding phenomenon is YouTube. In YouTube's infancy, K-pop content was unofficially distributed. The virality of K-pop videos on YouTube played a crucial marketing, distributional and advertising role in promoting K-pop as a popular entertainment form worldwide. But, of course, the effect of such videos was mutual: with YouTube's own popularity, its role as a global media archive, and its credibility as unfiltered (or uncensored), being one reason for it becoming a home for K-pop videos. Now YouTube is a self-reflexive staple in the campaign process of marketing new and old K-pop artists and productions. YouTube's ease of access made it possible for audiences to download and upload content, and to write in the comment streams below videos. These practices reposition Korea and Korean culture not only within the global cultural imagery, but also within processes of global capitalism, and within empire. An embedded marker of modernity's infrastructural commitment to technology, YouTube plays an indispensable role in the K-pop's worlding and/or un-worlding process.

This chapter examines the role YouTube plays in the global spread of K-pop by asking how this Western-originating medium benefits local industry and culture and alters the way we understand worlding to occur. K-pop culture, unlike the first Korean Wave in the early 2000s, is, in part, a pre-planned and well-organized cultural product demonstrating synergies among: (1) marketing strategies of the music industry (strategies of industries created out of empire); (2) a dispersed, yet strong, global fandom; and (3) the power of YouTube. Therefore, we investigate the close relationship between YouTube and K-pop and conduct an interview with a K-pop industry worker. By doing so, we aim to present multi-layered aspects of the transnational cultural K-pop phenomenon that deserves such complex and in-depth attention.

Rethinking subalternality

In the early 1990s, Spivak expressed concerns that postcolonial societies are worlded by a global culture from the West and that "subaltern" subjects cannot speak within this existing structure; nonetheless, she suggested that listening for subaltern voices is necessary. Research on globalization and global culture has expanded beyond earlier, more unilateral, conceptions of relationships between the West and the non-West, and between empire and colony, and in our case specifically research has expanded beyond homogenization and heterogenization. As Appadurai has argued, "the new global cultural economy … has to be understood as a complex, overlapping, disjunctive order, which cannot any longer be understood in terms of existing center–periphery models (even those that might account for multiple centers and peripheries)" (1990: 296). Thus, in discussing South Korea and K-pop an analysis of power that extends beyond the "West and the Rest" models of analysis allows for a complex understanding of inter-animating colonial and power relations and the mutual production of cultural tendencies. Globalization and global culture must therefore be regarded as mutually reinforcing, simultaneously existing, complex and multi-dimensional phenomena.

In his discussion of globalization of culture, Featherstone (1993: 171) echoes Appadurai's position, highlighting the importance of a "process" in the postmodern condition; he notes that the process of history should not be understood as a unitary one but as a complicated one binding together "the individual histories of particular nation states and blocs." Of course, here, the phrase "particular nation states and blocs" is not limited to traditionally privileged countries or regions. In fact, the idea that history was geared toward the unification of the world with Europe and the United States at the center in the nineteenth and twentieth centuries has dwindled, whereas non-Western groups have emphasized vernacular identity, economy and forms of artistic expression that have focused attention on local histories, representing them on a global stage. Asiacentric perspectives, for example, have drawn attention to the notion that the particularity of Asian-centered conceptions of communication requires the alteration of frameworks and theories of analysis to address a transformed global terrain (Miike 2008).

The economic and cultural success of Japan has demonstrated the possibility of change, and Hong Kong and Bollywood cinema further added to the reconfiguration of processes of globalization within and outside of Asia. Local cultures, regardless of whether or not they were worlded historically by imperial powers, permeated global markets and led to their appropriation within Western culture, appropriation that undoubtedly paralleled certain early colonial processes. Thus, globalization necessarily must be conceptualized so as to address the mutual interpenetration of culture between previously colonial and previously colonizing nations in order to account for globalizing processes that include the importation and exportation of vernacular culture.

Within broader processes of globalization, nation–state cultures may be significantly influenced by many cultures. Dasgupta (2006) provided a good example of such diversity: the circulation of yaoi culture in East Asia. Yaoi, a homosexual romance mostly written by female fans, is one of the manga (comics) subcultures in Japan (Sabucco 2003: 70). As it spread to other Asian countries, its original form was appropriated. For instance, the Hong Kong film *Bishônen* (1998), based on the yaoi theme and narrative structure, was created, and its popularity led to the making of a manga version in Japan. Actually, scholars like Dasgupta (2006: 59) noted that the Korean Wave (Hallyu) incorporates and repackages Asian cultures, a point that is now commonplace within scholarship by scholars studying the Korean Wave.[1] For instance, according to Choi (2006: 79), culture is (re)contextualized in particular times and places, meaning it has no essence: that of the Korean Wave, in this particular case. That is, a concatenation of cultures, according to Hyun (2012: 305–7), is part of the Korean Wave, a result of globalization processes.

Among many dimensions of the Korean Wave (which includes commodities across music, film, television, literature and retail markets generally), K-pop embodies contextualization and appropriation as component dimensions of the encounter with different cultures. Since the late nineteenth century, Korean music has been influenced by overseas music. Indeed, Viet Kieu (Vietnamese who are not currently living in Vietnam) popular music has significantly influenced mainland Vietnamese music, which has in turn re-influenced Viet Kieu music in the United States (Valverde 2003). In this sense, colonial processes are not even two-way, but complexly interwoven and reciprocal. With regard to Korea, specifically, Lie (2012) has historicized the foreign impact of Korean music. When Korean music first experienced its transition from premodern to modern, Western musical forms, such as "classical" music, ballads and *chanson,* and Japanese *enka* were introduced. In fact, Japanese *enka* grew from African and European music forms grounded in blues, jazz and country. During the U.S. occupation of Korea, American popular music flourished. U.S. Korean music consumers enjoyed jazz, blues, pop and rock via Armed Forces radio and television. In the 1960s and 1970s, the authoritarian regime tried to ban the spread of Western music because the West had already had a profound colonial influence on Korea; this caused the popularity of *trot,* a Korean version of Japanese *enka.* Since the late 1970s, diverse shifts in musical production to address the colonial and Korean production of culture were made: for example, Cho Young-Pil combined rock music, *trot* and *pansori* (traditional Korean music), while Shin Joong-Hyun and Kim Chu-Ja pursued a more Western pop style. Until the 1980s, as Shim (2006: 35) has written, *ppongjjak*, a different name for *trot* and Korean ballads, "characterized by mellow sounds and amorous lyrics influenced by Western styles," dominated. In 1992, a revolutionary song and a male band came to sudden prominence in Korean music history: the debut of Seo Taiji and Boys and the release of their first single, "I Know." Park (2006: 40), citing Howard (2002), posited that the hybridization of Korean popular music began burgeoning because of that band. They mixed many genres such as pop, hip-hop, soul, rock and roll, techno, punk, hardcore, *ppongjjak* and *pansori* and added dynamic dance as a critical part of their performance (Lie 2012: 349; Shim 2006: 36). Shim (2006: 37) appreciated the role of Seo Taiji in "transforming Korean pop music, elevating its status in society, and setting the standard for Korean dance music that would later suit the tastes of Asian fans," in the end becoming attractive to international fans. This short history of Korean music epitomizes the knotty interconnections among musical products. As King and Craig (2010: 5) put it:

> So, popular music from the developed West, itself the product of ethnic and class diversity, can be co-opted and reshaped by Celtic, Caribbean, African, and Asian performers, and incorporated by eclectic Western visionaries into world music projects, or adopted intuitively by young artists with little conscious awareness of or concern for the source. This music is then, *mutatis mutandis,* received and remoulded by performers worldwide and presented to their "local" audiences in the language they can best understand and with musical variations that play to the audience's understanding of itself.

That is, music and, by extension, culture, is little by little colored and transformed by diverse localities and consumed locally and globally; this dimension is what we wish to emphasize, while being careful not to overstate the politically revolutionary dimensions of this globalizing phenomenon.

What is important to stress is that the "origin" of musical style loses significance within reciprocal processes of cultural interchange. For this reason, Choi (2006: 93) stresses the variety of times and places from whence K-pop comes, claiming Korean Wave texts encompass dimensions from traditional, modern and postmodern times and from Korea, the United States, Japan and many other countries. To put it simply, the Korean Wave is an exemplar of contemporary global hybridity, just as Western culture itself is hybrid. Stuart Hall (1996) in his discussion of modernity, concluded, "Modern nations are all cultural hybrids," pointing out that even the West, which is commonly understood within historical Eurocentrism and modernity, is also radically hybrid (617).

According to King and Craig (2010: 6), the hybridity of different cultures is natural because the same technology used in the production or dissemination of the original culture is also used when other cultures produce or disseminate their own cultural products. Hence, they claimed:

> Subaltern groups (oppressed nations and races, disadvantaged minorities, and majorities) cannot be silenced ... Their voices, even though they may be manipulated and mediated by the artistic and business moguls of the

music, film, and television industries, are needed to invigorate the global popular culture that is then fed back to them and to everyone else.

In the rest of this chapter, we examine the proliferation of K-pop based on the concept that globalization and global culture facilitate hybridity; hence, the notion of culture both worlding and un-worlding simultaneously helps explain the phenomenon of K-pop.

The Korean Wave 1.0: unexpected, unprepared

The global prevalence of contemporary Korean culture is not a new phenomenon; the Korean Wave dates back to the late 1990s, when a few Korean dramas such as *What Is Love All About?* in 1997 and *Stars in My Heart* in 1999 attracted a substantial audience in China. That was when the word "Hallyu" was coined (Hyun 2012; Lie 2012; Shim 2006; Yang 2011).[2] The same cultural fever started sweeping through Japan in 2004, when *Winter Sonata* was televised. Middle-aged Japanese women were enthusiastic about the drama, and the fandom became a solid foundation for the introduction of other Korean cultural products to Japan.

Other genres also contributed to the popularity of Hallyu. H.O.T., a boy band, was introduced on Channel V, an Asian music television channel, and topped the pop charts in 1998 (Shim 2006: 28). Other singer groups such as NRG or Baby V.O.X. were successful within Asian markets.

As the zeal for Korean popular culture gradually cooled down, some agreed that the Korean Wave could not last for long or make tremendous inroads into other global regions as it had in Asia. Kim (2007: 210) had strong doubts about the sustainability and extensibility of the Korean Wave, which he explains as follows:

> The reason why the future of the Korean Wave is not quite as rosy as it was during its transpacific and trans-Asian beginnings stems from the generally accepted observation that the Korean Wave merely succeeded in carving out a niche market only within East Asia which are [*sic*] under the cultural influence of the U.S. As a matter of fact, some regard the Korean Wave as nothing but a repackaging of U.S. products with a "Korean" flavor and furthermore suggest that the accomplishments of the cultural fad were both unexpected and coincidental, in contrast to being intentional and well-prepared. Given this viewpoint, logically, the next common idea is that, in time, another cultural trend will arise and replace the Korean Wave, just as the Korean Wave itself had replaced popular culture in Hong Kong and Japan in the 1980s and 1990s.

Regardless of whether or not the critique was correct, Kim's diagnosis of the Korean Wave at the time seemed plausible. The Korean Wave was by no means anticipated by anyone: the content itself was not designed for foreign sale but for domestic consumption, and the artists, producers and marketers were not ready for overseas expansion. Hence, the relatively pessimistic outlook was not groundless.

As it turns out, however, the forecast was not accurate. As observed at the beginning of this chapter, the Korean Wave is booming. This new era of popularity and success is sometimes referred to as "the second Korean Wave" or "the Korean Wave 2.0" (Lie 2012: 352; Lim and Heo 2012: 456; Oh 2012: 206). This new Korean Wave has distinguished itself from its previous iteration through the centrality of Korean pop music vs. Korean dramas, which dominated the first wave. Moreover, unlike the earlier version which was popular in Korea and East Asia, popularity of Korean Wave 2.0 exists all over the world (Ahn 2011: 84).[3] The biggest difference is that, this time, everything and everyone has been ready for the Korean sensation.

K-pop paving the way to a global market

The self-examination and self-criticism of shortcomings in the achievement of the first Korean Wave by the Korean entertainment companies became the primary driver of the second Korean Wave. Drama and cinema productions made contracts with Hallyu celebrities for them to perform and shoot scenes in foreign locations in an attempt to expand into overseas markets. In some cases, they tried to collaborate with international producers, directors and actors to gain attention from other countries. Korean stars, of course, constantly sought ways to make their appearance on the global stage, which is more lucrative. It was the field of popular music that most successfully guided the second Korean Wave through such farsighted plans after intensive plans and preparations.

By the late 1990s, the ongoing major entertainment companies such as SM Entertainment, JYP and YG Entertainment had already established themselves. All of them had adopted a star-making system similar to the ones in Japan and the U.S. and produced a few singer groups that had been performing for years as singers and dancers. However, these performers were not ready to enter foreign markets (Park and Rhee 2011). For example, members of H.O.T., the first K-pop star group, were supposed to go into the Korean military, and could therefore only be issued a single passport, which severely limited their international travel to promote their identities and music. Furthermore, H.O.T. group members had language problems. S.E.S., another K-pop singer group, could not make it in the Japanese popular music market because a contract with a local Japanese agency restricted international promotion of the group. These trials and errors made the Korean agencies choose to take more long-term and aggressive measures.

Through "systematic production" from casting to debut, they tried to make their singers perfect (Ahn 2011). Teen trainees selected during early reviews of their talent spent five to ten years of training to become singers. That training included not only singing and dancing but also acting and personal development (Seo 2012: 63). To be successful in a global market, a variety of actions are taken. For instance, having foreigners or foreign residents as members of a group, teaching foreign language skills such as English, Chinese or Japanese before debut performances, and introducing a singing group in a foreign market first are strategies used to develop and prepare groups for international audiences.

What is most remarkable is that a number of international producers, composers and choreographers participate in the training process as well as in the production of albums, so that performances by K-pop singers can be made attractive to global audiences (Ahn 2011: 84; Son 2012: 66). Indeed, will.i.am, an American songwriter and producer and a member of the Black Eyed Peas who recently made a blockbuster solo album, *#willpower* (2013), produced 2NE1's American album, and Kanye West, an American musician, composed songs for JYJ. For a Japanese market, TVXQ received songs from Ryoji Sonoda, a Japanese lyricist and singer, and Big Bang did from Daishi Dance, a popular Japanese DJ (Oh and Park 2012: 379). For Girls' Generation's world debut album in 2011, Dominique Rodriguez, who joined in the albums of Michael Jackson and Lady Gaga, composed a title song, *The Boys* (Hwang 2013). Not only the production of albums but also their marketing are supported by global and local professionals. In an interview with one of us, a staff member working in one of the Korea entertainment companies mentioned, "Promotion and marketing in each country are strategically different. For promoting albums and artists, we get help from a Japanese company in Japan, global agencies in the U.S. or Europe, domestic experts for a Korean market." As the earlier section indicates, Korean music has developed, absorbing and mixing genres across the globe. These stories about strategies in the K-pop entertainment industry affirm that this hybridity is deepening within the current evolution of K-pop. According to Oh (2012: 208), the hybridity was intended to appeal to universal sentiments globally.

Along the way, the K-pop industry ceaselessly tried ways to succeed in a global market, while they trained their performers to get ready for meeting global expectations. An unexpected development enhanced marketers' attempts to popularize K-pop 2.0: the appearance of social networking sites (SNSs) such as YouTube, Facebook and Twitter (Ahn 2011; Seo 2012). These SNSs provided a convenient way of introducing K-pop artists and songs to people globally, ranging from Japan, China and other Asian countries to Europe, the Americas and Africa. Seo (2012: 63–4) highly touted the role of SNSs. Dividing the pre-SNS era and the SNS era, he remarked that it took four to five years for BoA and TVXQ to get established in Japan, while the first album of Girls' Generation reached first place in the Oricon Chart, a well-known music chart in Japan, on the same day it was released, thanks to SNSs. Among the online spaces, YouTube played a pivotal role (Ahn 2011; Lie 2012; Oh and Park 2012; Shim and Noh 2012; Yang 2011). Interestingly, the

French interviewees, whom Son (2012) met to investigate K-pop fandom, commonly agreed that YouTube allowed them to encounter and consume Korean cultural products, including Korean dramas and K-pop. As Oh and Park (2012: 369) stated, "YouTube is now opening up a new dedicated K-pop channel, as K-pop related videos have more than tens of millions of steady hits from Asia, Europe, and Americas every month." Not to mention the rise of Psy in 2012, even three years ago the music video of the song *Gee*, by Girls' Generation was widely watched, hitting almost 100 million views and generating 250,000 comments. Considering that Lady Gaga's "Poker Face" music video, released about the same time, had 150 million views and 150,000 comments, the achievement of Girls' Generation is huge. And in the survey of the number of views of K-pop music videos on YouTube, countries outside of Asia such as the United States, Canada, Saudi Arabia and France, occupy, according to Shim and Noh (2012: 127), the top ten places.

This sensational boom of K-pop on YouTube spread to the offline world and enabled K-pop singers to give stage appearances throughout the world. Not everyone would agree with the idea that YouTube is the most significant factor in the current wave of K-pop. Yet, no one can deny it is a highly significant factor in K-pop's global circulation and popularity: the K-pop content, reflecting all the efforts made to gain a global market, began booming in part as a result of the audience access YouTube provides.

Having established YouTube as significant in the global circulation of K-pop, it is possible to address the issue of colonialism and K-pop: Can we say that YouTube, a modern technology based on Western culture, contributes to un-worlding through its dissemination of K-pop? Or is it actually another instance of the West worlding third world countries? In the next section, we examine the ways in which YouTube benefits the transmission of K-pop.

K-pop's best friend – YouTube

YouTube is one of the revolutionary technologies that has transformed "ways to consume, create and share music" in the history of music (Cayari 2011: 2). Additionally, as we argue, YouTube significantly altered the status of K-pop in the world as a cultural force. On the relationship between YouTube and K-pop, KpopStarz (2012), a K-pop entertainment news website in New York, favorably commented:

> YouTube itself is very friendly towards K-pop. They created a K-pop genre in the music category, which only consists of genres such as pop, rock, R&b, rap, folk and Latin. K-pop is the first genre to be created for a particular country.

Here, we examine the features of YouTube – visual, global, consumer-led, and free of certain limitations and restrictions – in relation to how K-pop has taken advantage of them. First, YouTube reinforces the visuality of music. In fact, the audiovisual components of music emerged when MTV was launched in 1982. Since then, music has become something to both listen to and view, and the role of music video strengthened the spread of music (Holt 2011: 50; Schackman 2008: 7). As MTV gradually diverted its business focus on reality and competition shows, YouTube took over its role of providing a place to consume music videos (Schackman 2008: 9; Thornton 2010: 56). In this way, the visuality of music was central to YouTube's effectiveness, and consequently offered an opportunity for K-pop. As mentioned earlier, K-pop singers are trained in dancing and acting, as well as singing, and their hair and fashion styles are carefully designed. In a word, K-pop is performance-centered. Oh (2012) demonstrated the performative nature of K-pop in her interviews with U.S. audiences. Her informants answered that they were attracted by the ways in which music was visualized as a performance, combining powerful dances with the energies of young and passionate K-pop singers. These reactions mean that visual impression plays a significant role in the consumption of K-pop by fans globally (Oh 2012). Although viewers cannot always fully understand K-pop lyrics due to the language barrier, they are sometimes impressed by cool group dances or charming physical appearances of K-pop singers in the video. As an audio and visual medium, YouTube allows for the visuality of performance to be central to what makes K-pop circulable.

Second, YouTube is a transnational technology in ways older media could not be. Oh and Park (2012: 391) quoted an interview with Kim Young-Min, the CEO of SM Entertainment, in making this point: "Unlike TV and radio, YouTube is the first global mechanism that allows producers like us to advertise our music." The ease of download, as well as the ease of access through the Internet globally, makes possible broad audience consumption of K-pop (Cayari 2011): new (as well as repeat) visitors to sites, an easy-to-use search engine and the interlink with Google, its parent company, further facilitate access. As early as 2006, the K-pop industry quickly perceived the usefulness of YouTube, and major companies, including SM Entertainment and YG Entertainment, opened and operated YouTube channels.

Third, YouTube's most important value lies in its interactive capabilities: users can post comments in comment streams that can be read by anyone visiting a given video site, including the makers of videos and those who upload them. Additionally, "prosumers" can upload their own videos as well as consume them and others. Unlike traditional media YouTube does not work without "you," people to upload videos, view them, offer comments and read those comments. Out of YouTube comment streams is the potential to build virtual communities in cyberspace (Oh and Park 2012: 373). This ability to be involved in a participatory culture is incredibly valuable when it comes to the popularity of K-pop. International fans who enjoy imitating K-pop singers' performances upload their own self-filmed dance or musical covers.[4] In East Asian countries such as Thailand, the K-pop dance cover is, according to Seo (2012) and Oh (2012), hugely popular among younger generations and is proliferating throughout Europe and the United States. Even dance cover festivals are held and sometimes, through the events, promising, talented youngsters are picked up by K-pop agencies. Furthermore, flash mobs and dance parodies of K-pop performances are staged: millions of flash mobs and dance parodies of *Gangnam Style* have been uploaded onto YouTube. There are versions of *Gangnam Style* parodies country-by-country, occupation-by-occupation and school-by-school. The interviewee from a Korean entertainment company emphasized that these fan-made productions from the world actually spurred K-pop artists to enter a global stage.

Lastly, YouTube's limitations are minimal (Oh and Park 2012: 373) and relatively inexpensive. Cayari (2011: 21) noted the portability, availability and repeatability of YouTube features. YouTube significantly lowers various kinds of barriers to consuming music. The same applies to uploading videos onto YouTube. Uploaded videos can contain a wide variety of content, although copyrighted material, material conceived of as offensive, or (for instance) of concern for revealing military intelligence or guarded trade secrets can be and is restricted. Therefore, other than music videos, clips related to K-pop are uploaded, no matter what they are about, such as "TV music shows, their domestic and international lives, and music award ceremonies" (Shim and Noh 2012: 128). Moreover, as the interviewee at the entertainment company stated in an interview, "clips which cannot be televised in the traditional media are covered on YouTube." For example, "behind-the-scenes" stories, short interviews, fan-shot content: all of them may function to shorten the emotional distance between singers and fans.

In brief, YouTube is "a key factor in the K-pop fever," and therefore top K-pop agencies launch competitive YouTube channels and maintain them with a separate division (personal communication with the interviewee). Thanks to such efforts, K-pop content grows, and its transnational fan bases increase. At the end of last year (2012), KpopStarz (2012) reported: "The 3 big management companies SM, YG, and JYP have together recorded 2,280,000,000 views on YouTube, which is 3 times the number in 2010. According to Google Korea, there are fans in such locales as Cuba and Sierra Leone."

Yes, YouTube is very friendly toward K-pop. The current success of K-pop can be significantly attributed to YouTube. If YouTube plays such a significant role in the circulation and consumption flow of K-pop transnationally, then what does this mean for thinking through the worlding of culture?

YouTube re-worlding culture

YouTube started off as a video-sharing website but now is one of the most important online spaces for the public exchange of information in which virtual communication, community and culture are nurtured, and real live communities outside of cyberspace can also be forged.[5] YouTube has become an essential medium for the transnational distribution of certain media products; prospective stars cannot afford to overlook YouTube in preparing to market songs, videos and the like, including commercials for virtually every product. High-profile stars such as Britney Spears have social media teams that maintain her social networking sites and interact with fans across the globe (Kaplan and Haenlein 2012: 27). Even "unknowns" can have a similar (and or better) presence on YouTube than already well-known celebrities like Britney Spears. As a result, plenty of YouTube stars such as Matt Harding, Justin Bieber and Judson Laipply have been born (Cava 2011). The popularity of these self-made YouTube stars could not have been possible without YouTube.

The new technology offers the same chance for postcolonial subjects, at least subjects who have access to the Internet and other technologies, such as cameras, required for production. While some may argue South Korea is not "postcolonial" in the way that Algeria, the Philippines and India are post-colonial, K-pop singers have made good use of YouTube as a way to circulate Korean culture and identities. Earlier, we briefly mentioned what King and Craig (2010) claimed, by quoting an excerpt of a quotation by them. Here we quote them in full: "The same technology that imports the alien mega-culture into Asian societies and disseminates its localized variants at home also exports these variants back out into worlds beyond" (ibid.: 6). Their point is clearly affirmed in the K-pop case. Korean popular music has been worlded by Western music; undoubtedly and indisputably, this is the case. However, that worlding is not one-way, and contemporary new media facilitate the multi-directionality of cultural flow. In other words, Spivak's notion of worlding assumes a *pre-Internet* and *pre-YouTube logic* in which cultural flow is unidirec-tional, akin to an import/export model in which colonial cultural influence only flows in one direction. However, our chapter, and the focus we provide in our study of K-pop, suggests that through the multi-directionality of flow K-pop simultaneously influences Western culture, transforming its contents, ideologies and power. K-pop music reveals Korean cultural diversity, and Korea's own hybridity; as well, K-pop circulates local particularities and local idiomatic expression and customs. Its reproduction by cover artists, performing karaoke transnationally, co-opts and reshapes K-pop products, rendering them newly rearticulated to other cultural expressions, forms, identities and social positions. While a medium originating in empire, YouTube contains the possibility of the re-worlding of that empire – a re-worlding, a process by which multi-layered and multi-rooted cultural influences function to create or add diverse meanings within a given place beyond the operation of its original concept, worlding that posits an imperial and unidirectional dominance – and, possibly and ultimately, its decolonization. By decolonization, we mean the re-imagining and restructuring of existing systems of domination that are remnants of historical colonizing practices and structures. Thus, given the relatively open-ended nature of YouTube, postcolonial ideas, arts and practices can circulate that help to undo historical colonial ones. In the future, it must be incorporated by Western directors or adopted by artists ignorant of its origins (King and Craig 2010: 5). In the process, the border between worlding and un-worlding diminishes or, at least, the meanings become more blurred, as possibilities for shifting power relations and social positions emerge.

We should not be overly optimistic about cultural hybridization; at the same time, we should not allow excessive vigilance based on West/East binarity and colonial mentality to rule out other possibilities. In the piece titled "Globalization as Hybridization," Nederveen Pieterse (1995) admitted that "relations of power and hegemony are inscribed and reproduced *within* hybridity for wherever we look closely enough we find the traces of asymmetry in culture, place, descent" (57). "At the same time," he underscored the point that nevertheless, "it's important to note the ways in which hegemony is not merely reproduced but *refigured* in the process of hybridization" (57). This is clear in the proliferation of K-pop. On YouTube, international fans watch music videos, post comments and present their dancing bodies to share the joy of consuming K-pop together. In the communication process, they exchange information on K-pop songs and singers. In some cases, their interest in K-pop culture is extended to the Korean language and the country of Korea and leads to a decision to learn more about Korean culture and to visit the country. For instance, Cha (2012) reported: "as K-Pop lures more and more foreign travelers to Korea, the government and local entertainment companies are jumping on the bandwagon." Some K-pop entertainment companies set up their own travel agencies to encourage this boom. In the process of actively consuming K-pop and Korean culture, global fans might re-identify residual imperial culture; this hybridity, however, makes them feel closer to the local culture and they continue to participate in re-worlding their culture. By re-worlding, we suggest that consuming K-pop has the potential to undermine traditional colonial relations; further, the consumption of K-pop has the potential not to re-world Korea, as the first world has done historically, but to re-world the first world with the culture of Korea, a previously colonial nation.

Nederveen Pieterse (1995: 63) added that the processes of globalization, "past and present, can be adequately described as processes of hybridization." This might not always have been the case historically, since imperial literatures continue to circulate in postcolonial spaces. But, we are witnessing simultaneous processes of re-worlding as well, processes that have actually taken place throughout human history but are more obvious or more easily noticed and foregrounded within virtual transnational technological spaces perhaps. One example of this re-worlding is K-pop's re-worlding of culture through the medium of YouTube.

Notes

1 Cho Hae-Joang (2005), for instance, analyzes first- and second-wave discourse, suggesting not only the way the Korean government's discourse about the Korean Wave changed over time, but also how discourse about the Korean Wave included ideas about both Korean and Asian culture and economics.
2 According to Lee (2012: 61), some suggested that the word "Hallyu" was first officially used by the Ministry of Culture and Tourism in 1999, although most believe that it derives from China.
3 This does not necessarily mean that the new Korean Wave is restricted to K-pop. According to Lee (2012), the number of countries that air Korean dramas is increasing, including countries in Eastern Europe, the Middle East and Africa. Also, films, games and animation characters are actively consumed at a global level (Lim and Heo 2012: 456).
4 The ability to perform existing songs as well as videos of artists has allowed for a transnational form of karaoke, allowing broad audiences to give input on cover performances.
5 Jung-sun Park (2004), for example, studies the creation of a transpacific Korean community and the complex transformation of cultural flow within Korean and Korean American youths who consume Korean Wave popular culture.

References

Ahn, S. (2011) "Girls' Generation and the New Korean Wave," *SERI Quarterly* (October): 80–9.
Appadurai, A. (1990) "Disjuncture and Difference in the Global Cultural Economy," *Theory, Culture & Society*, 7(2–3): 295–310.
Cava, M. (2011) "YouTube 2.0 Helping New Stars Redefine TV," *USA Today*, June 2. http://usatoday30.usatoday.com/life/lifestyle/2011-06-03-YouTube-creators-camp-Michelle-Phan-Joel-Jutagir_n.htm (accessed March 7, 2013).
Cayari, C. (2011) "The YouTube Effect: How YouTube Has Provided New Ways to Consume, Create, and Share Music," *International Journal of Education & the Arts*, 12 (6): 1–28.
Cha, F. (2012) "Harnessing K-pop for Tourism," CNN Online, April 17. http://travel.cnn.com/seoul/visit/harnessing-k-pop-tourism-386868 (accessed March 7, 2013).
Cho, H. (2005) "Reading the Korean Wave as a Sign of Global Shift," *Korea Journal*, 45(4): 147–82.
Choi, W. (2006) "Korean Interpretation of 'Modernity' and Change of Topography in Popular Culture: with the 'Korean Wave' as a Momentum," *Discourse201 (Damron201)*, 9(4): 75–103.
Craig, T. and King, R. (2010) *Global Goes Local: Popular Culture in Asia*, Honolulu: University of Hawaii Press.
Dasgupta, R. (2006) "The Film Bishōnen and Queer(N)Asia through Japanese Popular Culture," in M. Allen and R. Sakamoto (eds) *Popular Culture, Globalization and Japan*, New York: Routledge.
Featherstone, M. (1993) "Global and Local Cultures," in J. Bird, B. Curtis, T. Putnam, G. Robertson and L. Tickner (eds) *Mapping the Futures: Local Cultures, Global Changes*, New York: Routledge.
Hall, S. (1996) "Modernity: An Introduction to Modern Societies," in S. Hall, D. Held, D. Hubert and K. Thompson (eds) *Modernity: An Introduction to Modern Societies*, Malden: Blackwell.

Holt, F. (2011) "Is Music Becoming More Visual? Online Video Content in the Music Industry," *Visual Studies*, 26(1): 50–61.

Hwang, J. (2013) "Dominik, a Composer for Girls' Generation's Song 'The Boys' Singed Hyu Map Contents," January 4. Newsjeju Online, http://www.newsjeju.net/news/articleView.html?idxno=110025 (accessed March 7, 2013).

Hyun, N. (2012) "The Identity of Korean Wave in the Transcultural Era: Focused on Conceptional Analysis," *Journal of Philosophical Thoughts* (*Sidae-wa Cheolhak*), 23(3): 301–27.

Kaplan, A. and Haenlein, M. (2012) "The Britney Spears Universe: Social Media and Viral Marketing at its Best," *Business Horizons*, 55: 27–31.

Kim, S. (2007) "The Korean Wave and East Asian Cultural Networks," *Journal of World Politics* (*Segye Jeongchi*), 7: 192–235.

King, R. and Craig, T. (2010) "Asia and Global Popular Culture: The View from He Yong's Garbage Dump," in T. Craig and R. King (eds) *Global Goes Local: Popular Culture in Asia*, Honolulu: University of Hawaii Press.

KpopStarz (2012) "Global K-Pop is Thanks to YouTube," December 2. http://www.kpopstarz.com/articles/17852/20121202/global-k-pop-is-thanks-to-youtube.htm (accessed March 7, 2013).

Lee, S. (2012) "Special Topic: Characteristics and Competitive Power of Korean Wave Dramas," *Comparative Korean Studies*, 20(1): 59–84.

Lie, J. (2012) "What is the K in K-pop? South Korean Popular Music, the Culture Industry, and National Identity," *Korean Observer*, 34(3): 339–63.

Lim, Y. and Heo, S. (2012) "The Proliferation of Korean Wave in Japan (*Ilbon-eseo Hally moonhwa Hwaksan-gwa Insik Yeon-gu*)," paper presented at The International Association of Area Studies Spring Conference (*Kookje-jiyouk-hakhoe Choon-gye-haksool-daehoe*) in East Asia, Seoul, June 2012.

Miike, Y. (2008) "Toward an Alternative Metatheory of Human Communication: An Asiacentric Vision," in M. Asante, Y. Miike and J. Yin (eds) *The Global Intercultural Communication Reader*, New York: Routledge.

Nederveen Pieterse, J. (1995) "Globalization as Hybridization," in M. Featherstone, S. Lash and R. Robertson (eds) *Global Modernities*, Thousand Oaks: Sage.

Oh, I. and Park, G. (2012) "From B2C to B2B: Selling Korean Pop Music in the Age of New Social Media," *Korean Observer*, 43(3): 365–97.

Oh, S. (2012) "Attractiveness Factors in K-Pop: Focused on American Consumer of K-Pop in U.S.A.," *Journal of KSSSS* (*Jookwanseong Yeongu*), 24: 205–23.

Park, H. (2006) "A Study on the Korean Appropriation of Global Culture and Postcolonial Identities: A Case Study on Korean Popular Music," *Media and Society* (*Eollongwa Sahoe*), 14(3): 35–72.

Park, J. (2004) "Korean American Youth and Transnational Flows of Popular Culture across the Pacific," *Amerasia Journal*, 30(1): 147–69.

Park, Y. and Rhee, D. (2011) "SM Entertainment, Race for the Global Entertainment," *KBR*, 15(2): 65–87.

Sabucco, V. (2003) "Guided Fanfiction: Western 'Readings' of Japanese Homosexual-themed Texts," in C. Berry, F. Martin and A. Yue (eds) *Mobile Cultures: New Media in Queer Asia*, Durham: Duke University Press.

Schackman, D. (2008) "World Fusion? Global Communication about Music Videos on YouTube," paper presented at the International Communication Association in North America, Quebec, August 2008.

Seo, M. (2012) "Lessons from K-Pop's Global Success," *SERI Quarterly*, 5(3): 60–6.

Shim, D. (2006) "Hybridity and the Rise of Korean Popular Culture in Asia," *Media, Culture & Society*, 28(1): 25–44.

Shim, D. and Noh, K. (2012) "YouTube and Girls' Generation Fandom," *Journal of Korean Contents (Hankook Contents Hakhoe Nonmoonji)*, 12(1): 125–37.

Son, S. (2012) "Local Context and Global Fandom of Hallyu Consumption: The Case of Korean Connection in France," *Journal of Media and Economy (Media Gyeongje-wa Moonhwa)*, 10(1): 45–85.

Spivak, G. (1993) "Can the Subaltern Speak?," in P. Williams and L. Chrisman (eds) *Colonial Discourse and Post-Colonial Theory: A Reader*, New York: Columbia University Press.

Thornton, N. (2010) "YouTube: Transnational Fandom and Mexican Divas," *Transnational Cinemas*, 1(1): 53–67.

Valverde, K. (2003) "Making Vietnamese Music Transnational: Sounds of Home, Resistance, and Change," *Amerasia Journal*, 29(1): 29–49.

Yang, H. (2011) "Cultural Exchange, Hallyu Culture, and Future of Hallyu: Focused on Capitalization and Post-commercialism," *Journal of Humanities (Inmoonhak Yeongu)*, 86: 381–406.

Chapter 13

The Korean Wave as a cultural epistemic

Anandam Kavoori

I have elsewhere suggested that a useful way to examine contemporary global media forms is to examine them as a "cultural epistemic" (Kavoori 2007 and 2009; Kavoori and Chadha 2009).[1] This episteme is constituted by wider "nodes" (modernism, postmodernism, postcolonialism and nationalism). "Culture," I have argued, is the connective tissue that co-creates these nodes. Much like water that takes the shape of its container, Culture has become the vehicle through which these paradigmatic/epistemic nodes of the world are being *visualized*.

In what follows, I will suggest that we use this model to *locate* the Korean Wave. This is not an essay about the specificities of the Korean Wave (a topic extensively addressed elsewhere in this volume) but a broad theoretical statement about its placement within a specific model of global media forms. What I will provide is a thumbnail sketch of each node followed by a programmatic statement as it applies to the Korean Wave.

Culture as modernism has historically assumed the primacy of the institutional and cultural/communicative practices that emerge within the socio-economic space of European industrial and urban growth, and then becomes transmuted as a mediated vocabulary for cultural and economic development globally. The benchmarks of this include those of industrial enterprise, economic valuation, political accountability and personal freedom. Thus, the work of culture as modernism has traditionally retained its use as a category of periodization and its wider use as a prescriptive for socio-economic development.

I would suggest that the Korean Wave, like other contraflows (for example, telenovelas, Bollywood), reiterates such a trajectory. In its embrace of the economics of industrial practice, through its emblematic reworking of older art/drama forms, through its explicit location as a key element in state policy (a process mirrored in the economic/cultural work of post-independence Indian cinema) and, above all, in its direct, unproblematic assertion of the value of cultural production, initially for local/national, and now increasingly for transnational and diasporic, consumption, the Korean Wave embodies a hybrid but thoroughly nationalized modernism.

Culture as postmodernism is reflected in the emergence of not only a new kind of social and economic accounting (culture as consumption) but also a specific semiotic universe (a globally interconnected, rapidly mobile landscape of signifiers) and new vocabularies for cultural mediation (for example, hyper-tourism, micro-media, cybersex). At the heart of this process is the articulation of identity politics (race, class, gender, sexuality, ethnicity, etc.), which is reflexively engaged within the associated realms of technology, performance and cross-cultural transference (across both state and non-state actors).

I believe the Korean Wave represents many of these elements but some that are especially worth noting. First, is the sheer mobility of its texts (across pop, cinema, television and viral video), the second is its contradictory vocabulary that simultaneously effects simulation, dissonance, actualization, eroticization and ideological affiliation. Third, is its reworking of "traditional" identity politics (specifically class and ethnicity) in a global setting where they become markers of a regional consciousness, historically marked as "oriental" but now increasingly imprinted with a national marker – constituted in the Asian case by the national cinemas of India and China and the viral culture of Korea.

Culture as nationalism has historically been defined as the communicative ethos of new states (and those yet to be born) and the emergent values of "renewal" in third world states as they grapple with conditions of global capitalism. At the other end of the spectrum, this relationship animates the emergence of global ethnicities (for example, the category of "Asian" or "Latino") and functions as a discursive touchstone for state mobilizations over national identity and regional nationalisms. Anderson's notion of "imagined communities" has functioned as the key organizing principle for a considerable body of research on nationalism and national identity in relation to the media (along with relevant ideas from the work by Gellner and Hobsbawm).

In the context of the Korean Wave, three broad areas of relevance may be identified. First, is the indelible link between nationalism and ethnicity in a global context articulating issues of cultural identity and identity politics (the panoply of viral culture around Psy is especially central to such work). The second is the role of the work of *popular culture as cultural policy*, both as a means for national assertion on a global stage and as the oft-stated soft power equation to the spread of media hardware (especially LG and Samsung). Finally, there is the role of the Korean language itself as a mobilizer of a national identity, seen in the emergence of language videos (typically explaining the latest viral video) and blogs focusing on wider cultural narratives that embed these videos and which have become of interest to wider pan-national and diasporic fan communities.

Culture as capitalism is evident in the emergence of "consumption" as a key category in understanding global (mediated) relations. Capitalism assumes through the cultural value of consumption the aura of inevitability – in the sense of both a globally connected, historically contingent matrix of economic and social relations and its current "naturalization" by nation-states for cultural/economic development. Further animating this relationship is the multi-faceted presence of capitalist values in a variety of contexts (the

The Korean Wave as a cultural epistemic   217

"marketplace" of both goods and ideas, for example) and guises (as state policy; as corporate strategy and new belief systems – for example, the idea of "pleasure" in mass-mediated youth subcultures).

The role of the Korean Wave in this equation is especially useful to consider. Specifically, the usability of the classic questions of hegemony and ideology in a global context, where the issue with the Korean Wave is less one of internal cultural/institutional mechanisms (of aesthetic constitution) as for the ideological work of the Korean Wave. At the heart of this question is the intimacy of global capitalism with national hegemonies, especially as they deal with state-sponsored events and media campaigns. Related to this is the question of political agency (of both corporations and national policy-making bodies) and economic effect (in the creation of markets/products). Finally, the broadest issue relates to the role of the Korean Wave in the economics of political life and inversely in the politics of economic life – where the key issue (as in other postcolonial societies rapidly embracing market liberalization) is the steady erosion of the public sphere by the forces of corporatization with or without the enabling work of the nation-state.

Culture as postcolonialism emerges in a complex of ways – as a category that signals communicative transference between the modern and the postmodern in the non-Western world, or as a vehicle for the presentation of ethnic identity politics in the West; but most commonly, postcolonialism becomes the trademark of a global de-territorialization that moves people in search of jobs, trademarks in search of people, power in search of new territories (physical and psychological), and most crucially, the mobilization of "identity" in search of itself.

The Korean Wave is grounded in two key areas. One is the entirety of its movement (across television, film and viral culture) as a global wave (simultaneously national, regional, transnational and diasporic). This has been manifest in the work of the Korean Wave in animating and reworking the categories of identity (especially around gender and ethnicity); in developing a specific model for personal (national) expression within a global frame of reference – *becoming Korea* so to speak. Finally, the Korean Wave allows us to reframe questions of subalternity and agency from one of unreflexive domination (as in "cultural imperialism") to those of hybridity and mélange – even as it stays close to its roots as the language of national renewal and cultural affirmation.

What I have suggested above is one way to think theoretically about the Korean Wave, as a complement to other frameworks. These are conceptually broad – and necessarily incomplete – strokes by which we can problematize the Korean Wave as a global cultural epistemic.

Note

1 This chapter draws on arguments and materials published by the author in recent years (Kavoori 2007 and 2009; Kavoori and Chadha 2009).

References

Kavoori, A. (2007) "The Word and the World: Re-thinking International Communication/Defining the IC Prism," *Global Media Journal*, 2(2): 3–18.

——(2009) *The Logics of Globalization*, Lanham: Rowman & Littlefield.

Kavoori, A. and Chadha, K. (2009) "The Cultural Turn in International Communication: Mapping an Epistemic," *Journal of Broadcasting and Electronic Media*, 53(2): 336–46.

Chapter 14

The Korean Wave and "global culture"

Yudhishthir Raj Isar

This chapter explores how the Korean Wave phenomenon illustrates trends and raises issues of a general nature framed in the perspective of a sociology of culture on a worldwide canvas that is also informed by economic geography. The trends and issues discussed are all directly linked to the tropes of the "global" which are *de rigueur* nowadays (and indeed that term anchors the present volume's subtitle) and which for that very reason require unpacking. They revolve notably around the anxieties, perceptions and expectations generated by the processes of contemporary accelerated globalization (rather than globalization *tout court*, as will be explained below) that appear to have transformed the cultural world and have also come to dominate our analytical discourse. The experience of the Korean Wave relates to all these questions in a variety of ways. Some of these will be explored below, in the light of the author's experience in co-editing Sage's Cultures and Globalization Series, notably the second and third volumes, entitled respectively *The Cultural Economy* and *Cultural Expression, Creativity and Innovation* (Anheier and Isar 2008 and 2010). But first it would be useful to unpack both the "global" and "globalization."

What is the "global"?

Before taking up the ways in which the Korean Wave is germane to cultural theorizing today, let us unpack the notion of the "global" in relation to culture and cultural expression (Isar 2012a and 2012b). "Global culture" was among the various ideas associated with the term "global" that was much used at the end of the 1980s and still retains substantial purchase in the institutional discourses of international cultural politics and diplomacy. But what is the "global"? Does the term refer simply to phenomena encountered everywhere in the world? Or to phenomena that dominate the planet because of globalization? Or is the "global" a higher level of human organization and process, a new whole at the planetary level that is more than the sum of its parts, and endowed with an ethos of its own? Such questions are never more than partially answered.

Different readings of the global go hand in hand with various understandings of the term "culture," some of which have become prominent "scripts" in rhetoric, policy and practice all over the world. The leading usage today is of culture as a particular way of life, whether of a people, a nation-state, an ethnic or other identity group, a historical period or, sometimes, of the human species itself (Williams 1988). This is closely followed by a narrower idea of culture as the works and practices of intellectual and artistic activity, in other words, culture as the arts (this understanding of the arts also includes the inherited traces of past human creativity, now called "cultural heritage," hence this meaning is often expressed as "arts and heritage"). Distinctly less current nowadays is the oldest historical usage of the term, which was that of a general process of intellectual, spiritual and aesthetic development (as in talk of a "cultured" person). The three usages are often combined or conflated, sometimes within the space of the same written paragraph or oral utterance.

Against this semantic backdrop, the existence of a global culture is sometimes affirmed, sometimes rejected. Is there or can there ever be such a thing? For analysts and laymen alike, the question of the degree and significance of such a global culture may relate to one or the other of the senses mentioned above. On occasion the question implies a concatenation of the different understandings. Sociologists such as Anthony Smith find the very notion to be a practical impossibility, except when it is taken to be the culture of planet Earth as a whole, for the differences between different segments of humanity in terms of lifestyles, systems of values and beliefs, etc. are too great and the shared elements are too general (Smith 1990). Others, such as Mike Featherstone (1990), accept that a globalization of culture is occurring but reject the idea that a global culture akin to that of the nation-state writ large is emerging at all. Yet others argue that a planetary culture has indeed crystallized, but simply as a shared frame of reference for norms, attitudes and behaviors. Anthropologists hold that affirmations and claims of cultural diversity are forms of resistance to homogenizing forces (Hannerz 1996; Sahlins 1994). These claims and affirmations themselves constitute a new cultural system at a world level, whose core value is the affirmation of cultural distinctiveness.

From the global to globalization

Different visions of globalization underpin the different viewpoints on the question of global culture. Lechner (2007) sums up globalization as three processes: (1) the ever-wider diffusion of symbolic products, including ideas; (2) a growing repertoire of shared knowledge and knowhow that result from social relations and activities that span the globe; (3) an increasing volume of shared norms and principles – human rights, for example – that concern how the world does or should work (each of these processes involves one or more readings of "culture"). The question of global culture cannot be discussed independently of either the forms globalization takes in the cultural domain or

The Korean Wave and "global culture" 221

the mutual interactions between cultural processes and global processes. Many scholars such as Held *et al.* (1999) refer to this as "cultural globalization": movements, flow and interactions of a cultural nature, e.g. the worldwide proliferation of internationally traded cultural goods and services, or the global ascendancy of consumer culture as well as popular cultural icons and artifacts.

Several important points need to be made in connection with this debate. First, the processes of cultural globalization, as indeed of globalization *tout court*, are not new: empires, world religions, secular ideologies, transport and communications infrastructure have all been at work for centuries shrinking the dimensions of time and space. It is only that today they have been greatly strengthened, deepened and accelerated (Chanda 2007). As Albrow notes (1997), our contemporary awareness of globality – consciousness of the world as a whole – draws attention to processes that previously were either embryonic or went unnoticed. Second, there are different interpretations of the power as well as the virtues of globalization; these in turn color understandings of the global human condition. *Hyperglobalizers* look favorably upon a homogenization of the world's cultures along the model of American mass culture and consumerism. The historian Frederick Cooper calls this "the Bankers' Boast" (Cooper 2005: 93). *Skeptics* lament the erosion of "thick" national cultures and point to the "thinness" and ersatz quality of globalized culture (for Cooper, this tune is "the Social Democrat's Lament"). *Transformationalists* (for Cooper they are a "Dance of the Flows and the Fragments") shift attention to the intermingling of cultures and the emergence of hybrids and networks. A third point, forcefully made by Alexander (2005), is that the very notion of globalization and its associated terms have become collective representations, energizing symbols that raise strong normative hopes, even when we think we are reasoning analytically. As Friedman has noted (1994), globalization involves the formation of global institutional structures that organize an already existing global field as well as global cultural forms, that is, forms that are either produced by or transformed into globally accessible objects and representations.

In the view of many analysts, there is also a blinkered "presentism" to many such conceptions, as well as unjustified totalizing pretensions (Cooper 2005). Taking a historical perspective, Nederveen Pieterse points out that globalization has unfolded in different stages – ancient, modern and contemporary – and enjoins us to use the term "contemporary accelerated globalization" for the phenomena discussed here. He cites Clark's observation that "today's globalization process differs from that of earlier times in three ways: the volume of materials moved is larger; the speeds with which they are moved are faster; and the diversity of materials (matter, energy, information) moved is greater" (Nederveen Pieterse 2009: 28). Discussing the flows of influences between cultures, he also argues:

> Italian Renaissance artists such as Raphael, Flemish painters and artists such as Albrecht Dürer found followers in Mughal India. The adoption of

Mughal motifs in seventeenth-century European painting, then, also echoes European influences in Mughal miniatures and is thus an interlacing of cultural influences – interculturalism moving in circles.

(2009: 131).

Empirically, cultural globalization can be mapped, as by Held *et al.* (1999), under several categories: the global infrastructures of telecommunications and language; multinational corporations producing cultural goods and services and their worldwide marketing networks; radio and the music industry; cinema and television; tourism. The movements and flows of contemporary globalization may be measured in terms of their extensity or geographical range; the intensity of the interconnections among them; the velocity of net-worked interactions and, finally, their impact, which is the feature that is the most difficult to conceptualize and map. These impacts are bound to be shaped by different kinds of processes. In some cases, patterns of cultural consumption may be *imposed*; in others the process is more one of *diffusion*. It could in other cases be a matter of *emulation*; in yet others of *interpenetration*, where hybrids and fusions of expressive repertoires and languages occur. In yet other instances, globalization provokes sharp *resistance*, whereby local culturalist claims and identities are magnified and essentialized. These diverse interactions produce different kinds or degrees of globalization in the cultural arena: thick (high extensity, high intensity, high velocity and high impact), with the Internet, mass tourism as cases in point; diffused (high extensity, high intensity, high velocity and low impact), e.g. global art markets; expansive (high extensity, low intensity, low velocity and high impact), e.g. elite cultural networks or thin (high extensity, low intensity, low velocity and low impact), e.g. international cultural organizations.

Despite these differences, all analysts seem to agree that globalization is a contradictory, disjunctive process and one that is full of paradoxes. With regard to culture and cultural expression, individuals and societies experience these contradictions and paradoxes each in their own different ways. Some may want above all to preserve their indigenous cultures. Others on the other hand may want to jettison them in favor of the globally dominant cultural models that are there to be imitated. Is this the Korean Wave option, as it appears to have been also in the case of Japanese popular culture? Some, notably in the global South, appear to be taking a compromise stance, seeking to balance their own cultural patterns against those emanating from other locations in the globalized world they want to belong to, by creating diverse flows of symbols and meanings.

A dialectic of sameness and difference

Contributors to the Cultures and Globalization Series, like most recent writers on the subject, have confirmed that the interface between cultural change and globalization is more complex than it appears in the popular imagination. Rather than reinforcing old, historically anchored hegemonies, the forces of globalization are helping to destabilize them. The interaction has become a two-way street. At a general level, the Korean Wave testifies to this dynamic interaction. Its rise and flourishing give the lie to fears of cultural domination. Indeed it would have greatly comforted a prescient Indian thinker, Mahatma Gandhi, who wrote famously almost a century ago: "I do not want my house to be walled in on all sides and my windows to be stuffed. I want the cultures of all lands to be blown about my house as freely as possible. But I refuse to be blown off my feet by any. I refuse to live in other people's houses as an interloper, a beggar or a slave" (1921: 170).

For many others in the postcolonial twenty-first century, across the global South, the Korean Wave demonstrates that they can indeed live happily in their own houses and contribute to those global cultural winds. Today, all peoples have become as culturally self-conscious as Gandhi was, if not more so, as notions of the "global," along with terms such as "globalization," "globality" and "globalism," have become prisms through which "major disputes over the collective human condition are refracted: questions of capitalism, inequality, power, development, ecology, culture, gender, identity, population ... " (Nederveen Pieterse 2009: 7). The key parameter on which such questions hinge is imbalances and/or divides. Given the prevalent world patterns of market domination, the question arises as to how other societies might emulate the Korean Wave example, not in full measure to be sure, but at least to some degree, as the complex interplays between cultures and globalization processes are at once unifying and divisive, liberating and corrosive, homogenizing and diversifying; as they transform patterns of sameness and difference across the world, and modify the ways in which cultural expression is created, represented, recognized, preserved or renewed.

A much used term, *glocalization*, adapted from a Japanese management theory term that refers to the capacity to "think globally, act locally" and popularized by Roland Robertson (1992), is apposite here. It has the virtue of pinpointing the dialectical relationship that has emerged between the universal and the particular, one that bridges both. The central dynamic of the global culture, then, is the twofold process of the particularization of the universal and the universalization of the particular. In other words, globally defined values and practices are increasingly adapted at the local level, just as, globally, the celebration of particularistic difference becomes a value in itself. The local is itself a global product. Although the broad ways of life idea of culture is the principal axis along which global culture thinking has unfolded here, it is inextricably tied to the narrower, expressive culture reading. Indeed increasingly – and this vision is wholly contemporary – cultural expression is seen in an instrumental way, as the assets or resources that belong to a collectivity, in the service of an intensive practice of identity (Friedman 1994). Hence, the arts and heritage are not valued for their own sake, for their intrinsic value, but because they embody, express and represent those various particular – local – ways of life that it is desirable to "protect," or "affirm," or "promote." This often takes the form of advancing the "soft power" discourse in the framework of a national cultural diplomacy or nation-branding policy and indeed has done very visibly in the case of the Korean Wave. The usage is a bit loose, however, blurring the distinction made by Joseph Nye (2004), the inventor of the term, between the mere deployment of cultural forms to make a nation "look good" as it were and ensuring that recognition of and respect for these forms promote acceptance of that country's value preferences, or strengthen the country's influence in the geopolitical and like domains. The core question is whether the culture of X can help in getting others to want what X wants.

Reading this landscape of contemporary culturalism, Marshall Sahlins saw the emergence in the late twentieth century of a world – or global – culture as such, which was characterized by simultaneous homogenization and diversification. While an actually existing world system, understood as the planetary reach of Western capitalism, had no doubt engendered a culture consisting of standardized commodities destined for mass consumption, this process itself had engendered a new kind of repluralization. Both processes were partly the result of many centuries of earlier globalization, and of the incompleteness of this process. For one thing, the colonialist expansion of the West was often resisted and filtered, and the external cultural influences mediated and redirected in distinct patterns of appropriation by different peoples – as amply demonstrated by the syncretism of many features of contemporary Indian culture. Westernization was attractive in different degrees and ways. In some cases, Western lifestyles and values were goals pursued in order to be "modern"; but in the case of cargo cults and other religious expressions of dependence on external "life-force," Western objects and practices were wholly encompassed by indigenous strategies (Friedman 1994). Often resisted while it lasted, in the immediate postcolonial situation, Western cultural hegemony was self-consciously reversed.

Toward multiple creativities

These last considerations call to mind the cultural imperialism model, which privileged the United States as a central and organizing actor in the international cultural and media economy. In the context of the Korean Wave it is perhaps useful to consider the dynamics involved in the light of a typology put forward by Diana Crane (2002).

Her *cultural flows or network model* sees the transmission process as a set of influences that do not necessarily originate in the same place or flow in the same direction. Receivers may also be originators. In this model, cultural globalization corresponds to a network with no clearly defined center or periphery but shifting configurations. Globalization as an aggregation of cultural flows or networks is a less coherent and unitary process than cultural imperialism and one in which cultural influences move in many different directions to bring about rather more hybridization than homogenization.

The reception model argues that audiences vary in the way they respond actively rather than passively to mass-mediated culture, and that different national, ethnic and racial groups interpret the same materials differently. Hence, the different responses to cultural globalization by publics in different countries, a phenomenon one observes readily in many developing countries where "cultural pride" is strong. This model does not view globally disseminated culture as a threat to national or local identities. Culture does not transfer in a unilinear way. Movement between cultural areas always involves interpretation, translation, mutation, adaptation and "indigenization" as the receiving culture brings its own cultural resources to bear, in dialectical fashion, upon cultural imports. The cultural imperialism model failed to account for the diverse ways in which audiences make use of foreign media.

Finally, a *negotiation and competition* model, based on the recognition that globalization has stimulated a range of strategies on the part of nations, global cities and cultural organizations to cope with, counter or facilitate the culturally globalizing forces. They include strategies for preserving or rejuvenating inherited cultural forms, processing and packaging the local for global consumption. In this perspective, for example, globalization is increasingly impelling cities, regions and nations to not only "protect" but also position and project their cultures in global space. The cultural imperialism approach overlooked the growing influence of domestic media producers and failed to acknowledge the increasing prominence of transnational media production centers in cities such as Mumbai, Hong Kong, São Paulo or Lagos. It focused on national cinemas and national broadcasting systems, paying little attention to the increasingly complex and trans-border circulations of popular media.

Against the idea of dominant power emanating from a single source, Curtin (2008) among others identifies the complex and contingent forces and flows at work, as the number of media producers, distributors and consumers has grown dramatically, first in Europe and then in Asia, with China and India together adding almost two billion new viewers. Although powerful global media conglomerates were active contributors to these forces and flows, local, national and regional media firms expanded rapidly as well. Rather than exhibiting patterns of domination and subordination, media institutions now appear to be responding to the push-pull dynamic of cultural globalization, as increasing connectivity inspires significant changes in textual and institutional practices.

Hence, the turn away from the idea of Western hegemony and toward the ways in which a larger set of processes operates trans-locally and interactively. In other words, rather than being an arena of centralized power, the world's increasingly interconnected cultural and media environment is more and more the outcome of messy and complicated interactions. These processes, observes

Curtin, have led to the use of such adjectives as fractal, disjunctive or rhizomatic to characterize a complex terrain of textual circulation, reception and appropriation. This is not to deny that human cultural variety is softening into a paler, and narrower, spectrum, as Geertz (2000) would have put it; yet as this is happening, a new dynamic for the production of new kinds of diversity has emerged, in which the affirmation of cultural difference is a self-conscious project. The global landscape of cultural production has become increasingly polycentric and polysemous. Globalization appears less and less to be resulting in a pattern of mass cultural uniformity, but in the emergence of a mosaic of cultural production centers tied together in complex relations of competition and collaboration across the globe (Scott 2008). The Korean Wave embodies this process.

Cultural production, creativity and innovation

The volume entitled *The Cultural Economy* (Anheier and Isar 2008) was dedicated *inter alia* to mapping the vibrancy of the cultural economy in different regions of the world. Hence, it was no accident that it included a chapter on the Korean Wave that discusses the factors of its emergence as a phenomenon at a time when different forces of contemporary globalization had already had a marked effect on the production, distribution and consumption of the cultural forms of economic activity (Choi 2008). While these forces have reduced the market reach and power of cultural producers in some cases, in many others – such as the Korean Wave – they have vastly extended this reach and power and helped bring them fully into the circuits of global trade, as already mentioned in the preceding section.

The experience of the Korean Wave also speaks to patterns of *spatial concentration and dispersion* in cultural production, as a growing number of cultural-products agglomerations in different places is accompanied by a growing differentiation of outputs, as individual centers struggle to mobilize their place-specific competitive advantages and as they build up reputations for particular kinds of product designs and forms of semiotic expression. And in this context there are two key factors – the geographic diversification of productive efforts and the socio-spatial fragmentation of demand – that both seem to resist the processes through which certain producers and/or agglomerations establish monopoly powers in certain global market segments.

The Korean Wave is also germane to issues explored in *Cultural Expression, Creativity and Innovation* (Anheier and Isar 2010). What does creativity mean in a globalizing economic, cultural and artistic landscape? How does creativity manifest itself empirically, and what are the economic, sociological and cultural factors that help account for variations in creativity across genres, fields, regions and societies over time? What institutions, organizations and professions as well as artistic, political or economic interests are behind such milieus, and how are they interlinked? Is the changing "map" of creativity related to the various drivers and patterns of globalization? Addressing such questions from the non-Western perspective meant envisioning creativity as more a matter of "social authorship" than transubstantiation of the soul or expression from within, as has long been recognized with respect to all the cultural traditions of Asia. Yet, there has been a tendency to think of creativity and innovation as things ineffable, embodied only in the individual, as the emanation of an inner inspiration. But recent thinking – and cases such as the Korean Wave – open up the analytical frame to include the socio-cultural context, interpreting creativity in conjunction with collective action and defining it as a process in which novelty is recognized and acknowledged collectively.

To be sure, creativity continues to manifest itself as an individual product, in which latent and manifest talents, expertise and serendipity combine in often seemingly unpredictable ways. Yet, alongside and perhaps gradually superseding this image of the individual genius kissed by the muse is a new one: it is based on the understanding that the likelihoods of creativity to emerge, of creative acts to be recognized, and of both leading to innovation, yielding sustained change, are all closely linked to the organization of economy and society as well as patterns in the cultural domain itself. The experience of the Korean Wave bears out this insight.

New repertoires of cultural expression are emerging, increasingly in a spirit of hybridity and intercultural fusion and moving across all boundaries. The Korean Wave is one of them. Yet like all the others, we need to question the fullness of the interculturality involved. Are the globalized consumer industries of the global North molding motifs as well as tastes here as well? Or are other loci of cultural production such as Korea or Bollywood achieving genuine parity on the global scale? Are they exerting significant transnational influence through hybrid forms that work with, or blend in with, Western and other forms and repertoires reinterpreted in terms of locally specific perceptions, understandings and styles? The example of the Korean Wave does demonstrate how creative industries can play to existing local strengths, taking advantage of skills and forms of expression that are intrinsic to each specific place and often unique to it. Or that the dynamics that generate creative places are not exclusive to key "metropolitan" centers. In fact, recent history is replete with examples of how new material, products or expressions from diverse places – in music alone, for instance, reggae, zouk, rai, salsa, samba, tango, flamenco, bhangra, fado, gamelan, juju or qawwali – have entered the global space of flows, some of them before Korean musical creations. Other creative pursuits have emerged endogenously simply to meet demand locally, where they remain necessarily constrained in their scope and influence – such as urban, regional and national media, broadcasting and publishing industries. Examples abound: Tanzanian hip-hop; West African community radio; Taiwanese publishing; television production in Mexico; and film industries around the world from Lebanon to Brazil to Burkina Faso (Gibson 2012).

These cases also embody, together with the Korean Wave, the manner by which, in the arts and arts practice, communication, exchange, fusion and

228 Yudhishthir Raj Isar

hybridization among and between different repertoires and forms are proliferating today. How practice has taken on an increasingly inter- or transcultural dimension, often through the merging of traditions where audiences are confronted with the specific as well as the universal truth by virtue of performances that blend various cultures. Premonitions of this particular global circumstance came as early as Goethe's early nineteenth-century vision of the dawning age of *Weltliteratur*, in which writers and poets should become the first citizens of a global Republic of Letters. Performance can now take place anywhere, for any type of audience – as is once again the case with the Korean Wave – and this itself turns the global dimension into a central part of the spectacle, as the world views itself (Albrow 1997).

This form of global consciousness can be understood in terms of the third reading of culture set out earlier, the general idea of refinement or "civilization." One aspect of the global civilization idea, as distinct from earlier ideas of "universality," is that the West is once again becoming, as it was earlier in human history, only one element in world society; it will increasingly have to take on board references and constructs which the West itself has played little or no part in making. In the meantime, however, Western-originated ideas have been globally appropriated. Applied to culture in the other two senses as well, this requires us to recognize and contribute towards the elaboration of a true "Culture of cultures" – as a phenomenon both profoundly mixed and essentially plural, and as a way of changing the whole world for the better.

To conclude then, by paraphrasing Chris Waterman, the Korean Wave, like many other contemporary forms of cultural flow, embodies the individual and collective act of

> thinking-through-making, a mode of labour that apprehends the conjurings of imagination and marshals them into palpable visual, tactile, sonic and textual patterns, squeezed through the sieves of historical and social circumstance, shaped by ideology, identity, and aesthetics, and fine-tuned to the particularities of place and media. Once cast into the world, any creative act or work takes on a social life of its own, in a complex interaction with pre-existing regimes of evaluation and interpretation, systems of cultural consolidation and dissemination, and all manner of unintended consequences.
>
> (Waterman 2010: 273–4).

References

Albrow, M. (1997) *The Global Age: State and Society Beyond Modernity*, Stanford: Stanford University Press.

Alexander, J. (2005) "Globalization as Collective Representation: The New Dream of a Cosmopolitan Civil Sphere," *International Journal of Politics, Culture and Society*, 19: 81–90.

Anheier, H. and Isar, Y.R. (eds) (2008) *The Cultural Economy*, The Cultures and Globalization Series 2, London: Sage.

——(eds) (2010) *Cultural Expression, Creativity and Innovation*, The Cultures and Globalization Series 3, London: Sage.

Chanda, N. (2007) *Bound Together: How Traders, Preachers, Adventurers and Warriors Shaped Globalization*, New Delhi: Penguin Viking Books India.

Choi, J. (2008) "The New Korean Wave of U", in Y.R. Isar and H. Anheier (eds) *The Cultural Economy*, The Cultures and Globalization Series 2, London: Sage.

Cooper, F. (2005) *Colonialism in Question: Theory, Knowledge, History*, Berkeley and Los Angeles: University of California Press.

Crane, D. (2002) "Cultural Globalization from the Perspective of the Sociology of Culture," paper presented at the Symposium, *Statistics in the Wake of Challenges Posed by Cultural Diversity in a Globalization Context*, UNESCO Institute of Statistics, Montreal, October 21–23, 2002.

Curtin, M. (2008) "Spatial Dynamics of Film and Television," in H. Anheier and Y.R. Isar (eds) *The Cultural Economy*, The Cultures and Globalization Series 2, London: Sage.

Featherstone, M. (1990) *Global Culture: Nationalism, Globalization and Modernity*, London: Sage.

Friedman, J. (1994) *Cultural Identity and Global Process*, London: Sage.

Gandhi, M.K. (1921) *Young India*, January 6.

Geertz, C. (2000) *Available Light: Anthropological Reflections on Philosophical Topics*, Princeton: Princeton University Press.

Gibson, C. (2012) "Building Creative Economies, Widening Development Pathways," Contribution to the UN Creative Economy Report 2013, unpublished typescript.

Hannerz, U. (1996) *Transnational Connections: Culture, People, Places*, London: Routledge.

Held, D., McGrew, A., Goldblatt, D. and Perraton, J. (1999) *Global Transformations: Politics, Economics, and Culture*, Cambridge: Polity.

Isar, Y.R. (2012a) "Culture, Media, Global," in *The Encyclopedia of Global Studies*, Thousand Oaks: Sage.

——(2012b) "Global Culture," in B. Chimni and S. Mallaravapu (eds) *International Relations: Perspectives for the Global South*, New Delhi: Pearson.

Lechner, F. (2007) "Cultural Globalization," in R. Robertson and J. Scholte (eds) *Encyclopedia of Globalization*, London: Routledge.

Nederveen Pieterse, J. (2009) *Globalization and Culture: Global Mélange*, Lanham: Rowman & Littlefield.

Nye, J. (2004) *Soft Power: The Means to Success In World Politics*, New York: Public Affairs.

Robertson, R. (1992) *Globalization: Social Theory and Global Culture*, London: Sage.

Sahlins, M. (1994) "Goodbye to Triste Tropes: Ethnography in the Context of Modern World History," in R. Borovsky (ed.) *Assessing Cultural Anthropology*, New York: McGraw Hill.

Scott, A. (2008) "Cultural Economy: Retrospect and Prospect," in H. Anheier and Y.R. Isar (eds) *The Cultural Economy*, The Cultures and Globalization Series 2, London: Sage.

Smith, A. (1990) "Towards a Global Culture," in M. Featherstone (ed.) *Global Culture: Nationalism, Globalization and Modernity*, London: Sage.

Waterman, C. (2010) "Closing Reflections," in H. Anheier and Y.R. Isar (eds) *Cultural Expression, Creativity and Innovation*, The Cultures and Globalization Series 3, London: Sage.

Williams, R. (1988) *Keywords: A Vocabulary of Culture and Society*, London: Fontana.

Index

Aion 151, 156, 157
Allkpop.com 2, 13
Americanization 149
Appadurai, Arjun 201
Asia as method 15, 44, 49, 54
Asian American 120, 121, 124, 125, 128, 131
Asian female in the U.S. 107–12, 115–17
Asian identity 136, 137, 143
Asian modernity 79
Asian pop culture 120, 128, 131
Asian values 16, 23, 135, 138, 141, 142, 144
Asianism 15, 16

banal inter-nationalism 51
Beast 171
Benjamin, Walter 165–67
Bhabha, Homi 149, 150
BoA 107–8, 110, 112–13, 117
Boys Over Flowers 7
brand nationalism 50–51

censorship 189, 195
chaebol 8, 96–97, 100–101, 105
   chaebol-funded films 10
chogukjeok 179
civilization 228
collective regional identity 135, 136
computing 60, 63
Confucian values 84
Consalvo, Mia 159
consumptive desire 100
contra-flow 12, 15, 85, 86
cosmopolitanism 18–23, 89–90
   consumer cosmopolitanism 18, 20, 39
   cosmopolitan openness 21, 87
   cultural cosmopolitan 18, 21
   imagined cosmopolitanism 18
   pop cosmopolitans 19

cover dancer 21, 169
creativity 220, 224, 226, 227
cross-border dialogue 43, 44, 47–50, 53–54
culture 220, 228
cultural change 222
cultural citizenship 124, 126
cultural difference 21, 89
cultural distribution 225, 226
cultural diversity 3, 14, 18, 21, 41
cultural economy 226
cultural export 6
cultural expression 219, 222, 227
cultural globalization 122, 131, 148–49,
   160–61
cultural hybridization 120, 129
   in East Asia 45–47
cultural identities 3, 10, 17, 18, 22, 23,
   87, 223
cultural imperialism 41, 149, 159
cultural industries 189, 190
cultural inter-nationalism 49–53
cultural modernities in East Asia 46–49
cultural policy 11, 185–97
cultural production 226

dance tracker 168–69
decolonization 15
democratization 186, 188, 190
developmental state 186–87
de-Westernization 43, 44, 53
digital diasporas 19, 88
digitization 135, 137
dominant culture 135, 138, 146

East Asian culture 137, 139, 146
East Asian (im)migrants 135, 136, 137, 138,
   139, 145
East Asian media culture connection 43–54

Index 231

East Asian pop culture studies 44–45, 52, 54
emotion 7, 75–77
    A-ha! emotion 75–76
empire 58, 61, 68, 70–71
English 14, 17
entrepreneurial business 13
entrepreneurial self 8
ethnic media 88
ethnic space 122, 124, 125, 126, 128, 132
Europe 135, 136, 137, 138, 139, 142,
    145, 146

F4 97–100
Facebook 165, 179
family 81, 83–85
fans 9, 12–15
    digital fan culture 12–15
    fan clubs 2, 13
    fandom 13–14, 19
    overseas fans 194–96
fansubbing 13
fantasies 108–9
Friend (Chingu) 10

Gangnam Style 2, 8, 20, 33, 34, 167,
    177–79, 199, 209
Girls' Generation (SNSD) 2, 8, 20, 113–16,
    171–72, 175
global capitalism 18, 80
global culture 219, 220
    global consumer culture 18, 19, 20
global financial meltdown (in 2008) 95
global governance of media culture
    connectivity 49–53
globalism 223
globality 221, 222, 223
globalization 145, 149, 157–58, 201, 204,
    211, 219, 220, 221, 222
glocal 222, 223

Hallyu 13, 121, 124, 128, 135–36,
    138–40, 142, 144–46, 150, 152, 185,
    202, 204–5
    digital Hallyu 2
    Hallyu 2.0 167, 169, 179
han 40, 85
Hana Yori Dango 93
hardware 60–61, 63, 67–68, 70
hegemony 121, 122, 129, 130
Hollywood 9, 10, 63, 70, 121, 122, 130
hybridity 10, 11, 17, 23, 148–50, 152, 156–57,
    159–61, 221, 222, 225, 227, 228

hybridization 11, 17–18, 148–50, 152–53,
    155–57, 159–61, 203, 211
hyper-connectivity 22

ICT 65–66
identity 3, 10, 17, 18, 22, 23, 87, 120, 126,
    127, 131, 132, 223
idol 107–10, 113–14, 116–17
image 107–11, 113, 115, 117
imagined community 123, 127, 132
individualization 75, 81–82
    female individualization 81–82
innovation 226, 227
inter-Asian referencing 15, 43–54
intercultural communication 222, 228
internationalization of Korean culture
    189–91
Internet 2, 12, 14, 23, 37, 75, 79,
    87–88, 90

Japanese popular culture 4, 9, 19, 38
Jewel in the Palace (Dae Jang Geum) 7, 36
Joint Security Area 10
JYP Entertainment 110–13

K-culture 192–93, 196
K-pop 8, 106–8, 110, 113–15, 117,
    135–37, 139–40, 143–44, 199–211
Kancheong Style 178
KBS2 94
Kim, Youna 19, 21, 37, 75–76, 78–82,
    84, 87
Korean American 121–23, 125–26,
    128–33
    youths 120–21, 123–24, 126–28,
    130–32
Korean cinema 148, 152, 154–55, 160
Korean culture 189, 196
Korean culture industry 3–4, 39
Korean government 3–4, 11, 18, 35
Korean language 12, 35, 36
Korean-ness 18
Korean popular culture 121, 123–24,
    127–28, 131
Korean Wave 1, 58–60, 120–21, 123,
    135–36, 138–40, 142, 144–46, 185,
    200, 202–5
    and modernism 215
    and postmodernism 215
    and nationalism 216
    and postcolonialism 217
    and state policy 216, 217

232   Index

anti-Korean Wave 40
 hating the Korean Wave 86
Korean Wave projects 191–93

Lineage 151, 156, 157
local identities 149, 160

mammonism 100
manga 9, 13, 93, 104, 105
market 121, 123, 131
masquerade 153, 156
media 121–23, 128, 130–32
media consumption 137
media education 103
media imperialism 16, 58–62, 64–68, 70–71
Meteor Garden (*Liuxing Huayuan*) 47
MMORPGs 151, 156–57, 161
movies 60–61, 63
multi-directional flow 13
music 63, 68
music video 106–7, 109–12,
   114–15

nation branding 12, 34, 39
national border 135, 137
national culture 187–89, 196
national identity 90
national image 12
nationalism 41, 90
 cultural nationalism 41
 diasporic nationalism 75, 87, 90
 pop nationalism 75, 85
national/transnational 135, 136, 137,
   144, 145
NCSOFT 151, 157, 158
neoliberalism, neoliberalization 4, 58–59,
   61–62, 67–68, 186, 188
Nobody 110–11, 113
nomadic sensibility 87
North Korea 2, 7, 23, 37, 80–81
 black market 99
 defectors 94
Nye, Joseph 5, 22, 31–33

online culture 135, 137, 139
online games 11
orientalism 20, 109

pan-Asian community 135
participatory culture 12–13
periphery/center 121, 130, 131
Planet Hallyuwood 11

popular culture 187–89, 196
popular pleasure 76
postcolonial 109, 201, 210–11
power 3, 11, 17, 18, 21, 22, 23, 31,
   85–86
 consumer power 19
propaganda 66, 68
Psy 2, 8, 20, 33, 34, 199, 207
Pusan International Film Festival 10

race 107, 108, 110
 racial, racialized 107–10, 112, 116, 117
 racialization 21
racism 16, 89, 90
Rain (*Bi*) 20
reflexivity 75, 77–78, 80
 everyday reflexivity 75, 77–78
regionalism 40, 135, 136, 145
resident Koreans in Japan 52
re-worlding 209, 210, 211

segyehwa 35, 123, 130
sexuality 20, 107–10, 112, 114, 117
Shiri 10
Singapore 165, 173–79
Singaporean Style 178
Singlish 177
SM Entertainment 113–14, 199, 205,
   208, 209
social media 12, 13, 23, 135, 137–40,
   145–46
social networking sites (SNSs) 2, 14,
   206, 210
soft power 3, 5, 12, 22, 31–33, 60,
   63, 71
software 62–63, 67–68, 70
Soompi.com 2, 13
sound tracker 168–69
Spivak, Gayatri 199, 200, 201, 210
star chaser 169
star system 8
state 121, 123, 130, 131
 state control 186–87, 189
subaltern, subalternity 201, 203

T-ara 170–72, 174
technology 120, 122, 131
telephony 60–61, 64
television 60–62, 65, 69
television dramas 6
The Boys 114
The Thieves 156

tourism 12, 35, 36
tradition 81, 83–85
    de-traditionalization 83
    re-traditionalization 84
translation communities 13
transnational consumerism 195–96
transnational (im)migrants 120, 122, 126, 132
transnationalization 152
trans-Pacific cultural flows 120–21, 128, 130–32
Twitter 179

universality 222, 223, 228
urban middle class 5
    middle-class consumerism 5
U.S. pop market 106–10, 112–13, 116–17

Winter Sonata 6, 34, 36, 48, 53, 77, 85
Wonder Girls 110–13
worlding 199, 200, 204, 207, 209, 210, 211

YouTube 8, 17, 33, 106, 111–12, 115, 167, 169, 172, 174, 176, 179, 199–200, 206–11